iLife® '09

PORTABLE GENIUS

12/2009
$ 21.47 w shipping

iLife® '09

PORTABLE GENIUS

by Guy Hart-Davis

WILEY

Wiley Publishing, Inc.

iLife® '09 Portable Genius

Published by
Wiley Publishing, Inc.
10475 Crosspoint Blvd.
Indianapolis, IN 46256

www.wiley.com

ISBN: 978-0-470-41732-4

Manufactured in the United States of America

10 9 8 7 6 5 4 3 2

For general information on our other products and services or to obtain technical support, please contact our Customer Care Department within the U.S. at (800) 762-2974, outside the U.S. at (317) 572-3993 or fax (317) 572-4002.

Wiley also publishes its books in a variety of electronic formats. Some content that appears in print may not be available in electronic books.

Library of Congress Control Number: 2008943642

WILEY

About the Author

Guy Hart-Davis is the author of more than 50 computing books, including *Mac OS X Leopard QuickSteps*, and the coauthor of *iMac Portable Genius*.

Credits

Senior Acquisitions Editor
Jody Lefevere

Project Editor
Chris Wolfgang

Technical Editor
Dwight Spivey

Copy Editor
Scott Tullis

Editorial Manager
Robyn B. Siesky

Business Manager
Amy Knies

Senior Marketing Manager
Sandy Smith

Vice President and Executive
Group Publisher
Richard Swadley

Vice President and Executive Publisher
Barry Pruett

Project Coordinator
Kristie Rees

Graphics and Production Specialists
Jennifer Henry
Andrea Hornberger
Ronald Terry

Quality Control Technician
John Greenough

Proofreading
Penny Stuart

Indexing
Broccoli Information Mgt

Contributing Writer
Paul McFedries

This book is dedicated to Rhonda and Teddy.

Acknowledgments

I'd like to thank the following people for making this book happen:

- Jody Lefevere for getting the book approved and signing me up to write it.
- Chris Wolfgang for shaping the outline, cutting the chapters down to size, and running the editorial side.
- Dwight Spivey for reviewing the book for technical accuracy and making many helpful suggestions.
- Paul McFedries for invaluable help updating the book for iLife '09.
- Scott Tullis for copy-editing the book with a light touch.
- Andrea Hornberger for laying out the book in the design.
- Penny Stuart for scrutinizing the pages for errors.
- Broccoli Information Management for creating the index.

Contents

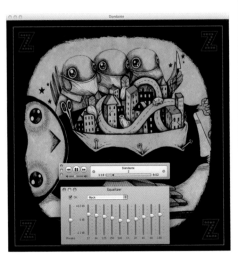

chapter 2

How Do I Get My Photos
into iPhoto?   46

chapter 3

How Do I Organize, Edit, and
Share My Photos? 68

How Do I Import Video into iMovie? 122

chapter 5

How Do I Turn My Content into
a Movie?   154

chapter 6

How Do I Finish My Movie and Share It? 180

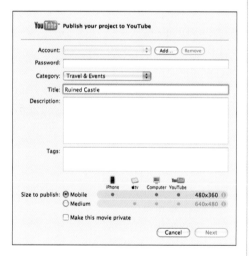

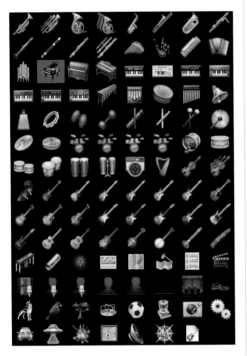

chapter 9

How Can I Make My Song Sound
Great and Then Share It?   272

chapter 10

How Do I Build a Web site
with iWeb? 296

How Do I Publish Blogs and
Podcasts with iWeb? 332

Introduction

 Your Mac is a fantastic tool for enjoying multimedia, and the iLife suite of applications lets you create and share your own multimedia content with the whole wired world.

iLife '09 Portable Genius shows you how to get the most out of the iLife applications. Here's a taste of what you can do with this book:

- **Enjoy music and videos in iTunes.** Exploit iTunes to the full by setting it and your iPod to deliver high audio quality, building a powerful, easy-to-use media library, creating videos that work with iTunes, getting the most out of playlists, and using your iPod or iPhone to carry files.

- **Bring your photos into iPhoto.** Import your digital photos directly from your digital camera or a removable memory card — or from another folder on your Mac or your network. Use Image Capture to scan printed photos so that you can use them on your Mac.

- **Organize, improve, and share your photos.** Quickly organize your photos into iPhoto Events and tag them with keywords so that you can instantly find the photos you want. Use iPhoto's new Faces feature to automatically identify the key people in your photos and the Places feature to organize photos by location. Once you've cropped and adjusted your photos so that they look exactly as you want them, you can create powerful slide shows, share your photos with other people on your network or the Internet, or simply use them to enhance your copy of Mac OS X.

- **Import your video footage into iMovie.** Bring your video clips into iMovie from your DV camcorder or from your digital camera. Swiftly and effortlessly review your clips, mark the footage you want to use in your projects, and organize related clips into Events so that you can retrieve them easily.

- **Build a movie from your clips.** Grasp iMovie's slick, nondestructive method of handling edits, and learn when to edit in the Event Browser and when to edit on the Storyboard.

Build the movie on the Storyboard by arranging the clips and editing them to fit. If you want, add still photos — and enliven them with custom Ken Burns effects.

- **Finish, polish, and share your movie.** Give your movie a professional finish by adding themes, titles and transitions and creating a custom sound track complete with music and sound effects. You can then share the movie with friends by creating a file or a DVD or with the world by posting it to YouTube, your MobileMe Gallery, or your Web site.

- **Set up a music studio on your Mac.** Perhaps the best feature of iLife is the way it packs a complete music studio into your Mac. As soon as you've connected your musical keyboard and any physical instruments you're using to your Mac, you're ready to start making music with GarageBand—or learning to play an instrument or a song with GarageBand's help. If your song needs a kick-start, fire up the Magic GarageBand feature to quickly lay down a backing track that you can play or sing along with.

- **Record a song.** To create a song quickly in GarageBand, you can build tracks out of loops, changing them so that they exactly meet your needs. You can then add in your own performances playing either a Software Instrument via your keyboard or a real, physical instrument such as a guitar or drum kit. You can even create your own custom Software Instruments to get exactly the sounds you want.

- **Mix a song and share it.** Even the best performance may need editing, and GarageBand makes it easy to remove mistakes or cut together the best parts of several takes. You can then mix the song, adjusting the balance, panning, and effects on each track so that it fulfils your artistic vision. When the song is finished, you can export it to iTunes; add tags, lyrics, and artwork there; and finally share the song on the Internet.

- **Build your own Web site quickly and easily.** The best place to showcase the photos, movies, and music you create with the iLife applications is by reaching a worldwide audience on the Web. The iWeb application lets you quickly create great-looking Web sites from your content. You can even add Web widgets such as interactive Google Maps, AdSense advertisements, YouTube videos, and RSS feeds.

- **Add blogs and podcasts to your Web site.** If you have rapidly changing information that you need to share, you'll love iWeb's features for adding blogs and podcasts to your Web site. You create the blog entries in iWeb and the podcasts in GarageBand, and can post them to your Web site with minimal effort. You can also add your podcasts to the iTunes Store, which lets you reach a huge audience worldwide.

- **Burn custom DVDs of your movies and photos.** Despite the Internet, DVDs remain a great way of sharing and enjoying movies and photos. iDVD gives you all the features you need to create professional-looking DVDs with customized menu screens and compelling content. And if you need to create a DVD in a hurry, you can use the Magic DVD feature to do the grunt work for you — or use the OneStep DVD feature to burn a movie straight to DVD from your DV camcorder.

How Can I Best Enjoy Music and Videos in iTunes?

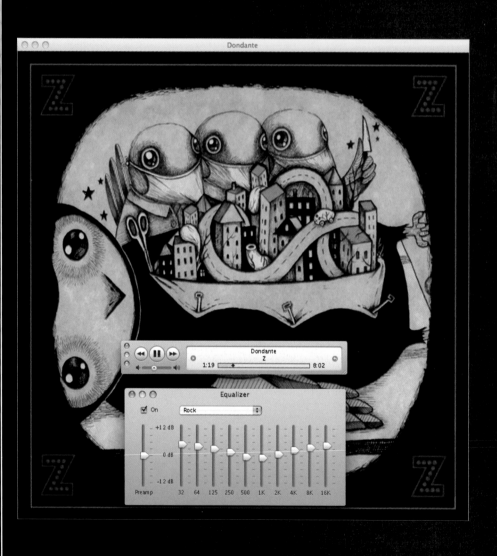

You can start playing music and videos within minutes of launching iTunes, but to get the very best out of iTunes, you'll need to explore its advanced features. Do you want to make sure that iTunes gives you the highest audio quality that your Mac can deliver — and that you get the best possible sound on your iPod as well? What about building an iTunes library that lets you quickly find the songs you like? You'll probably want to create both unchanging playlists and playlists that update themselves automatically with fresh songs, back up your iTunes library in case disaster strikes your Mac, and use your iPod to carry or transfer essential files as well as your songs and videos.

Getting High-Quality Audio on iTunes and an iPod

If you love music, you'll love the audio quality that iTunes and an iPod can deliver. But to get the very best out of your Mac and iPod, you need to choose the right settings in iTunes and on the iPod.

Setting iTunes to deliver high audio quality

You need to do three things to set iTunes to give you high-quality audio:

- Set iTunes to create high-quality audio files from CD
- Choose essential playback settings in iTunes
- Apply equalizations to your songs

Setting iTunes to create high-quality audio files from CD

Here's how to get the best audio quality when you import songs from CD.

1. **Choose iTunes ⇨ Preferences to open the Preferences dialog box.**

2. **Click General in the toolbar to open the General preferences (see figure 1.1).**

1.1 iTunes' General preferences let you control which action iTunes takes when you insert a CD.

3. **Tell iTunes what to do when you put a CD in your Mac.** I find that Show CD is the best choice because it lets you fix any incorrect tag information before you import the CD. Your alternatives are Begin Playing, Ask To Import CD (the default), Import CD, Import CD And Eject, and Show CD.

4. **Select the Automatically retrieve CD track names from Internet check box if you want iTunes to download track names for you.** This is the easiest way to get CD information, but it's a good idea to check that the information is correct before you apply it.

5. **Click the Import Settings button to display the Import Settings dialog box (see figure 1.2).**

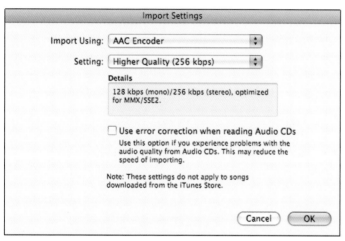

1.2 iTunes' Import Settings control the quality of the music you get in iTunes on your iMac and on your iPod or iPhone. If you want high-quality audio, you need to change the default settings.

6. **In the Import Using pop-up menu, choose the encoder for creating the audio files.** See the sidebar "Picking the Best Encoding for Your Needs" for advice.

7. **Choose a quality setting for the encoder in the Setting pop-up menu.** iTunes offers preset choices for all encoders except Apple Lossless Encoding. To choose custom settings, click Custom and work in the dialog box that iTunes displays. Figure 1.3 shows the MP3 Encoder dialog box for choosing custom settings for encoding MP3 files.

8. **Select the Use error correction when reading Audio CDs check box if you find your song files contain pops, skips, or dropouts caused by the drive reading them incorrectly, or if you simply want to be sure of getting quality audio files.** Using error correction slows down the importing speed, so you may prefer to clear this check box and test whether the song files come out clean.

8. **Click OK to close the Import Settings dialog box, and then click OK to close the Preferences dialog box.**

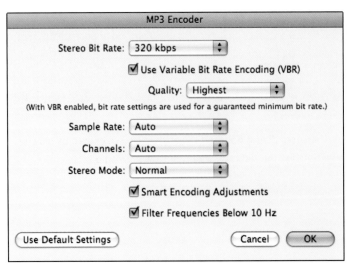

1.3 Custom dialog boxes such as the MP3 Encoder dialog box let you choose exactly the encoding settings you want.

Choosing essential playback settings in iTunes

Your next step is to choose three settings that make a huge difference to how iTunes plays back the songs. Follow these steps:

1. **Choose iTunes ⇨ Preferences to open the Preferences dialog box.**

2. **Click the Playback button to display the Playback preferences (see figure 1.4).**

3. **Select the Crossfade Playback check box only if you want to use the cross-fading feature.** This fades from the end of one song to the beginning of the next. If you use this feature, drag the slider to set the number of seconds (from 1 to 12), depending on how much of each song you want to lose.

4. **Select the Sound Enhancer check box if you want to use Sound Enhancer.** This feature performs several audio tricks, such as increasing the stereo separation of the left and right tracks and adding harmonics. Sound Enhancer can make music sound more lively, but at the cost of authenticity. If you use this feature, drag the slider to set the degree of enhancement.

5. **Select the Sound Check check box if you want iTunes to normalize your songs.** *Normalization* involves evaluating the songs in your library for loud and quiet points and reducing the difference between the two. This helps to avoid getting your ears blasted by a loud song that follows a quiet one, but it makes the music much less dynamic and compelling.

Note Explanations of what the Sound Enhancer actually does tend to vary, but if you've ever used a Loudness button on an old stereo, you may see a similarity between that and Sound Enhancer. But where most Loudness features could only be either on or off, you can adjust the amount of difference the Sound Enhancer makes by dragging its slider.

6. **Click OK to close the Preferences dialog box.** Test the settings you've chosen by playing various types of songs, and change the settings if you don't like the results.

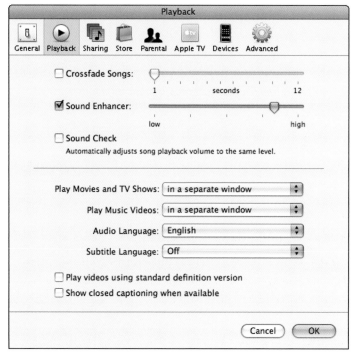

1.4 In the Playback preferences, choose whether to crossfade playback, use Sound Enhancer, and use Sound Check.

Genius Turn off Sound Check so that you can enjoy your songs with as full a dynamic range as the sound engineer has given them. Unfortunately, to pack songs with enough punch to penetrate our cluttered consciousness on the radio or in public, sound engineers all too often now compress the dynamic range, which makes the music seem louder overall but removes the difference between the "loud" and "quiet" parts.

Picking the Best Encoding for Your Needs

CDs contain music files in an uncompressed format designed for use on CDs. To copy the songs from CDs to your Mac, you use an *encoder* to convert the files to a format suitable for computers. iTunes comes with five encoders, so you can pick the one that's right for your needs. For some of these encoders, you can also adjust the quality setting, or *bitrate*, which also affects the file size.

iTunes comes set to import songs from CD using the Advanced Audio Coding (AAC) encoder at the 128 Kbps bitrate. This is good for general-purpose recording with modest file sizes, but if you want high audio quality, either choose the Higher Quality (256 Kbps) setting, or use the Custom dialog box to set the highest available bitrate, 320 Kbps.

If you use a Mac and an iPod or iPhone, AAC is usually the best format to choose. iTunes, iPods, and iPhones can play AAC files, but most other hardware and software players can't. If you need to play your song files on other players, use the MP3 format instead. MP3 has lower quality than AAC at the same bitrate, so choose at least the Higher Quality (192 Kbps) bitrate for MP3. For best results, use the Custom dialog box to set the highest available bitrate, 320 Kbps.

If you have lots of hard disk space on your Mac and want superior audio quality, try the Apple Lossless Encoding encoder. *Lossless* means that, unlike the AAC and MP3 encoders, Apple Lossless Encoding does not discard any of the data contained in the original music — so the song file should be perfect. Apple Lossless Encoding files take up much more space than AAC and MP3 files, so they're not great for iPods and the iPhone. In fact, the iPod shuffle can't even play Apple Lossless Encoding files.

Your last two choices of encoder are WAV and AIFF. These are essentially the same thing: uncompressed audio data, but with different instructions at the beginning of the file. WAV and AIFF both give perfect audio quality but lack the tag information that portable music players need; besides, WAV and AIFF files are so large that few will fit on any but the most capacious portable players.

Applying an equalization to the music you're playing

Your third move toward making songs sound the way you like them is to use the Equalizer. You can either apply an equalization to the music as you listen, just as you might do with a graphical equalizer on a stereo or boom-box, or apply an equalization to any song in your library (see the next section).

iTunes' Equalizer is easy to use. These are the moves you need to know:

- Choose Window ⇨ Equalizer or press ⌘+Option+2 to toggle the display of the Equalizer (see figure 1.5).

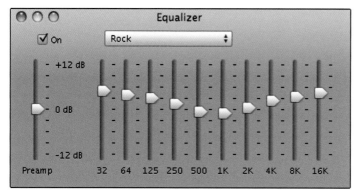

1.5 Use the Equalizer to make songs sound the way you like them.

- Select the On check box to turn the Equalizer on, and then choose the equalization you want from the pop-up menu.

- To create a custom equalization, drag the frequency sliders to produce the sound you want. If you want to boost the amplification, drag the Preamp slider up; to reduce the amplification, drag the slider down. Open the pop-up menu, choose Make Preset, type the name in the Make Preset dialog box (see figure 1.6), and then click OK.

- To rename or delete an equalization, open the pop-up menu and choose Edit Presets. In the Edit Presets dialog box (see figure 1.7), select the equalization, and then click Rename (to rename it) or Delete (to delete it). Click Done when you're ready to close the dialog box.

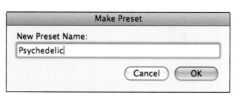

1.6 You can easily create a custom preset to apply an equalization.

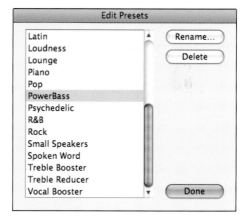

1.7 Use the Edit Presets dialog to rename a preset or delete it.

Note Custom equalizations don't carry through to the iPod or iPhone, so if you use one of these devices, it's best to experiment with iTunes' built-in equalizations before creating your own.

Applying an equalization to a particular song

Applying an equalization as you're listening works well, but what's much handier is applying an equalization to each song in your library. This way, whenever you play the song, iTunes uses that equalization automatically. So does your iPod or iPhone (as long as the equalization you choose is one of the built-in ones).

You can apply an equalization to any song in your library in one of these ways:

- **Single song.** Ctrl+click or right-click the song, choose Get Info, and then click the Options tab of the Item Info dialog box (see figure 1.8). Open the Equalizer Preset pop-up menu, choose the equalization, and then click OK.

1.8 Choosing an equalization for a single song in the Item Info dialog box.

- **Single song.** Add the Equalizer column to the current view by Ctrl+clicking or right-clicking an empty column heading (after the last column) and choosing Equalizer from the menu. (You can also replace an existing column by Ctrl+clicking or right-clicking its column heading and then choosing Equalizer.) You can then apply an equalization to a song by using the pop-up menu as shown in figure 1.9.

1.9 Add the Equalizer column to a view to give yourself the easiest way to apply an equalization to a song.

- ⬤ **Multiple songs, an album, or all an artist's songs.** Select the songs or the album, Ctrl+click or right-click, and choose Get Info to open the Multiple Item Information dialog box. For an artist, click the artist, and then press ⌘+I to open the Multiple Item Information dialog box. Click the Options tab, open the Equalizer Preset pop-up menu, choose the equalization, and then click OK.

Genius

Which equalizations sound best to you will depend on the type of music you listen to, the type of speakers or headphones you use, and the state of your ears, not to mention your personal preferences. Bear in mind that the names of the built-in equalizations are merely suggestions — so if you find you like to listen to speed metal using the Jazz equalization, feel free to do so.

Choosing suitable iPod settings

To get the highest audio quality on your iPod, you need to load high-quality songs, such as those you've ripped from your CDs as discussed earlier in this chapter. You need to turn off the Sound Check feature on your iPod (or iPhone) to prevent it from normalizing the sound. You may also need to apply equalizations on the iPod.

All iPods and iPhones include decent-quality headphones, but you can improve the audio quality by buying higher-quality headphones that you find comfortable. If you're thinking of upgrading your headphones, also look into buying a headphone amplifier because this can greatly improve the sound you get out of your iPod or iPhone.

Turning off Sound Check on the iPod or iPhone

If you want songs to sound good on your iPod or iPhone, turn off the Sound Check feature to prevent the player from robbing the songs of dynamic range by normalizing the sound.

Here's how to turn off Sound Check on the various models of iPod and on the iPhone:

- **Sixth-generation iPod or iPod nano.** Choose Main menu ⇨ Settings ⇨ Sound Check, and then press the Select button to switch between On and Off.

- **iPod shuffle.** Connect the iPod shuffle to your Mac, then click it in the Devices category in the Source list to display its control screens. On the Settings tab, clear the Enable Sound Check check box, and then click Apply.

- **iPod touch.** Press Home, touch Settings, touch Music, and then touch the Sound Check slider to move it to the On position or the Off position.

- **iPhone.** Press Home, touch Settings, touch iPod, and then touch the Sound Check slider to move it to the On position or the Off position.

Applying equalizations on the iPod or iPhone

If you've applied one of iTunes' built-in equalizations to each song, as discussed earlier in this chapter, your iPod or iPhone automatically applies those equalizations when you listen to the songs.

Keeping Audio Quality High on an iPod shuffle

To keep audio quality high on the iPod shuffle, clear the Convert higher bit rate songs to 128 Kbps AAC check box in the Options area of the iPod's Settings tab. Converting songs to 128 Kbps AAC reduces the amount of space the songs take up, but it costs you audio quality. You lose even more quality if the song you're converting was encoded using an encoder other than AAC (for example, MP3). The conversion also makes synchronization take longer, which is seldom welcome.

When you've applied a custom equalization to a song, however, you'll find that it's not available on your iPod. In this case, you can change the equalization on the iPod or iPhone manually. You may also need to do this for songs whose equalizations are available, simply because songs sound differently through headphones than through your Mac's sound system.

Here's how to apply an equalization on the iPod or iPhone:

- **Sixth-generation iPod or iPod nano.** Choose Main menu ⇨ Settings ⇨ EQ. Scroll to the equalization you want, and then press the Select button.

- **iPod touch.** Press Home, touch Settings, touch Music, and then touch EQ. On the EQ screen, touch the equalization you want, and then touch Music to return to the Music screen.

- **iPhone.** Press Home, touch Settings, touch iPod, and then touch EQ. On the EQ screen, touch the equalization you want, and then touch iPod to return to the iPod screen.

Building a Powerful, Easy-to-Use Library

To make your iTunes library as powerful and easy-to-use as possible, store it in a folder that has plenty of space, and make sure that folder contains the file for each song in the library. For faster searching and enjoyable playlists, tag the files with accurate information, rate the songs so that iTunes knows which you like, and trim off any unwanted parts of songs.

Normally, you'll want to store all your songs in a single library so that you can play them easily. But if need be, you can create multiple iTunes libraries, each containing a different collection of songs.

Choosing where to store your library

iTunes normally comes set to handle your library like this:

- Put all your music and video files in the same folder within your Home folder.

- Keep the folder organized by artist folder, album folder, track number, and track title — for example, /Bruce Springsteen/Greatest Hits/01 Born to Run.m4a. (If there's a disk number, such as Disk 1 of 2, iTunes includes that too.)

- Make a copy of each file you add to the library from another folder, instead of linking to the file in that folder.

This behavior is convenient for many people, but if you have a large iTunes library or your Mac has a small hard disk, you may run short of space. You may also want to store your iTunes library in a different folder so that you (or others) can access the media files from other computers on your network.

Here's how to check and change where iTunes is storing your library and choose other key settings.

1. **Choose iTunes ⇨ Preferences and then click the Advanced button to display the Advanced preferences (see figure 1.10).**

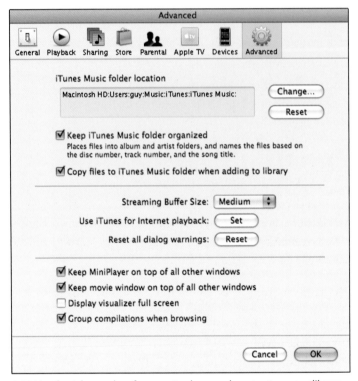

1.10 Use the Advanced preferences to choose where to store your library.

2. **Look at the iTunes Music folder location box to see which folder iTunes is storing your music in.** If you want to change the folder, click the Change button, select the new folder in the Change Music Folder Location dialog box, and then click Open.

3. **Select the Keep iTunes Music folder organized check box if you want iTunes to organize the folder and filenames.** This setting is usually helpful, but it does mean that when you change a tag such as a song name, iTunes changes the filename to match as well.

4. **Select the Copy files to iTunes Music folder when adding to library check box if you want iTunes to copy each file you add from another folder.** If you want iTunes to create a link to the file in that folder instead, clear this check box.

5. **Click OK to close the Preferences dialog box.**

Getting all your media files in the same folder

If you want to be able to back up your iTunes library in a single action, use the Consolidate Library command to make sure all your media files are stored in the same folder.

Caution   There's no easy way to undo consolidation, so before you consolidate your iTunes library, make sure that the drive on which you're storing your iTunes library has plenty of space to hold all the files. The easiest way to see how much space your iTunes library takes up is to click the Music item in the Source list, click All in the Artists list and the Album list, and then look at the readout at the bottom of the iTunes window. Repeat the process for Movies, TV Shows, and any other items that appear in the Source list, and then add the figures together.

When you give this command, iTunes copies any files that are stored outside your iTunes Music folder into the iTunes Music folder. Normally, it's a good idea to select the Keep iTunes Music folder organized check box in the Advanced preferences before you consolidate your library, allowing iTunes to rename folders and files and generally keep your library straight.

After this preparation, consolidating your library is easy, but copying the files may take some time. Follow these steps:

1. **Choose File ➪ Library ➪ Consolidate Library.** iTunes displays the message box shown in figure 1.11.

2. **Click Consolidate.** iTunes copies those files that are located outside your iTunes Music folder into the folder. If you've selected the Keep iTunes Music folder organized check box, iTunes renames files whose names differ from their tag information.

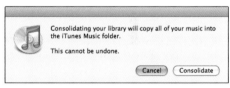

1.11 iTunes double-checks that you want to consolidate your iTunes library because there's no easy way to undo a consolidation.

Tagging songs after adding them to your library

After you've added a song to your library, you can easily change its existing tags or add missing tag information.

If you need to change a tag that's displayed in whichever iTunes view you're using, you can simply edit it in place like this.

1. **Click once to select the song.**

2. **After a short pause, click again to put an edit box around the field (see figure 1.12).** If you don't pause between the clicks, iTunes registers a double-click and starts playing the song.

☑ Don't You (Forget Abo...	4:21	Simple Minds	Glittering Prize	11/13/2005 8:57 AM
☑ Leilani	3:03	Game Theory	Tinker to Evers to Chance	11/9/2005 9:04 PM
☑ Creeping Death	5:08	Apocalyptica	Plays Metallica By Four Cellos	11/16/2005 4:50 PM
☑ Too Little Too Late	4:22	Metric	Live It Out	7/18/2006 3:53 PM
☑ Cadillac Coming	4:38	James Ray	Best	1/13/2006 12:37 PM

1.12 The quickest way to edit a single tag is to open an edit box in the iTunes list.

3. **Click to position the insertion point, type the change, and then press Return to apply the change.**

Genius

If none of iTunes' genres seems right, create a genre of your own. Either open the Genre pop-up menu and choose Custom, or simply drag across whichever genre is currently displayed to select the text. Type the name of the genre you want to create. You'll then be able to use this genre for other songs too.

To change several tags on a single song, use the Item Information dialog box like this:

1. **Ctrl+click or right-click the song and choose Get Info to open the Item Information dialog box.**

2. **Click the tab that contains the tags or settings you want to change.** For example, to control how iTunes sorts the songs, click the Sorting tab (see figure 1.13) and use the boxes on it.

Genius

Select the Gapless Album check box if you want to mark the songs as being gapless. This setting turns off cross-fading and is good for live albums, classical music, and spoken-word audio.

1.13 The Sorting tab of the Item Information dialog box lets you add extra information for sorting without changing the tags that appear in the iTunes interface.

3. **When you finish changing the tags and settings, click OK.**

Understanding the less obvious tags

Most of the tag fields, such as Name and Artist, are easy to grasp. Here's a quick run-down of the more puzzling ones:

- **Album Artist.** The artist name that you want to use for the album, where it's different from the artist name for the song. For example, you might use Various Artists as the album artist for a compilation album.

- **Grouping.** This tag lets you group the movements in a classical music work, but you can use it for other purposes too. For example, instead of creating a Psychedelic Rock genre, use the Rock genre and put Psychedelic in the Grouping tag; or add Grouping tags such as Party or Workout to songs of different genres so that you can pick them out across different genres.

- **BPM.** Beats per minute — the tempo of the song.

17

Genius

To find out the beats per minute of songs and add this info to the tags, use a tool such as Tangerine from Potion Factory (www.potionfactory.com/tangerine/) or beaTunes (www.beatunes.com).

● **Sort tags (Sort Name, Sort Artist, Sort Album Artist, Sort Album, Sort Composer, and Sort Show).** These let you control how iTunes sorts songs (and shows) without changing the information iTunes displays. For example, you may want to sort your Beethoven music by "Beethoven" rather than by the names of the various orchestras and conductors. By adding **Beethoven** to the Sort Artist tag, you can do so.

To change one or more tags on multiple songs at once, use the Multiple Item Information dialog box like this:

1. **Select the songs whose tags you want to change.** For example, click the first song, then ⌘+click each of the other songs.

2. **Ctrl+click or right-click in the selection and choose Get Info to open the Multiple Item Information dialog box (see figure 1.14).**

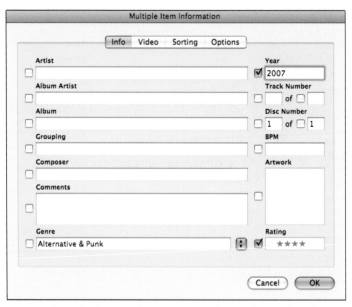

1.14 Use the Multiple Item Information dialog box to change shared tag information on several songs at once.

18

3. **Change the tags that apply to all the songs you selected, and then click OK.** When you change a tag, iTunes selects the check box next to it so that you can easily track the changes you've made.

Note To add artwork (such as a CD cover picture) to several songs at once, drag the picture to the Artwork box on the Info tab in the Multiple Item Information dialog box. Amazon.com includes cover pictures for many CDs, but you can also add your own pictures if you prefer.

Genius If you want to apply tags to your songs automatically, visit the Doug's AppleScripts for iTunes Web site (http://dougscripts.com/itunes/) and look through the Managing Track Info scripts.

Trimming off unwanted parts of songs

Do you ever find yourself always skipping the beginning or end of a song? If so, don't suffer through it — use this trick to trim off the unwanted part of the song.

1. **Play the song, and note the time at which you want the song to start or stop.**

2. **Ctrl+click or right-click the song and choose Get Info to open the Item Information dialog box, and then click the Options tab (see figure 1.15).**

3. **Click in the Start Time box or the Stop Time box, and then type the time you want the song to start or stop.** Use the format *minutes:seconds.thousandths* — for example, 3:24.000. Note that it's a period between the seconds and thousandths, not a second colon.

4. **Click OK to close the dialog box.**

5. **Play the song again and make sure the cutoff is right.** If not, open the Item Information dialog box again and adjust it.

6. **Right-click the song and choose Create *Format* Version.** (*Format* here is the encoding format you've chosen in iTunes — for example, Create AAC Version.) iTunes creates a new version of the file minus the parts you chose to exclude.

7. **If you want, remove the original song file from your iTunes library, leaving the new file.**

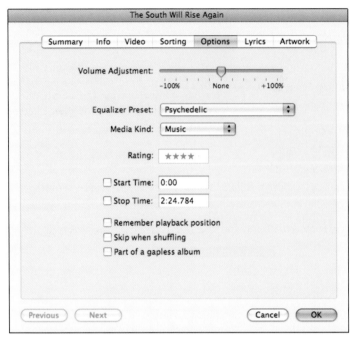

1.15 On the Options tab of the Item Information dialog box, you can set the start time or end time for a song. You can then trim the song file to use this start time or end time.

Genius

You can also use this trimming technique to split a song into different parts, which can be useful when you've recorded a live performance and want to keep only parts of it. First, create a duplicate copy of the song. The easiest way to do this is to Ctrl+click or right-click the song, choose Show In Finder, press ⌘+D to duplicate the song file, and then drag the duplicate to your iTunes library. In iTunes, trim off the first part of the song from one file, leaving the second part, and then trim off the second part of the song from the other file, leaving the first part.

Separating your music with multiple iTunes libraries

Normally, iTunes puts all your songs into a single library. But here's a neat feature: You can create separate music libraries if you want. For example, you may prefer to keep your classical music separate from your popular music, put a library on an external drive to save space on your Mac's hard drive, or maintain a family-friendly library as well as one that includes harder-edged material.

Creating a new iTunes library

First, create a new library. Here's how to create one:

Choose iTunes Library

iTunes needs a library to continue. You may choose an existing iTunes library or create a new one.

Quit   Create Library...   Choose Library...

1.16 The Choose iTunes Library dialog box is your springboard for both creating and selecting separate iTunes libraries.

1. **Quit iTunes if it's running. Press ⌘+Q or choose iTunes ⇨ Quit iTunes.**

2. **Hold down Option and click the iTunes icon on the Dock to display the Choose iTunes Library dialog box (see figure 1.16).** Keep holding down Option until the dialog box appears — a quick Option+click doesn't usually do the trick.

3. **Click the Create Library button to display the New iTunes Library dialog box (see figure 1.17).**

1.17 Give your new iTunes library a descriptive name so that you can easily identify it.

4. **Type a descriptive name for the library (for example, Chill-Out Music) in place of iTunes' suggestion (iTunes 1, iTunes 2, and so on), choose the folder in which to store the library, and then click the Save button.**

5. **iTunes opens using the library you just created, so no songs appear in it.** You can now add songs to the library as usual:

   ● **Insert a CD and rip its songs to audio files.**

- **Drag audio files from a Finder window to the library.**

- **Choose File ⇨ Import, select the folder containing the files, and then click Open.**

After you've added songs to the library, you can use the library as normal. For example, you can play songs back, add them to playlists, or create Smart Playlists that draw on the library.

Note

iTunes suggests saving each library in the folder specified in the Advanced preferences. By default, this is the ~/Music/iTunes/ folder unless you change it. If you've got plenty of hard disk space, this folder is a good choice. But if you want to put the new library in another folder, expand the New iTunes Library dialog box and navigate to that folder.

Selecting the library you want to load

To switch from one library to another, you use the Choose iTunes Library dialog box you saw a moment ago.

1. **Quit iTunes if it's running.** Press ⌘+Q or choose iTunes ⇨ Quit iTunes.

2. **Hold down Option and click the iTunes icon on the Dock to display the Choose iTunes Library dialog box.** Keep holding down Option until the dialog box appears.

3. **Click the Choose Library button to display the Open iTunes Library dialog box.**

4. **Select the library you want, and then click the Open button.**

When you want to switch to another library, simply quit iTunes, and then hold down Option as you restart it.

Note

If you open iTunes without holding down Option, iTunes opens the last library you used.

Enjoying Music and Visualizations with iTunes

As soon as you've got a good selection of songs in iTunes, you can relax and enjoy them — together with iTunes' stunning visualizations if you like.

iTunes could hardly be simpler to control with the mouse, but you can also control it using the keyboard — even when iTunes isn't the active window.

When iTunes has the focus (is the active application), you can control it using the keyboard shortcuts shown in Table 1.1. (If iTunes doesn't have the focus, the quickest way of switching the focus to iTunes is to hold down ⌘ and press Tab until the iTunes icon is selected, then release ⌘.)

Table 1.1 Keyboard Shortcuts for Controlling iTunes

Action	Keyboard shortcut
Play/pause	Spacebar
Next song	Right Arrow or ⌘+Right Arrow
Previous song	Left Arrow or ⌘+Left Arrow
Rewind	⌘+Option+Left Arrow
Fast forward	⌘+Option+Right Arrow
Next album in the current list	Option+Right Arrow
Previous album in the current list	Option+Left Arrow
Increase the volume	⌘+Up Arrow
Decrease the volume	⌘+Down Arrow
Mute or unmute iTunes	Option+Left Arrow
Display or hide iTunes main window	⌘+Option+1
Display or hide Graphical Equalizer	⌘+Option+2
Zoom to or from mini player	⌘+Ctrl+Z
Minimize iTunes	⌘+M
Select the Find box	⌘+Option+F
Turn the Visualizer on or off	⌘+T
Switch the Visualizer to or from full-screen mode	⌘+F

Sharing Music

Enjoying music on your own is great, but even better is sharing the music you like with other people — and letting them share music with you.

iTunes lets you share music in two different ways. First, you can share all or part of your library with other iTunes users on your local network, and they can share with you. Second, you can share a playlist with the whole wired world by publishing it to the iTunes Store.

How to Get Exactly the Visualizations You Want

The Visualizer is great, but you can make it even better by using the following secret key presses to adjust the behaviors, color schemes, and color themes:

- Press W to start the next behavior, or Q to revert to the previous behavior.
- Press A to change to the next color scheme, or press S to go back to the previous scheme. The color scheme is a set of colors within the color theme (see the next paragraph).
- Press Z to switch to the next color theme, or X to switch back to the previous theme. The color theme is the overall mix of colors, so pressing these keys produces a bigger difference than changing the color scheme.

When you find a Visualizer configuration you like, save it by pressing a key combination from Shift+0 to Shift+9 (which lets you save ten different configurations). Press the number without Shift to launch that configuration.

Press R to switch to a random configuration, or press D to reset the Visualizer to its defaults.

Press F to toggle the frame rate display on and off, T to toggle frame-rate capping at 30 frames per second, and I to toggle the display of song information on and off.

Genius

iTunes lets your Mac share music with five other computers per day. Any further computers see a message saying that your Mac is not accepting sharing or that it accepts only five different users each day, so please try again later.

Sharing music on the network

Your first step for sharing music is to share it with other iTunes users on your local network. Sharing works with iTunes on both Macs and PCs.

Setting iTunes to share music and look for shared music

You can set up sharing and looking for music others are sharing in a single step:

1. **Choose iTunes ⇨ Preferences to open the iTunes Preferences dialog box.**
2. **Click the Sharing button to display the Sharing preferences (see figure 1.18).**

1.18 Setting up sharing and looking for shared music in iTunes' Sharing preferences.

3. **Select the Look for shared libraries check box if you want iTunes to show the songs other people are sharing.**

4. **Select the Share my library on my local network check box if you want to share some or all of your songs.** iTunes enables the controls beneath this check box so that you can choose which songs to share:

   ● To share all your songs, select the Share entire library option button. To share only a selection of songs, select the Share selected playlists option button, and then select the check box for each playlist you want to share.

   ● If you want to protect your shared songs with a password, select the Require password check box and type the password in the box next to it. A password is useful on a larger net-work where you need to stay within iTunes' five-computers-a-day limit for sharing. On a smaller network (for example, at home), a password may be a hindrance rather than a help.

5. **Click the General button to display the General preferences, and then type the name you want to give your shared library in the Library Name box.** This is the name under which your shared songs appear in the Source list on other people's computers.

6. **Click OK.** iTunes closes the dialog box and starts sharing the songs you chose.

Changing the selection of playlists you're sharing

If you chose to share some playlists rather than share all your music, you can quickly share another playlist or stop sharing a playlist you're sharing. Ctrl+click or right-click the playlist in the Source list (see figure 1.19), and then click Share to either remove the check mark next to it (if the playlist was shared) or to place a check mark next to it (if the playlist wasn't shared).

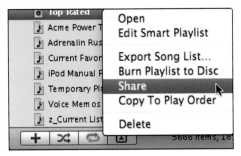

1.19 The quick way to share or stop sharing a playlist is to Ctrl+click or right-click it and choose Share from the menu.

Playing songs that other iTunes users are sharing

Once you've selected the Look for shared libraries check box (as discussed earlier in this chapter), iTunes automatically displays the library names in the Shared category of the Source list (see figure 1.20). If the Shared category has a sideways disclosure triangle next to it, click the triangle to display the shared libraries.

Click a library to display its contents in your current iTunes window, or double-click it to display its contents in a new window.

If the library is password-protected, iTunes displays the Shared Library Password dialog box (see figure 1.21). Type the password, select the Remember password check box if you want iTunes to remember it so you don't have to type it again, and then click OK.

1.20 Libraries others are sharing appear in the Shared category of the Source list.

After you connect to a shared library, you can find and play music using the same techniques as for your own library. For example:

- Click the disclosure triangle next to the library to toggle the display of its playlists on or off. If you display the playlists, you can click a playlist to show only its contents, as in figure 1.22.

1.21 Connecting to a shared iTunes library that's protected by a password.

1.22 Browsing a single playlist in a shared library.

- Choose View ⇨ Show Browser to display the browser so that you can browse by artist or album.

- Search for songs using the Search box.

- Sort the shared songs or playlists into a different order by clicking the column headings.

- Clear the check box of any song you don't want to play.

However, because of copyright restrictions, you can't copy songs to your Mac, add them to playlists, or burn them to CD or DVD.

When you finish using a library, disconnect from it by clicking the Eject button next to its name in the Source list.

Sharing an iMix playlist on the iTunes Store

When you create a great playlist, you may want to share it more widely than people on your local network. To put the playlist in reach of every iTunes user on the planet, publish it as an iMix on the iTunes Store.

Genius

There's one serious limitation to sharing playlists as iMixes: Because you're sharing the list and order of songs rather than the song files themselves, you can include only songs that are available on the iTunes Store. This limitation makes sure that anybody who downloads your iMix can listen to all the songs, so it's reasonable enough — and iTunes warns you when songs you've included in your playlist will be removed from the iMix.

When you've created a playlist that you want to make into an iMix:

1. **In the Source list, click the playlist.**

2. **Choose Store ➪ Create An iMix.** Unless you're already signed in to the iTunes Store, iTunes displays the Sign In To Publish Your iMix dialog box.

3. **Sign in as usual using your Apple ID or your AOL screen name and password, and then click the Publish button.** iTunes displays the iMixes screen, showing which songs from your playlist are available for the iMix. Figure 1.23 shows an example.

1.23 Set up your playlist as either a regular iMix or a Sport iMix, give it a catchy title, and provide a description.

4. **Check through the songs left in the iMix after the iTunes Store has removed those that aren't available.** If the iMix won't work in its reduced form, click Cancel, return to iTunes, and then fix it.

5. **If the iMix is best for sports, click the Sport iMix option button instead of the iMix option button.**

6. **Change the title for the iMix in the Title box if necessary.** You may want to give the iMix a more explicit and descriptive name on the iTunes Store than your playlist needed on your Mac.

7. **Type a description for the iMix in the Description box.** This is optional, but a good description helps draw listeners to your iMix.

8. **Click Publish.** iTunes displays the iMix Received screen to let you know that it has published the iMix to the iTunes Store.

9. **Click Done.** If you want to see your iMix on the iTunes Store, wait until you receive the e-mail message telling you that the iMix has been posted, and then click the link in the message.

Note The iTunes Store keeps each iMix for a year before removing it automatically.

Playing music through AirTunes

If you have an AirPort Express wireless access point, you can plug your speakers into it and play music through them from iTunes. You can send the music from any computer running iTunes — Windows PCs as well as Macs — either across the wireless network or via a wired Ethernet network.

To play music across a wired network, you need to turn on the AirTunes over Ethernet feature like this:

1. **Click the Desktop, choose Go ⇨ Utilities, and then double-click AirPort Utility to open AirPort Utility.**

2. **Click the AirPort Express in the list box, and then click Manual Setup to reach the configuration screen.**

3. **Click the Music button in the toolbar.**

4. **Select the Enable AirTunes over Ethernet check box.**

5. **If you want to restrict use of the speakers to people who know a password, type the password in the iTunes Speaker Password box and the Verify Password box.**

6. **Click Update.**

7. **Press ⌘+Q or choose AirPort Utility ⇨ Quit AirPort Utility.**

To start playing the music through AirPort Express, click the Speakers pop-up menu button in the lower right corner of the iTunes window, and then choose the AirPort Express from the menu. The Speakers pop-up menu button (see figure 1.24) appears only when iTunes detects an AirPort Express within striking distance.

1.24 Use the Speakers pop-up menu to switch between your computer's speakers and speakers connected to an AirPort Express.

Genius

What's even better than playing music through AirPort Express is playing music through AirPort Express *and* speakers connected to your Mac at the same time. To do this, click the Speakers pop-up menu in iTunes, and then click Multiple Speakers. The Remote Speakers dialog box opens. Select the check box next to each set of speakers you want to play music through, and then click Close.

Note

If the Speakers pop-up menu button doesn't appear in iTunes even when an AirPort Express is available, choose iTunes ⇨ Preferences, and then click the Devices button to display the Devices preferences. Select the Look for remote speakers connected with AirTunes check box to make iTunes look for the AirPort Express. While you're here, you can also select the Disable iTunes volume control for remote speakers check box if you want to prevent iTunes from controlling the volume on the speakers, and select the Allow iTunes control from remote speakers if you want the remote speakers to be able to control iTunes. Click OK when you've made your choices.

Making Videos That Work with iTunes

To enjoy iTunes as fully as possible, you'll want to use it to watch videos too. You can buy movies, TV shows, and music videos from the iTunes Store, but most likely you'll want to create your own videos as well.

Note

The Apple TV can also play any video that you can play on an iPod.

Creating videos from iMovie

If you've created your own movies in iMovie, you can easily export versions that you can play in iTunes or on an iPod. Follow these steps:

1. **Launch iMovie, and then open the movie you want to export.**

2. **Choose Share ⇨ iTunes to open the Publish your project to iTunes sheet (see figure 1.25).**

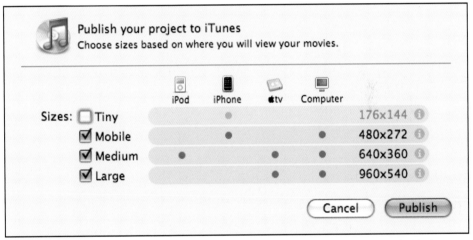

1.25 iMovie makes it easy to create versions of your movies that will play in iTunes, on the iPod or iPhone, or on Apple TV.

3. **Select the check box for each size you want to create.** The blue dots show which of the four devices — iPod, iPhone, Apple TV, and Computer — the sizes are suitable for.

Note

Even though it plays on the iPhone, the Tiny size looks poor on almost any device. The Mobile size gives far better results, but the file size is five times as large.

4. **Click Publish.** iMovie exports the version or versions you chose, adds it or them to iTunes, and activates iTunes.

5. **In iTunes, click the Movies category in the Source pane, and then test the movies you created.**

Note

See Chapters 4, 5, and 6 for detailed coverage of iMovie.

Creating videos from DVDs

Another tempting possibility is to create videos from your DVDs. That way, you can play the videos from iTunes without needing the DVD, enjoy them on an iPod or iPhone during your commute, or connect the iPod or iPhone to a TV via a cable and share them with your friends.

For legal reasons, Apple doesn't provide tools for creating videos from DVDs. Instead, you need to use a third-party application such as HandBrake (http://handbrake.fr). After ripping files from the DVD, drag the files to your iTunes library to add them to it.

Making the Most of Playlists

Listening to an entire album at a time is easy enough, but often you'll want to make your own arrangements of songs. iTunes lets you create unchanging playlists, in which you choose the songs and their order, and Smart Playlists, in which iTunes chooses the songs and their order for you.

Creating unchanging playlists

Sometimes you'll want to create playlists that contain only the songs you choose, in exactly the order you prefer them. For example, you might create a playlist for working out or running, with different tempos and rhythms to drive on your efforts; or you might create a chill-out playlist.

Displaying iTunes Content on an Apple TV

If you have an Apple TV, you can connect it to your wired or wireless network so that you can play back content from iTunes on your TV's screen and speakers.

First, pair your Apple TV with iTunes like this:

1. Turn on your TV and the Apple TV.

2. On your Mac, double-click the Source list in iTunes to expand it (if it's collapsed), and then click Apple TV. iTunes prompts you for the passcode for the Apple TV.

3. Type the passcode that appears on the TV screen into iTunes, and you'll be in business.

Now that the Apple TV is paired with iTunes, you can browse your iTunes library and your iPhoto library from the Apple TV. Select the content you want to play back — for example, a TV show from iTunes or a slideshow from iPhoto — and set it playing.

Here's how to create an unchanging playlist like this:

1. **Start a new playlist in one of these ways:**

   - Click the Create a Playlist button (the + button) in the lower left corner of the iTunes window (see figure 1.26).

   - Choose File ⇨ New Playlist or press ⌘+N.

   1.26 You can start a playlist by clicking the Create a Playlist button.

   - Select the first few songs you want to add to the playlist, and then either drag them to open space at the bottom of the Source list or choose File ⇨ New Playlist from Selection. Alternatively, press ⌘+Shift+N.

2. **In the edit box that iTunes displays, type the name you want to give the playlist, and press Return.**

3. **Drag songs to the playlist.** You can also drag an entire album, an artist, or an existing playlist to the new playlist.

4. **Click the playlist to display its contents, then drag the songs into the order you want.**

Creating Smart playlists

Unchanging playlists are easy and fun, but what's often even better is having iTunes build Smart Playlists for you — playlists that iTunes fills with songs matching the criteria you set. You can either keep the iTunes' initial selection of songs or let iTunes update a Smart Playlist automatically with new songs you add to your library.

Here's how to create a Smart Playlist. The example produces a playlist of favorite songs from the years 2000 to 2005 drawn from the Rock genres, and excluding any song that's marked as being in a compilation album.

1. **Choose File ⇨ New Smart Playlist or Option+click the Create Playlist button in the lower left corner of the iTunes window (see figure 1.27).** iTunes opens the Smart Playlist dialog box.

2. **Set up the first condition for the playlist.**

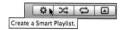

Create a Smart Playlist.

1.27 Option+click the Create Playlist button to start creating a new Smart Playlist.

Genius

You can also start creating a new Smart Playlist from the keyboard by pressing ⌘+Option+N.

● **Open the first pop-up menu and choose the field you want to use for the first condition.** For the example, choose Year. Figure 1.28 shows the choices that become available when you do this.

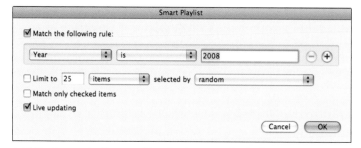

1.28 Setting up the first condition for the example playlist.

● **Open the second pop-up menu and make a suitable choice from the list.** Your choices here depend on the field you selected in the first pop-up menu. In the example, you can choose from "is," "is not," "is greater than," "is less than," and "is in the range"; choose "is in the range." The first line of the Smart Playlist dialog box changes to provide two boxes so that you can enter the range of years.

- **In the third control or set of controls, enter the details of the condition.** In this example, enter the years **2000** and **2005**, giving the condition "Year is in the range 2000 to 2005" (see figure 1.29).

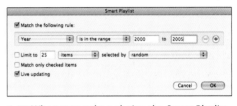

3. **If necessary, click the Add button at the right end of the first line of controls to add a second line, and then**

1.29 When you make a choice, the Smart Playlist dialog box changes as necessary to show the relevant options.

choose settings for the second condition. These are the settings you would choose to create the example playlist:

- **Open the first pop-up menu and choose Genre.**

- **In the second pop-up menu, leave the default selection — Contains — selected because this is what you need.**

- **In the text box, type** rock. If iTunes automatically suggests Rock as you type, press the Right Arrow key to accept the suggestion.

4. **If necessary, add further conditions.** The example playlist needs two more conditions (see figure 1.30):

- Rating is in the range ★★★★ to ★★★★★ (four stars to five stars).

- Compilation is false.

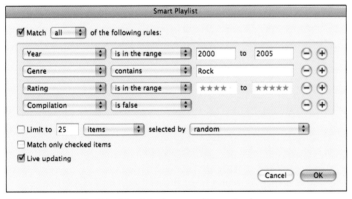

1.30 The Smart Playlist with all its four conditions in place.

5. **If you want to limit the playlist to a certain length or number of songs, select the Limit to check box and specify the limit.**

- **Type the number in the first box, and then choose Minutes, Hours, MB, GB, or Items in the first pop-up menu.**

- **In the second pop-up menu, choose how to select the songs — for example, by least often played, by highest rating, or simply at random.**

6. **Select the Match only checked items check box if you want to include only songs whose check boxes you've selected.** This setting lets you clear a song's check box and be sure it won't show up in your Smart Playlists.

7. **Select the Live updating check box if you want iTunes to update the Smart Playlist for you automatically.**

8. **Click OK to close the Smart Playlist dialog box.** iTunes creates the playlist, gives it a default name (such as Rock), and displays an edit box around the name.

9. **Type the name you want to give the Smart Playlist, then press Enter.**

Organizing Your Playlists into Folders

iTunes automatically adds each playlist to the Playlists category in the Source list, putting the Smart Playlists (with their distinctive cog icon) first in alphabetical order and then the regular playlists, also in alphabetical order.

When you've created more than a handful of playlists, you may find the Source list growing awkwardly long. To cut it down to size, you can create playlist folders and put your playlists in them. If you want, you can create a whole structure of playlist folders and subfolders.

To create a playlist folder, choose File ⇨ New Folder or press ⌘+Option+Shift+N. Type the name for the folder in the edit box that iTunes displays around the default name ("untitled folder") and press Return.

To create a subfolder, just click the existing folder first before giving the New Folder command.

When your folder is ready, drag a playlist to move it to the folder. Within the folders, iTunes sorts the Smart Playlists first, and then the playlists, both in alphabetical order.

To rename a playlist folder, double-click its name to display an edit box. Type the new name and press Return.

To delete a playlist folder, Ctrl+click or right-click it and click Delete.

To create a new playlist or Smart Playlist within a folder, click that folder, and then give the New Playlist command or New Smart Playlist command.

Creating Genius playlists

When you want to create a Smart Playlist quickly, you can use iTunes' Genius feature. The Genius is essentially a pre-configured Smart Playlist that analyzes the song you pick as a starting point and chooses a set of related songs.

Using the Genius could hardly be simpler:

1. **In your library, or in a playlist, select the song on which you want to base the Genius playlist.**

2. **Click the Start Genius button in the lower-right corner of the iTunes window (see figure 1.31) or the Genius symbol in the iTunes track readout at the top of the window.**

1.31 Click the Start Genius button to create a playlist based on the current song.

3. **iTunes creates the Genius playlist (see figure 1.32) and starts it playing.** Adjust the playlist as needed:

1.32 You can quickly change the number of songs in the Genius playlist or refresh it with new songs.

● To change the number of songs, open the Limit to pop-up menu and choose a different number: 25 songs, 50 songs, 75 songs, or 100 songs.

● To refresh the playlist but keep it based on the same song, click the Refresh button.

● To base the playlist on a song in the playlist, click that song, and then click the Start Genius button.

● To save the playlist, click the Save Playlist button. iTunes saves the playlist under the name of the first song. To change the name, double-click it in the Source list, type the new name, and then press Return.

Burning Discs and Backing Up Your Library

When you've created a playlist, you can burn it to a CD so that you can play it on just about any CD player in the world. You can also create a higher-capacity MP3 CD that will play on MP3 CD players and computers.

iTunes also lets you burn a DVD containing a playlist or a series of DVDs containing a backup of your full library.

Burning a playlist to CD

Here's how to burn a playlist to disc:

1. **In the Source list, click the playlist you want to burn to CD.**

Note iTunes gives the CD the same name as the playlist, so if you want to give the CD a different name, rename the playlist before burning the CD. You can restore the playlist's original name after the burn if you want.

2. **Click the Burn Disc button that appears toward the lower right corner of the iTunes window.** iTunes displays the Burn Settings dialog box (see figure 1.33).

3. **Choose the burning speed in the Preferred Speed pop-up menu.** Usually, it's best to choose Maximum Possible to let iTunes use the burner's fastest speed; but if you find the discs you burn contain errors, try throttling back the speed.

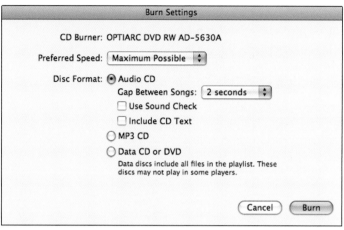

1.33 iTunes' Burn Settings dialog box lets you tell iTunes which type of CD you want to create.

Genius If your Mac has two or more burner drives, you can use the CD Burner pop-up menu in the Burn Settings dialog box to choose which drive to use. If your Mac has a single burner drive (as most Macs do), CD Burner appears as a readout rather than a pop-up menu.

4. **Select the option button for the type of disc you want to create:**

- **Audio CD.** This is the type of CD you can play in any CD player, from a basic boom-box to a top-of-the-line deck. An audio CD can contain up to around 80 minutes of audio. The audio is uncompressed, so it's full quality.

- **MP3 CD.** This is a CD that contains only MP3 files — you can't include other types of audio files (such as AAC or Apple Lossless Encoding files). The amount of music an MP3 CD can contain depends on the MP3 bitrate, but you can get up to about 11 hours at decent quality (128 Kbps) or fewer hours at higher quality. MP3 CDs play only in MP3 CD players and computers, not regular CD players.

- **Data CD or DVD.** This is a computer CD or DVD that happens to contain only audio files. You use this type of disc for backup or file transfer. Data CDs or DVDs play only on computers, not in regular CD players or in most regular DVD players.

5. **If you chose to create an audio CD, choose the next three options:**

- In the Gap Between Songs pop-up menu, choose the number of seconds for iTunes to put between songs: Either choose None, or a number of seconds between 1 second and 5 seconds. A gap of 2 seconds or so helps when you're ripping the CD with iTunes or another audio program.

39

- Select the Sound Check check box only if you want to even out the volume across the CD. The advantage of this normalization is that you don't get a CD with some songs far quieter than others. The disadvantage is that normalization compresses the dynamic range of the songs, which makes them sound less dramatic and can make the CD seem monotonous.

- Select the Include CD Text check box to put CD text — artist and song information — on the CD. Some CD players (especially car CD players) can display CD text, which is handy for keeping track of what you're listening to.

6. **Click Burn to close the Burn Settings dialog box.**

7. **When iTunes prompts you to insert a blank disc, do so.** iTunes then burns the playlist to the disc.

8. **Eject the disc and label it.**

Genius

Before you give the disc to someone else or file it away for backup, test it to double-check that the burn was successful. If you burned an audio CD, test it either in your Mac or any CD player. If you burned an MP3 CD, use your Mac or an MP3 CD–capable CD player. If you burned a data CD or DVD, use your Mac or another computer.

Note

To help discourage copyright infringement, iTunes lets you burn any playlist to disc only seven times. Once you hit this limit, you can create another playlist and burn that one up to seven times. The replacement playlist can contain the same songs in the same order as the original, so this limitation is only an inconvenience.

Burning a playlist to DVD for backup or file transfer

iTunes can also burn a playlist to DVD as long as your Mac has a DVD burner drive. DVDs are great for backing up your library or for transferring files from your Mac to another computer. You can't play music from audio DVDs in most non-computer DVD players.

Here's how to burn a DVD:

1. **Click the playlist in the Source pane, and then click the Burn Disc button.**

2. **Choose the Data CD or DVD option button in the Burn Settings dialog box.**

3. **Insert a disc when iTunes prompts you to do so, and then click the Data DVD button in the confirmation dialog box that appears (see figure 1.34).**

4. **If the playlist you've chosen is too long to fit on the DVD, iTunes warns you (see figure 1.35).** Click the Cancel button if you want to slim down the playlist until it fits on the DVD. Click the Data Discs button if you don't mind breaking the playlist among two or more DVDs.

1.34 iTunes double-checks that you want to create a data DVD.

5. **When the burn is complete, eject the disc and label it.** Then put it back in your Mac and make sure its contents are all present and correct.

1.35 iTunes warns you if the playlist won't fit on the DVD you've provided.

Note

If you've chosen a low-capacity, single-layer DVD by mistake, cancel the burn so that you can eject the disc and substitute a higher-capacity, dual-layer DVD.

Ejecting a Disc After Canceling a Burn

If you cancel a burn, the disc stays in your Mac, but it appears in neither the Devices list in iTunes nor in the Sidebar in the Finder. To eject the disc, use Disk Utility like this:

1. Click the Desktop or the Finder icon on the Dock, and then choose Go ⇨ Utilities to open a Finder window showing the Utilities folder.

2. Double-click Disk Utility to open Disk Utility.

3. In the left box, click the entry for the DVD drive, and then click the Eject button on the toolbar.

4. Choose Disk Utility ⇨ Quit Disk Utility to quit Disk Utility.

Exporting and Importing Playlists

Another way of sharing a playlist is to export it from one computer and import it on another. When you export a playlist, iTunes simply creates a list of the songs in the playlist — it doesn't include the song files themselves. Then when you import the playlist on another computer, iTunes adds to it only the songs that are available on that computer.

These restrictions mean that exporting and importing playlists work best when you're using the same library. For example, if you put the same set of songs on your MacBook and your iMac, you can export a playlist from the iMac and use it on the MacBook without problems.

Here's how to export a playlist:

1. **Click the playlist in the Source list.**

2. **Choose File ⇨ Library ⇨ Export to open the Save dialog box.**

3. **Change the playlist's name if necessary, and select the folder in which to save the file.**

4. **Choose XML in the Format pop-up menu.** XML is the best choice when you're sharing a playlist with another computer running iTunes. The other formats — Plain Text and Unicode — are useful for exporting playlists to applications that can't read XML.

5. **Click Save.**

To import a playlist, choose File ⇨ Import, select the playlist in the Import dialog box, and then click Open. If the playlist contains songs that your library doesn't have, iTunes warns you.

Restoring your music library from backup

After restoring your music library by inserting your first backup disc in your Mac's optical drive and following the prompts, you may need to delete extra copies of playlists. iTunes puts the playlists from each backup into a separate folder named Restored Playlists and the date (in YYYY-MM-DD format) and time (in HH:MM:SS format), so you end up with folders named like this:

- Restored Playlists 2008-12-11 11:12:44

- Restored Playlists 2008-12-11 11:20:53

Check that the latest playlists are the ones you want, and then delete the rest. (If you delete the wrong ones, no great worry — you can restore them again from your backups if necessary.)

Genius

If you have an iPod high enough in capacity to store your entire library, you can use your iPod as a backup. Unless you lose (or damage) both your iPod and your Mac at the same time, you can restore your library to your Mac from the copy your iPod contains. But you can't use iTunes to restore your library from your iPod. Instead, you need to use third-party software such as iPod Access (www.ipodaccess.com), iPodRip (www.thelittleappfactory.com), or Senuti (www.fadingred.org/senuti) to restore the library from the iPod to your Mac.

Using Your iPod to Carry Files

Your iPod is great for playing back music and (except for the iPod shuffle) video, but you can also use it to carry files with you. This is handy both for keeping your essential documents with you and for transferring large files from one computer to another.

Here's how to set up your iPod for carrying files:

1. **Connect your iPod to your Mac.** If iTunes isn't already running, Mac OS X launches it. Your iPod appears in the Devices category in the Source list, and iTunes displays the control screens for the iPod.

2. **Click the Summary tab (for an iPod classic or iPod nano) or the Settings tab (for an iPod shuffle).** Figure 1.36 shows the Summary tab for an iPod classic.

3. **Select the Enable disk use check box.** iTunes displays a dialog box warning you that you need to eject the iPod manually (see figure 1.37).

4. **Select the Do not warn me again check box, and then click OK.** The dialog box closes.

5. **Click Apply.** iTunes turns on disk mode for the iPod and synchronizes the iPod.

1.36 To use your iPod to carry files, select the Enable disk use check box on the Summary tab or Settings tab.

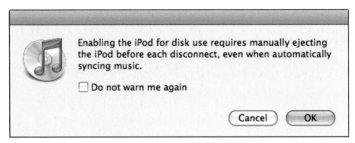

1.37 Tell iTunes you're prepared to eject your iPod manually before you disconnect it.

Your iPod now appears as a drive in the Finder (see figure 1.38), and you can store files and folders on it as you would any other removable drive.

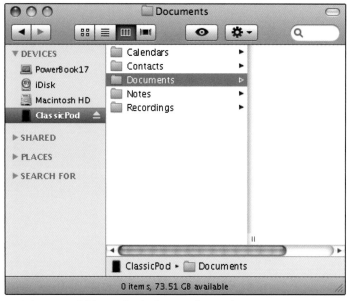

1.38 Creating a folder on the iPod in a Finder window.

Caution When you display the iPod's contents in a Finder window, you'll see several folders, such as Calendars, Contacts, and Notes. You won't see your songs and videos, which are hidden in an invisible folder named iPod_Control. Don't store your files in one of the iPod's folders. Instead, create one or more folders of your own.

After you enable disk mode on your iPod, you must eject it before you disconnect it. To eject the iPod, click the Eject button next to its item in the Source list in iTunes or in the Sidebar of a Finder window.

Genius If you have an iPod touch or an iPhone rather than one of the smaller iPods, you can't use this technique to store and move files. Instead, look at third-party software such as DiskAid (www.digidna.net/diskaid) or PhoneView that lets you put files on an iPod touch or iPhone.

How Do I Get My Photos into iPhoto?

Constrain: 2304 × 3072   Cancel   Apply

You've taken the photos with your digital camera, so now you're ready to add them to your iPhoto library. Importing photos from a digital camera takes only moments, but you can also import photos from folders on your Mac (or other computers) or directly from e-mail messages. And if you have hard copies of photos (or other documents), you can add them to your library too by using Image Capture. First, though, we'll take a moment to explore the

Navigating the iPhoto Interface

iPhoto packs a ton of power into an easy-to-use interface, so first make sure you know what's what in iPhoto. Figure 2.1 shows the main iPhoto window with the key elements labeled. Most of the action takes place in this window, but you can open a photo for editing full screen so that you can see as much of a photo as possible.

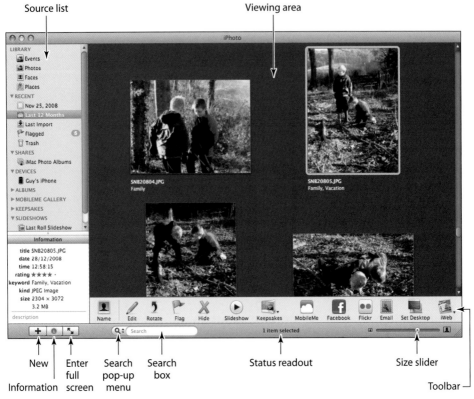

2.1 The main iPhoto window.

Here's what the main elements in the user interface do:

- **Source list.** This pane shows your iPhoto library, recent items, libraries other people are sharing on your network, any connected devices (such as a digital camera), photo albums, MobileMe Gallery, keepsakes (such as books), and slideshows you've created. You can click the gray disclosure triangle to the left of a category to expand or collapse its contents.

- **Viewing area.** This is where you view your photos, either as small thumbnail versions or taking up the whole area. Drag the Size slider to change the size of the thumbnails. From here, you can open a photo for viewing or editing.

- **Toolbar.** This contains buttons for manipulating the photo or photos you've selected.

- **Information pane.** This shows information about the photo, photos, or other item you've selected.

Setting iPhoto's Preferences So You Can Work Quickly

Before you start importing photos, take a few minutes to choose suitable settings for iPhoto's preferences. Like most applications, iPhoto has several screens of preferences, and having the right settings enables you to work much more quickly and comfortably.

Choose iPhoto ⇨ Preferences to display the Preferences dialog box, and then click the General button to display the General preferences if they're not automatically displayed. Then work through the following sections, choosing settings in the six categories of preferences as you go.

Choosing General preferences

The General preferences (see figure 2.2) are essential to working quickly and easily in iPhoto, so you'll want to check or change all the settings.

On the Sources line, choose whether to show the Last 12 Months album in the Source list. (An *album* in iPhoto is simply a way of grouping photos.) If you want, change the number of months this album shows. For example, if you take many photos, two or three months may be a better choice than 12 months.

Select the Show item counts check box if you want the number of photos to appear next to each item in the Source list.

In the Double-click photo area, select the Edits photo option button or the Magnifies photo option button to tell iPhoto what to do when you double-click a photo.

On the Rotate line, select the clockwise-rotation option button or the counterclockwise-rotation option button to specify the standard direction of rotation. You can reverse the rotation by Option+clicking the Rotate button on the toolbar.

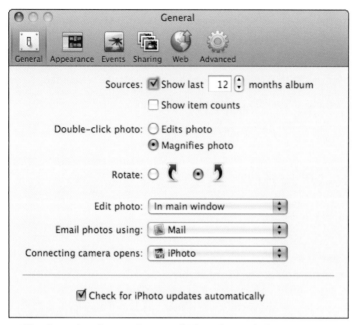

2.2 The General preferences let you tell iPhoto how to behave.

In the Edit photo pop-up menu, choose how you want to edit your photos. The first two options — In main window and Using full screen — use iPhoto. The last option lets you use another application, such as Adobe Photoshop. Choose the last item on the menu, which appears as "In application" until you choose an application. iPhoto displays an Open dialog box. Select the application you want to use, and then click Open. The application then appears in the Edit photo pop-up menu — for example, "In Adobe Photoshop CS."

In the Email photos using pop-up menu, make sure that iPhoto has selected your preferred mail application for sending photos — for example, Mail or Microsoft Entourage.

In the Connecting camera opens pop-up menu, choose the application you want Mac OS X to fire up when you connect a camera. If you use iPhoto for managing your photos, iPhoto is the best choice here. The alternatives are normally Image Capture and No application.

Select the Check for iPhoto updates automatically check box if you want iPhoto to check for updates when you launch it. Clear this check box if you prefer to use Software Update to check for updates.

Choosing Appearance preferences

In the Appearance preferences (see figure 2.3), choose how you want iPhoto to display and organize the photos.

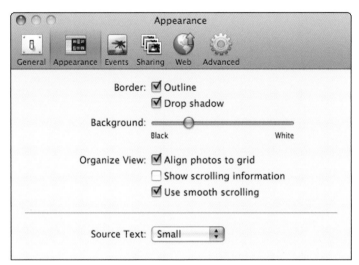

2.3 In the Appearance preferences, you can choose the border style, background color, how to organize the view, and the size of text in the Source list.

Experiment with the Border settings — you can apply an outline, a drop shadow, or both — and the Background slider. iPhoto shows the changes immediately while you work in the Preferences dialog box, so you can quickly find settings that suit you.

Select the Align photos to grid check box if you want iPhoto to use a rigid grid alignment rather than display each photo at a size that fits best.

Select the Show scrolling information check box if you want iPhoto to display information about the current photos as you scroll down — for example, the month and year. Scrolling information is useful for locating photos within large albums or Events.

Select the Use smooth scrolling check box if you want iPhoto to scroll smoothly rather than in jumps.

Genius

Smooth scrolling in iPhoto appears not to work consistently for every mouse and every Mac, so you may find you get better results by turning smooth scrolling off.

51

Choose the size of the text in the Source list — Small or Large — from the Source Text pop-up menu.

Choosing Events preferences

Events preferences (see figure 2.4) let you control how iTunes handles Events. Events are the main means of dividing your photos into different groups. A photo can belong to only one Event, but you can move a photo from one Event to another as needed. iPhoto can automatically create Events for you when you import photos, but you can also create Events manually if you prefer.

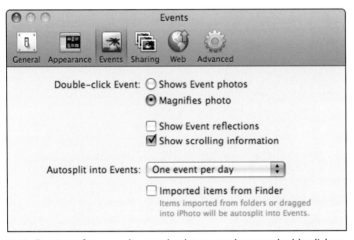

2.4 In Events preferences, choose what happens when you double-click an Event and decide whether to let iPhoto automatically split photos into separate Events when you import them.

In the Double-click Event area, select the Shows Event photos option button if you want to see all the photos in an Event when you double-click the Event. Select the Magnifies photo option if you want to jump directly to the photo to which you've browsed within the Event.

Select the Show Event reflections check box if you want to see a small reflection of the Event underneath it. This effect is visually cool but of no practical use.

Select the Show scrolling information check box if you want iPhoto to display the month and year as you scroll through Events. This information helps you find Events faster and more easily.

The most important setting in Events preferences is the Autosplit into Events pop-up menu, which lets you control how long an Event is. Choose One Event per day, One Event per week, Two-hour gaps, or Eight-hour gaps to determine how long the Events that iPhoto uses are.

Select the Imported items from Finder check box if you want iPhoto to split photos into Events when you drag them into iPhoto from a Finder window or use the File ⇨ Import to Library command.

Genius

If the photos you import from the Finder are collections from different dates, you'll do better to clear the Imported items from Finder check box and create such Events as you need manually. Otherwise, iPhoto creates separate Events for photos that belong together.

Choosing Sharing preferences

iPhoto's Sharing preferences (see figure 2.5) let you share your photos with other iPhoto users on your network and enjoy the photos they're sharing.

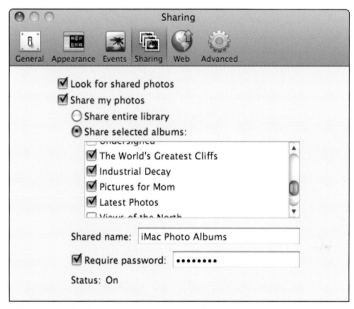

2.5 Choose whether to share some or all of your photos on the network and whether to look for photos others are sharing.

To see the photos others are sharing, select the Look for shared photos check box.

To share your own photos, follow these steps:

1. **Select the Share my photos check box.** iPhoto enables all the controls below this check box.

2. **Select the Share entire library option button if you want to share your entire library.** To share just some of it, select the Share selected albums option button, and then select the check box for each album you want to share.

3. **Type a descriptive name for your shared photos in the Shared name box.**

4. **If you want to password-protect your shared photos, select the Require password check box and type a password.**

Choosing Web preferences

iPhoto's Web preferences (see figure 2.6) let you choose and check the following:

- **Include location information for published photos.** Select this check box if you want iPhoto to include information about the location where a photo was taken when you publish that photo on MobileMe or the Web.

- **Check for new published photos.** In this pop-up menu, choose a setting to tell iPhoto how often you want to check for new photos that have been published on the Web. iPhoto lets you choose from Automatically, Manually, Every Hour, Every Day, and Every Week; the default setting is Automatically. If you choose Manually or one of the less-frequent settings, click Check Now to force iPhoto to check for new published photos right this moment.

- **iDisk Storage.** Use this readout to see how much of the available space on your iDisk you've used. If you're running out of space, click Buy More to launch Safari and open the MobileMe login page. There, you can log in to manage your MobileMe account and purchase more iDisk storage.

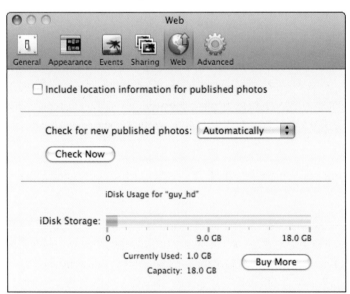

2.6 In the Web preferences, tell iPhoto whether to include location information in published photos and how often to check for new published photos. You can also check how much of your iDisk storage is left.

Choosing Advanced preferences

The Advanced preferences (see figure 2.7) contains only five settings, but they're important ones.

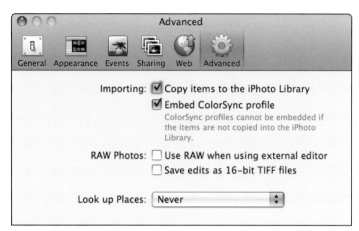

2.7 In the Advanced preferences, choose whether to copy items to your library and whether to embed ColorSync profiles in the photos, how to handle RAW photos, and whether to look up Places.

In the Importing area, select the Copy items to the iPhoto Library check box if you want iPhoto to make copies of photos you import from folders on your Mac or your network. This is iPhoto's normal behavior, and it's usually helpful because it puts all your photos in one place and makes backup simpler. But if you already have a ton of photos on your Mac and want to use the photos in their current folders, you can clear this check box to prevent iPhoto from making copies of them.

If you want to embed ColorSync profiles in your photos, select the Embed ColorSync profile check box. This check box is available only if you've selected the Copy items to the iPhoto Library check box, because iPhoto restricts your use of ColorSync profiles to photo files stored within iPhoto's own folders.

There are also two settings that apply only to RAW photos (see the sidebar "Understanding What RAW Image Files Are"):

- **Use RAW when using external editor.** Select this check box to use an external graphics editor (such as Photoshop or Aperture) for editing your RAW image files. With this check box selected, iPhoto passes the RAW image file to the external graphics editor instead of passing the JPEG or TIFF file that iPhoto uses (see the next option).

Genius

If you clear the Copy items to the iPhoto Library check box, iPhoto adds to your library only a reference to each photo you import — a pointer that tells iPhoto which folder the photo is located in. But if you edit the photo in iPhoto and save the changes, iPhoto creates a copy of the photo so that it can save the changes while leaving the original untouched. This setting doesn't affect files you import from your digital camera.

- **Save edits as 16-bit TIFF files.** When you import or edit a RAW image file, iPhoto normally saves the result as a JPEG file, which has lower quality but takes up less space. Select this check box to make iPhoto save the imported edited file as a 16-bit TIFF file instead, which is higher quality than the JPEG file.

Finally, use the Look up Places pop-up menu to tell iPhoto whether to look up the places in your photos. The choice is simple: Automatically or Never.

Note

ColorSync is a color-management feature built into Mac OS X. ColorSync helps you to standardize colors on different monitors and printers by providing various methods for matching colors visually. Embedding ColorSync profiles in your photos can help you to print the photos so that the prints have the same colors with which you view the photos on your Mac's screen.

Understanding What RAW Image Files Are

RAW image files are minimally processed image files that are also called *digital negatives* — the digital equivalent of negatives in film photography. You can set most digital SLR cameras and advanced models of digital compact cameras to produce RAW image files instead of converted image files in formats such as JPEG or TIFF.

A RAW image file contains every bit of data captured by the camera that took the picture rather than a converted and compressed form of that data. RAW image files are larger than converted image files and provide higher quality. They're mostly used by professional photographers, but you can use them either within iPhoto or with an external editor such as Apple Aperture or Adobe Photoshop.

RAW image files come in various formats. To see a list of the digital cameras that produce RAW image files you can use in iPhoto, see the Aperture 2 list at www.apple.com/aperture/specs/raw.html. (iPhoto supports the same list of cameras as Aperture 2.)

Customizing the toolbar

You can quickly customize the iPhoto toolbar by choosing View ⇨ Show in Toolbar and then click-ing the item you want to add or remove: Email, Set Desktop, Printing, Order Prints, MobileMe, Facebook, Flickr, Send to iWeb, Send to iDVD, and Burn.

Importing Photos

After you've chosen preferences, you're ready to import photos from your digital camera, a mem-ory card, a folder, or even an e-mail message.

Importing photos from your digital camera

Here's how to import photos from your digital camera:

1. **If the camera connects directly to your Mac via USB, connect it (and switch it on, if nec-essary).** Otherwise, remove the memory card from the camera and insert it in a memory card reader connected to your Mac.

2. **When Mac OS X notices the camera or memory card containing photos, it launches or activates iPhoto and prompts you to import the photos (see figure 2.8).**

Note   If you chose No application or another application than iPhoto in the Connecting camera opens pop-up menu in iPhoto's General preferences (as discussed earlier in this chapter), you must import the photos into iPhoto manually. See the next section for details.

3. **Type a descriptive name for the Event in the Event Name text box.**

4. **If you want, type a generic description for the photos in the Description text box.** You can give each photo its own description later.

5. **If you want iPhoto to split the photos into different Events by date and time, select the Autosplit Events After Importing check box.** iPhoto uses the Event length you set in Events preferences earlier in this chapter — for example, one day, or two hours.

6. **If the camera or memory card contains photos you've imported before, select the Hide photos already imported check box to make iPhoto hide these photos so you don't try to import them again.** Hiding the photos you've already imported also lets iPhoto show you the new photos on the camera or memory card more quickly.

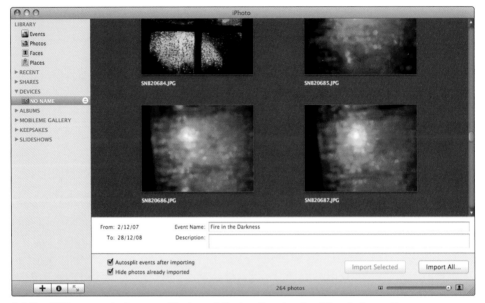

2.8 Mac OS X automatically opens iPhoto and displays thumbnails of the photos on the camera or storage card you've connected.

7. **Choose which photos you want to import:**

   • To import all the photos shown, click Import All.

   • To import only some of the photos, select them by dragging across a range or by clicking the first photo and then holding down ⌘ while you click each of the other photos. Then click Import Selected.

8. **iPhoto imports the photos you chose, and then prompts you to delete the photos from the camera or memory card (see figure 2.9).**

Importing Videos from Your Digital Camera

If your digital camera takes video files as well as still photos, you can easily import the videos into iPhoto along with the still photos. iPhoto shows a white camera icon in the lower left corner of the thumbnail for each video file. Otherwise, the procedure for importing videos is the same as for still photos.

Genius If you want to add the photos to a specific album, you can simply drag them from the camera or memory card to that album. In the album, iPhoto creates references to the photos, so they show up in it. iPhoto also adds the photos to your library as usual.

2.9 Choose whether to let iPhoto delete the photos from the camera or memory card.

Dealing with duplicate imported photos

When importing pictures from a camera, it's all too easy to import some of them twice — for example, because you forgot to reformat the memory card after putting it back in the camera.

iPhoto helps you avoid duplicate imports by warning you when you're about to import a digital photo you've already imported, even if you've changed the version that's already in iPhoto. Figure 2.10 shows an example of the warning.

Select the Apply to all duplicates check box if you want iPhoto to carry your decision through to all duplicate photos in the batch you're importing rather than prompt you to rule on each one. Then click Import if you want to import the photo anyway, Don't Import to skip importing it, or Cancel if you want to cancel the import.

2.10 iPhoto makes certain you know you're importing a duplicate photo. In this example, the version that's already in the library has been changed.

Ejecting the camera's volume

After importing all the pictures you want from the camera or the memory card, eject the camera or memory card by clicking the Eject button next to it in the Source list. Alternatively, Control+click or right-click the camera or memory card in the Source list and then click Eject. When iPhoto removes the camera or memory card from the Source list, you can safely unplug it.

Caution   Never unplug your digital camera or memory card reader without ejecting it. Doing so normally produces a Device Removal error message in Mac OS X, but it can also cause iPhoto or even Mac OS X to stop responding.

Importing photos with the Import command

If your photos are in a folder or on a CD or DVD rather than on a camera or a memory card, you can bring them into your library by using the Import command.

1. **Choose File ➪ Import to Library or press ⌘+Shift+I to open the Import Photos dialog box.**

2. **Select the photos you want to import.** You can import either an entire folder or one or more photos from within a folder.

3. **Click Import.**

Note   When you import a folder of photos from a Windows PC on your network, iPhoto may display the Unreadable Files dialog box telling you that a file named Thumbs.db could not be imported because it is in an unrecognized format. Don't worry — simply click OK and disregard the error. Thumbs.db is a database file Windows builds that contains thumbnail versions of the photos. You don't need to import this file into iPhoto.

Importing photos from the Finder or e-mail

Instead of using the Import command, you can simply select a photo — or several, or a folder containing photos — in a Finder window and drag it to the viewing area in iPhoto to add the photo or photos to your library.

If you receive a photo in the body of an e-mail message, you can drag the photo from your e-mail application (such as Mail or Entourage) to the viewing area in iPhoto.

If you receive a photo as an attachment in Mail, click and hold down the Save button on the attachment line, and then choose Add to iPhoto from the menu that appears. In other e-mail applications, you may need to save the attached photo to a folder, and then drag the photo from a Finder window to the viewing area in iPhoto.

Understanding Which Picture Formats iPhoto Can Handle

You can use several different photo file formats with iPhoto. These are the three file formats for which iPhoto provides full support:

- **JPEG.** A file format developed by the Joint Photographic Experts Group, JPEG is the most widely used format for digital photos. JPEG typically uses *lossy compression* (compression in which data is discarded) to reduce the file size of the photos but maintains high enough quality for general use. Many digital cameras take only JPEGs; others take JPEGs unless you change the file format.

- **TIFF.** The Tagged Image File Format uses either no compression or *lossless compression* (compression in which no data is discarded) to store images at full quality. Some digital cameras can create TIFF files as well as JPEG files.

- **RAW.** As discussed earlier in this chapter, a RAW file is a *digital negative* that stores minimally processed data. When you work with RAW files in iPhoto, iPhoto actually saves the results as a JPEG file or a TIFF file (depending on your choice in Advanced preferences).

These three file formats can all contain *metadata*, information about the photos such as the date and time they were taken, the camera and exposure used, and other details. You can view this information by choosing Photos ➪ Show Extended Photo Info or pressing ⌘+I. iPhoto can read metadata from all three formats but can write metadata only to the JPEG and TIFF formats.

You can import other types of photos into iPhoto, such as PNG (Portable Network Graphics) files, but iPhoto doesn't fully support them.

Scanning Photos Using Image Capture

To get photos that you have as prints (hard copies) into your iPhoto library, you need to create digital versions of the photos by using a scanner.

Mac OS X includes a powerful scanning application called Image Capture that you can use to control most scanners. However, if your scanner came with its own software, you may prefer to use that application instead because it may offer extra features that tie in with the scanner's capabilities.

Here's how to scan a picture using Image Capture:

1. **Turn on the scanner, and place the picture on the scanning surface.**

2. **Press the Start button or wake-up button on the scanner.** Your Mac notices the scanner and launches Image Capture.

3. **Image Capture makes the scanner run a quick scan of the picture to provide an overview, which it displays (see figure 2.11).**

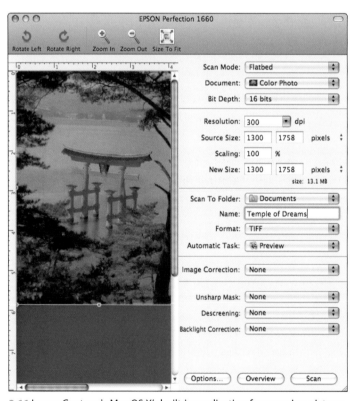

2.11 Image Capture is Mac OS X's built-in application for scanning pictures.

4. **If you need to rotate the picture, click the Rotate Left button or the Rotate Right button as needed.**

5. **If you need to zoom in to get the picture to a size at which you can crop it, click the Zoom In button.** Click the Zoom Out button if you need to zoom out again, or click the Size To Fit button to resize the picture to the biggest size at which the whole thing fits in the preview area.

6. **Drag across the preview to tell Image Capture which part of it you want to capture.**

7. **In the Scan Mode pop-up menu, choose the scan mode — for example, Flatbed or Transparency.**

8. **In the Document pop-up menu, choose Color Photo for a color scan or B/W Photo for a black-and-white scan.**

9. **In the Bit Depth pop-up menu, choose 16 bits (or higher, if your scanner offers it) for a high-quality scan or 8 bits for a modest-quality scan.**

Genius

Scan at a high bit depth and resolution to get as high-quality a file as possible. You can then create lower-resolution versions from iPhoto if you need them. Watch the little Size readout above the Scan To Folder pop-up menu to see the file size of the scanned image.

10. **In the Resolution pop-up menu, choose the resolution.** For good results in photographs, choose 300 dots per inch (dpi). Using resolutions higher than this will make the files much larger and also make the scans take longer, so it may not be worthwhile.

11. **If necessary, use the Source Size boxes to adjust the width and height of the area you're scanning.** You can choose pixels, inches, or centimeters in the pop-up menu to the right of the boxes.

12. **If you want to reduce the image, choose the percentage in the Scaling box.** Press Tab to move the focus away from this box, and the new width and height appear in the New Size boxes.

13. **In the Scan To Folder pop-up menu, choose which folder to store the scanned file in.**

14. **Type a name for the scanned file in the Name box.**

15. **Select the format in the Format pop-up menu.** Your choices are JPG, TIFF, PNG, and PDF. TIFF is the best choice for high-quality pictures you will use with iPhoto. JPG is the best choice for lower-quality pictures for use with iPhoto. PDF is good for scanning documents.

16. **In the Automatic Task pop-up menu, choose the application in which you want Image Capture to open the scanned file.** For example, choose Preview.

17. **If you need to tweak the colors on the image, open the Image Correction pop-up menu and choose Automatic or Manual instead of None.** If you select Manual, use the Brightness, Tint, Hue, and Saturation sliders that Image Capture displays (see figure 2.12) to produce the colors you want.

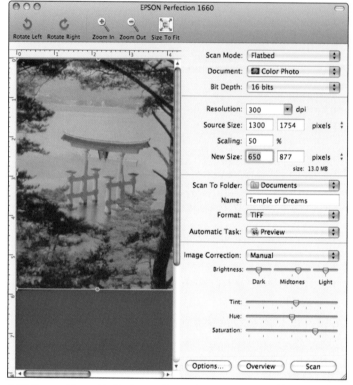

2.12 Choose Manual in the Image Correction pop-up menu if you need to adjust the colors in the picture you're scanning.

18. **If you need to adjust the sharpness of the picture, choose Low, Medium, or High instead of None in the Unsharp Mask pop-up menu.**

19. **If you need to remove cross-hatching from the scanned picture, open the Descreening pop-up menu, and choose General, Newspaper (85 lines per inch; lpi), Magazine (133 lpi), or Fine Prints (175 lpi).**

20. **If you need to improve the lighting of the picture, choose Low, Medium, or High in the Backlight Correction pop-up menu.**

21. **Click Scan to scan the picture.** Image Capture saves the file and then displays it in the application you chose in the Automatic Task pop-up menu so that you can see if the result is satisfactory. (If you chose None in the Automatic Task pop-up menu, Image Capture simply saves the file.)

22. **Scan further images as necessary, or quit Image Capture.**

Sharing a Scanner or Camera Using Image Capture

Image Capture makes it easy to share a scanner or camera among the Macs on your network.

Genius

If you install Bonjour for Windows on your Windows XP or Windows Vista computers, the PCs can also access the devices that the Macs are sharing via the Bonjour networking protocol. You can download Bonjour for Windows for free from www.apple.com/support/downloads/bonjourforwindows.html.

Start by setting up sharing on the Mac to which the scanner or camera is connected:

1. **Click the Desktop, choose Go ⇨ Applications, and then double-click Image Capture to open Image Capture.**

2. **If Image Capture displays a dialog box asking you to choose the device you want, click the device.**

3. **Choose Devices ⇨ Browse Devices to open the Image Capture Device Browser window.**

4. **Click Sharing to open the Sharing panel.**

5. **Select the Share my devices check box to enable the other controls in the Sharing panel (see figure 2.13).**

6. **If you want to share the scanner or camera via Bonjour Bookmarks in Safari, select the Enable Web Sharing check box.**

7. **Choose whether to accept the default name in the Shared name box or type a more descriptive name.**

2.13 Here's where you tell Image Capture to share a scanner or camera with other Macs and PCs on your network.

8. **If you need to prevent unauthorized users from using the scanner or camera, select the Password check box.** Type the password in the box.

9. **Click OK to close the Sharing panel.**

10. **Choose Image Capture ⇨ Quit Image Capture if you're ready to quit Image Capture.**

Now connect to the shared scanner or camera from another Mac like this:

1. **Click the Desktop, choose Go ⇨ Applications, and then double-click Image Capture to open Image Capture.**

2. **Choose Devices ⇨ Browse Devices to open the Image Capture Device Browser window.**

3. **If the Remote Devices category is collapsed, click the sideways disclosure triangle to expand it.** Under Remote Devices, expand the listing for the Mac that's sharing the scanner, and then click the scanner or camera (see figure 2.14).

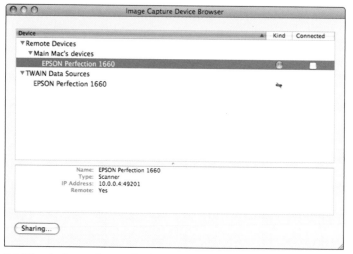

2.14 Use the Image Capture Device Browser to find a scanner or camera that one of your other Macs is sharing.

4. **Select the Connected check box.** If Image Capture prompts you for the password, type it, and then click OK.

You're now ready to use the scanner or camera across the network, just as if it were connected to your Mac rather than the remote Mac.

Note

If you see the message "Device is in use" when you try to connect to a remote scanner or camera, it usually means that Image Capture is open on the remote Mac. Close it, and you'll be able to use the scanner or camera.

How Do I Organize, Edit, and Share My Photos?

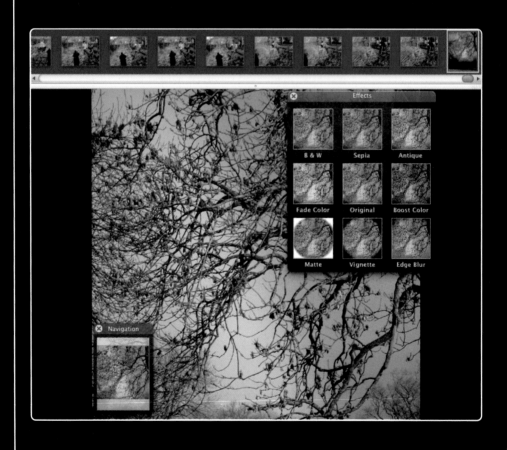

After importing your photos into your iPhoto library, you're ready to start making the most of them. One essential is to organize the photos effectively using iPhoto's Events, Faces, and Places tools, and to create albums so that you quickly put your hands on the photos you want. A second essential is to use iPhoto's powerful tools effectively to give your photos full power and impact. You may also want to separate your photos into two or more libraries for ease of use, and you'll almost certainly want to create compelling slideshows, share your photos with others, and use the photos extensively within the Mac OS X user interface.

Organizing Your Photos

You can quickly add large numbers of photos to your iPhoto library by using the techniques discussed in the previous chapter.

To get the most out of your library, you need to organize your photos effectively into Events and albums. iPhoto also lets you organize photos by people's faces using its face-recognition technology and by location using its Places feature.

To sort through your photos easily, you need to flag photos of interest, and add keywords, descriptions, and ratings to as many photos as possible.

Working with Events

iPhoto gives you four main ways of organizing your photos: by Event (which iPhoto capitalizes like that), by Faces, by Places, and by Album.

Understanding what an Event is

An *Event* is a way of organizing related photos together. Each time you import a set of photos from a digital camera or from a folder, iPhoto organizes them into Events by time and date. As you saw in Chapter 2, you can set iPhoto to create different Events for intervals of two hours, eight hours, one day, or a whole week.

Genius
To organize your photos, you can easily rename an Event or move photos from one Event to another.

In Events view, you see each Event represented by a single photo, the *key photo* (which you can choose). But you can position the mouse pointer over an Event to scroll through each of the Event's photos in turn. This is a great way of browsing quickly to the photo you want.

Genius
Events and albums can seem confusing at first. The big difference between the two is that a photo can appear in only one Event at a time, whereas you can add a photo to as many albums as you want.

Viewing an Event's photos

How you display the photos in an Event depends on the setting you chose for Double-click Event in Events preferences:

- **Double-click the Event.** If you've selected the Shows Event photos option button, either double-click an Event to display its photos or click the Show Photos button.

- **Click the Show Photos button on the Event.** If you've selected the Magnifies photo option button, click the Show Photos button on the Event (see figure 3.1).

When you display the photos within the Event, you see a small version of each photo (see figure 3.2). You can change the size by dragging the Size slider in the lower right corner of the iPhoto window.

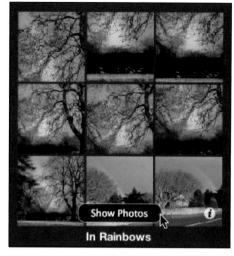

3.1 Hold the mouse pointer over the Show Photos button to display miniatures of the photos in the Event. Click the button to open the Event and display the photos.

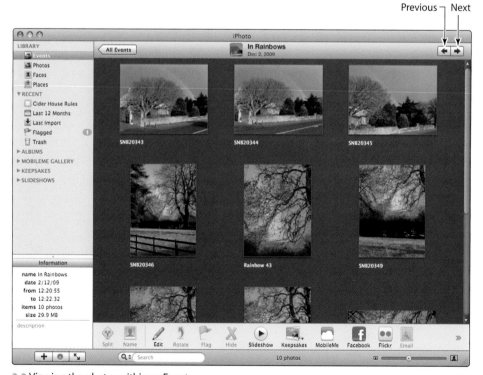

3.2 Viewing the photos within an Event

71

From here, you can double-click a photo to make iPhoto zoom in to the full area of the preview window and display the other photos as miniatures in a bar across the top of the window, or click a photo and use a toolbar button to manipulate it — for example, click the Rotate button to rotate the photo, or click the Edit button to open the photo for editing.

Click the All Events button when you want to go back to viewing all Events. Alternatively, click the Previous button to display the photos in the previous Event or the Next button to display those in the next Event.

Renaming an Event

iPhoto names each Event by dates, but often you'll want to give an Event a more descriptive name. You can rename an Event in any of these ways:

- **While browsing All Events.** Click the Event's name (*untitled event* until you change it) below its preview, type the name in the edit box that appears, and then press Return.

- **While browsing the Event.** Click the Event's name at the top of the window, type the new name, and then press Return.

- **Any time.** With the Event selected or opened, display the Information pane (if it's closed), select the name field, type the new name, and then press Return.

Setting the key photo for an Event

The photo that appears at the top of an Event's stack in the Events view is called the *key photo*. When iPhoto creates an Event for you, or when you create one yourself, iPhoto makes the first photo in the Event the key photo.

Sometimes this first photo will summarize the Event perfectly, but often you'll want to pick a key photo yourself. You can do so in three ways:

- **While browsing All Events.** Position the mouse pointer over the Event, then move the mouse until iPhoto displays the photo you want. Ctrl+click or right-click and choose Make Key Photo.

- **While browsing the Event.** Ctrl+click or right-click the photo and choose Make Key Photo. Or click the photo and then choose Events ⇨ Make Key Photo.

- **While browsing the Event.** Drag the photo to the icon just to the left of the Event's name at the top of the window.

Moving photos from one Event to another

Often, you'll need to move photos from one Event to another. You can do that easily like this:

1. **In the Source list, click Events to display all the Events.**

2. **Click one Event, and then ⌘-click the other Event.**

3. **Click the Show Photos button.**

4. **Drag one or more photos from one Event to the other (see figure 3.3).**

3.3 To move a photo from one Event to another, open both Events, and then drag the photo across the border.

Genius

To make it easier to manage photos, you may prefer to open an Event in a separate window. From the All Events screen, Ctrl+click or right-click the Event and choose Open in Separate Window, or click the Event and choose Events ⇨ Open in Separate Window.

Merging two Events together

If you find that iPhoto's automatic splitting has separated photos that you want to keep in the same Event, you can easily merge the two Events together. Here's what to do:

1. **In the Source list, click Events to display all the Events.**

2. **Click one Event, and then ⌘-click the other Event.**

3. **Click the Merge button on the toolbar or choose Events ⇨ Merge Events.** iPhoto displays a confirmation message.

4. **Select the Don't Ask Again check box if you want to merge more quickly in the future, and then click Merge.** iPhoto merges the photos into the first of the Events.

Splitting an Event in two

Other times, you'll need to split an Event into two or three. Follow these steps:

1. **In the Source list, click Events to display all the Events.**

2. **Open the Event you want to display.** Either double-click it or click the Show Photos button.

3. **Select the photos from which you want to create the new Event.** For example, drag through the photos.

4. **Click the Split button or choose Events ⇨ Split Event.** iPhoto creates a new Event containing the photos and names it *untitled event*. If the original Event contains photos both before and after the ones you selected, iPhoto creates two new Events, one containing the photos you selected and another containing the photos after them.

5. **Rename the new Event or Events.** Click the name, type the new name, and then press Return.

6. **Drag the photo you want to use as the key photo to the key photo box.**

Organizing photos with the Faces feature

Faces, one of the exciting new features in iPhoto '09, uses face-recognition technology to automatically identify the people in your photos. Here's how it works:

● **You teach iPhoto the name for a face.** You pick a face that's important to you and assign the name. The face must be human — Faces doesn't match animal faces, no matter how cute.

- **iPhoto scans your other photos for other instances of the same face.** iPhoto does this in the background as you do other things.

- **You check the photos iPhoto has found and confirm the ones that are right.**

Once you've identified the faces like this, you can quickly pull together albums, slideshows, or keepsakes featuring your favorite faces.

Genius

Faces is a terrific feature, but it's not all that accurate. While it can work apparent wonders, such as correctly picking one face out of a whole group, it also tends to give false positives — it's biased to finding matching faces in your photo library. Be prepared to vet every suggested match, or you'll get some surprises.

Teach iPhoto the name that matches a face

First, teach iPhoto the name for a face like this:

1. **Open the photo you want to use.** For best results, choose a picture that shows the person's face in close up, looking straight at the camera, and unobscured. The higher the resolution, the better. If you use a group photo, iPhoto picks out all the faces looking toward the camera; click the face for which you want to provide the name.

2. **Click the Name button on the toolbar.** iPhoto picks out the face and puts a white square around the area from above the eyebrows to below the mouth, including the eyes and nose but not the ears. Figure 3.4 shows an example.

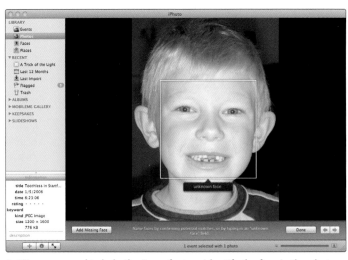

3.4 You may need to help the Faces feature identify the face in the photo. When you've done so, type in the name.

3. **If the square is in the wrong place, correct it.**

- Move the mouse pointer over the square so that iPhoto adds an X button to the upper-left corner, then click that button to remove the square.

- Click the Add Missing Face button at the bottom of the window. iPhoto adds a white square, this time with sizing handles around it, to the middle of the photo.

- Drag the square to the face, and then resize it if necessary. Drag a corner handle to resize it around the center. Option+click and drag a corner handle to keep the opposite corner stationary as you drag.

- When you've framed the face, click Done.

4. **Click the Unknown Face label below the frame, type the name, and press Return.** iPhoto adds the name and displays a right-arrow button next to it that you can click to see other photos in which iPhoto thinks this face appears.

Confirm the faces iPhoto has found

Now check the photos iPhoto has found and confirm which are right. Follow these steps:

1. **Click the right-arrow button next to the name you just added.** iPhoto selects the Faces item in the Source list, opens the Face for the name, and displays the faces it has found. Figure 3.5 shows an example.

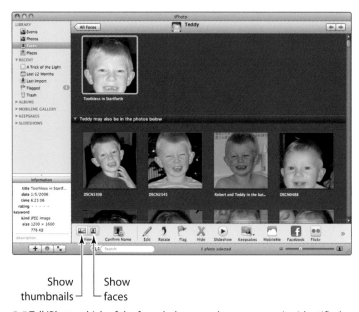

Show thumbnails Show faces

3.5 Tell iPhoto which of the faces belongs to the person you've identified.

2. **Click the Show Faces button if you want to zoom in on the faces in the photos.** Click the Show Thumbnails button if you want to see miniatures of the whole photos. Drag the Size slider if you want to make the photos larger or smaller.

3. **Click the Confirm Name button on the toolbar.** iPhoto adds a *click to confirm* button to the bottom of each photo.

4. **For each photo that's correctly identified, click the *click to confirm* button.**

5. **When you've finished confirming and denying photos, click Done.**

Genius

To confirm photos quickly, drag around them. iPhoto changes all the *click to confirm* buttons to show the person's name. If you realize you've chosen a photo you should-n't have, click the name button to change it to "Not *name*" — for example, "Not Bill."

Managing Faces

After you add one or more faces, you can manage them from the Faces corkboard (see figure 3.6). To display the corkboard, just click the Faces item in the Source pane.

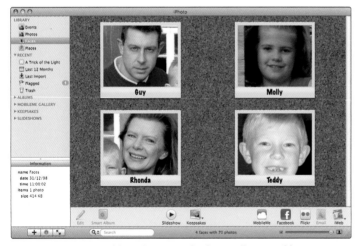

3.6 From the Faces corkboard, you can display a collection of faces.

From the corkboard, you can take the following actions:

- **Skim through the pictures.** Move the mouse pointer over one of the people, and then move the mouse around the picture to skim through the pictures.

- **Open a collection.** Double-click a collection to open it. You can then browse and work with the photos as usual. Click the All Faces button at the top of the window when you

want to return to the corkboard. Alternatively, click the Previous button or the Next button to display another collection.

◉ **Add information about the person.** Move the mouse pointer over the person's picture,
and then click the Information button (a circle with a lower-case *i* in it) that appears in
the lower-right corner. iPhoto displays a dialog box in which you can change the name
you assigned, add a full name, or add an e-mail address. Click the Done button when
you've finished.

Genius To delete a face, click Faces in the Source list, and then click the face you want to
delete. Press ⌘+Delete, and then click Delete Face in the Are you sure you want to
delete this person from Faces? dialog box.

Organizing photos by Places

iPhoto's new Places feature gives you another way to sort and organize your photos — by using
the location in which the photos were taken.

If your camera has GPS built in (as the iPhone's camera does, among various modern cameras), the GPS
information is recorded right in the photo, and the photo is ready for you to use Places. If your camera
doesn't have GPS, or if your pictures are older, you can simply add a location to them manually.

Genius If you know your camera has GPS (and you've turned the feature on), but Places
seems not to have noticed that the photos contain GPS information, open the
Advanced preferences (choose iPhoto ⇨ Preferences, and then click the Advanced
button) and choose Automatically in the Look up Places pop-up menu.

Adding a location manually

Here's how to add a location to a photo manually:

1. **Flip the photo over.** Move the mouse pointer over the photo so that an Information button
   appears in the lower-right corner, then click this button.

2. **Click in the Enter photo location box, and then click the New place button that
   appears.** iPhoto displays the Edit My Places dialog box (see figure 3.7).

3. **Use the controls to find the location you want to assign to the photo.** For example:

   ● Click in the search box, type the city name or zip code, and then press Return.

   ● Click the pushpin on the map, and then drag it to where you want it.

● Expand the circle around the pushpin by dragging the sizing handle on the right.

● Click Drop Pin if you want to place another pin on the same map.

● Type the name for the place above the city name.

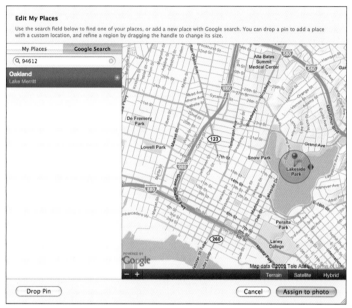

3.7 Use the Edit My Places dialog box to add a place and assign it to a photo manually. You can switch among Terrain, Satellite, and Hybrid views to find exactly the spot.

4. **Click Assign to Photo.**

5. **Click Done to flip the photo back over.**

Once you've added a place like this, you can choose it from the Enter photo location box to apply it quickly to another picture.

Viewing photos by place

After you or your camera has assigned location data to some of your photos in iPhoto, you can click the Places item in the Source pane to browse by place.

At first, Places displays a map showing marker pins in the locations your photos were taken. Double-click the map to zoom in on an area (see figure 3.8); keep double-clicking to zoom in closer. You can also drag the map to display the area you want, or drag the Map Size slider to zoom in or out.

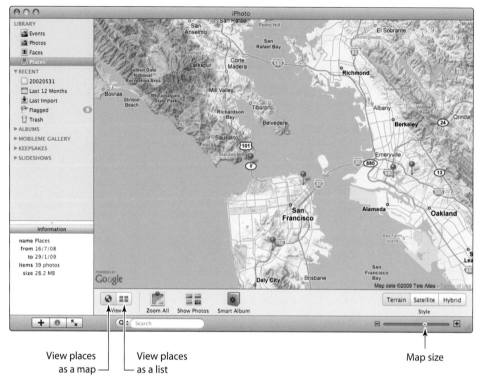

View places
as a map

View places
as a list

Map size

3.8 Click the Places item in the Source list and then zoom in on the pins that mark where your photos were taken.

To view the photos taken at a place, move the mouse pointer over a marker pin to pop up its name, and then click the arrow button to its right.

Instead of using the map to find photos, you can click the View places as a list button in the lower-left corner of Places and use the column browser to locate the photos. For example, click the country in the left column, the state in the second column, the city in the third column, and then the place in the fourth column. To switch back to the map, click the View places as a map button.

Organizing photos into albums

Organizing your photos into suitable Events (as described earlier in this chapter) gives you the basic structure of your iPhoto library. But you'll most likely want to create photo albums that draw photos from different Events. An album gives you an easy way of browsing related pictures in iPhoto. You can also use an album as the basis for a slideshow, calendar, book, or card.

iPhoto lets you create both standard photo albums (which don't change unless you change them) and Smart Albums, albums in which iPhoto selects the photos based on criteria you specify.

Creating a standard album

Here's how to create a standard album:

1. **Click the New button (the button bearing the + sign) at the lower left corner of the iPhoto window to display the dialog box shown in figure 3.9.** You can also choose File ▷ New Album or press ⌘+N to display this .

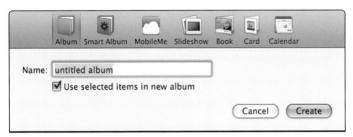

3.9 Beginning to create a new album.

2. **In the Album name box, type the name you want to give the album over the default name (for example,** *untitled album***).**

Note

If you want to include some photos from the current view in the new album you're creating, select them before giving the New command. iPhoto then selects the Use selected items in new album check box in the . If you've selected photos unintentionally before giving the New command, clear the Use selected items in new album check box.

3. **Click Create.** iPhoto creates the new album and adds it to the Albums category in the Source list. This category shows Smart Albums in alphabetical order followed by standard albums in alphabetical order.

4. **Add photos to the new album by dragging them from one of the collections in the Source list.** For example, you can click Events and add photos from Events, or click Faces and add photos from a person's collection.

Creating a Smart Album

If you want iPhoto to pick photos for you, create a Smart Album. This example shows you how to create a Smart Album that contains photos.

1. **Option+click the New button in the lower left corner of the iPhoto window to display the dialog box shown in figure 3.10.** Alternatively, choose File ⇨ New Smart Album or press ⌘+Option+N.

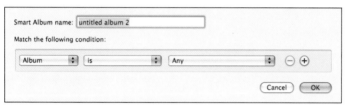

3.10 Beginning to create a new Smart Album

2. **In the Smart Album name box, type the name you want to give the Smart Album over the default name (for example,** *untitled album 2*).

3. **Use the line of controls under Match the following condition to set up the first condition for the Smart Album.** Here's what you would do to create the example Smart Album (see figure 3.11):

   - In the first pop-up menu, choose Date.

   - In the second pop-up menu, choose *is in the last*.

   - Type **6** in the text box.

   - In the third pop-up menu, choose months.

3.11 Creating the first condition for the Smart Album

4. **Add one or more further conditions as needed.** To add another condition, click the + button at the end of the current row. For the example Smart Album, you would create two more conditions, shown completed in figure 3.12:

   - Keyword is *Family*.

   - My Rating is in the range ★★★★ to ★★★★★ (four stars to five stars).

82

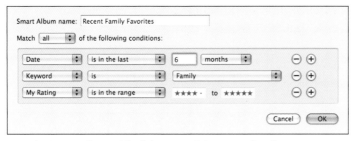

3.12 The Smart Album with all three conditions completed

5. **Click OK to close the dialog box.** iPhoto adds the new Smart Album to the Albums category in the Source list.

Deleting an album

When you tire of an album, you can delete it. Deleting an album removes only the album's links to the photos it contains; the photos themselves remain in your library.

To delete an album, Ctrl+click or right-click it, choose Delete Album, and then click Delete in the confirmation dialog box that iPhoto displays.

Renaming and duplicating albums

If you need to rename an album, just double-click its name, type the new name in the edit box that iPhoto displays, and then press Return.

To duplicate an album so that you can create another album from it, Ctrl+click or right-click the album and choose Duplicate. iPhoto gives the duplicate album the same name with a number added — for example, the duplicate of an album named Christmas is named Christmas 2. You can than rename the duplicate as just described.

Arranging your albums in order

iPhoto adds each new album you create to the bottom of the Source list. You can then move the album to a different position in the list as needed.

To sort the albums alphabetically, Ctrl+click or right-click any album and then click Sort Albums.

Arranging your albums into folders

If you create scads of albums, the Source list can become full enough to be awkward to navigate. To bring your albums under control, you can create folders and put the albums in them.

Folders are easy to use:

- **Create a folder.** Choose File ➪ New Folder or contort your hands and press ⌘+Option+Shift+N. iPhoto creates a new folder named untitled folder in the Albums category and displays an edit box so that you can change the name. Type the new name and press Return to apply it.

- **Create a folder within a folder.** Create a new folder, and then drag it to the folder in which you want to keep it.

- **Put an album in a folder.** Drag the album to the folder.

- **Rename a folder.** Double-click the folder's name, type the new name in the edit box, and then press Return.

- **Delete a folder and its contents.** Ctrl+click or right-click the folder and click Delete.

Caution

When you delete a folder, iPhoto deletes its contents (for example, albums) as well without double-checking. Choose Edit ➪ Undo Delete Folder immediately if you realize you've made a mistake. The photos in the albums are unaffected.

Adding keywords, titles, descriptions, and ratings

Each photo you bring into your library includes the file name the camera gave it, plus all the meta-data the camera includes — for example, the date and time the photo was taken, the camera used, the shutter speed and aperture used for the exposure, the GPS coordinates, and so on.

To help you identify your photos more easily, iPhoto lets you add a title, a rating, a description, and keywords to your photos. You can also add people's names and photo locations, as described earlier in this chapter.

Let's start with the information that's embedded in the photo itself.

Viewing the extended information for a photo

You can view the full range of info available for a photo by clicking it and choosing Photos ➪ Show Extended Photo Info or pressing ⌘+Option+I. iPhoto opens the Extended Photo Info window.

As you can see in figure 3.13, the Extended Photo Info window contains five sections — Image, File, Location, Camera, and Exposure — which you can expand or collapse by clicking the gray disclosure triangles. Some cameras include more information than others, but more recent cameras include the GPS Latitude and GPS Longitude data that Places needs.

While you've got the Extended Photo Info window open, you can click another photo in the iPhoto window to view its details. You can also move to another photo using the arrow keys on the keyboard.

When you've finished examining the details, click the close button (the red button in the upper left corner) to close the Photo Info window. You can also choose Photos ⇨ Hide Extended Photo Info or press ⌘+Option+I again.

Adding titles, descriptions, and ratings to your photos

To make your photos easy to find, you can give each photo a title and a description. Click the photo, click in the Information panel (see figure 3.14), and then type the text you want. If the Information panel is hidden, click the blue i button in the lower left corner of the iPhoto window to display it.

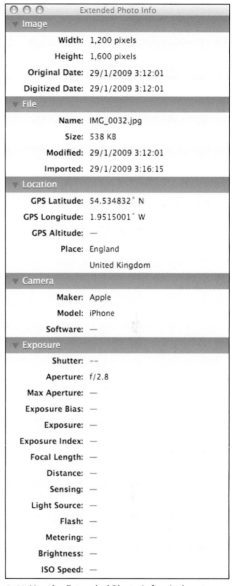

Extended Photo Info

Image
Width:	1,200 pixels
Height:	1,600 pixels
Original Date:	29/1/2009 3:12:01
Digitized Date:	29/1/2009 3:12:01

File
Name:	IMG_0032.jpg
Size:	538 KB
Modified:	29/1/2009 3:12:01
Imported:	29/1/2009 3:16:15

Location
GPS Latitude:	54.534832° N
GPS Longitude:	1.9515001° W
GPS Altitude:	—
Place:	England
	United Kingdom

Camera
Maker:	Apple
Model:	iPhone
Software:	—

Exposure
Shutter:	--
Aperture:	f/2.8
Max Aperture:	—
Exposure Bias:	—
Exposure:	—
Exposure Index:	—
Focal Length:	—
Distance:	—
Sensing:	—
Light Source:	—
Flash:	—
Metering:	—
Brightness:	—
ISO Speed:	—

3.13 Use the Extended Photo Info window to find out the details of the size, date, camera type, or exposure used for a picture.

Genius

You can rate a photo from the keyboard by pressing ⌘+1 (one star) to ⌘+5 (five stars). Press ⌘+0 (zero) to remove the rating.

85

To apply a rating of one star to five stars to a photo, click the appropriate number of stars in the Information panel.

Changing the date and time of a photo

Ideally, each photo gets the correct date and time stamp when the camera takes it, but it's all too easy to let battery failure reset the camera's clock to its default date and then take a stack of photos before noticing the date is wrong.

Luckily, you can change the date for one or more selected photos in iPhoto either in the Information pane for the photo or by choosing Photos ➪ Adjust Date and Time and working on the Adjust date and time of selected photos sheet (see figure 3.15). Select the Modify original files check box if you want to apply the date change to the original files rather than to iPhoto's copies.

3.14 Use the Information window to give a photo a title and description that will help you find it. You can also apply a star rating.

3.15 iPhoto lets you adjust the date and time of one or more photos.

You can also change the date or time by using the Batch Change feature, described next.

Making batch changes to photos

If you find you need to change the date, time, or description on two or more photos at once, use the Batch Change feature like this:

1. **Select the photos you want to affect.**

2. **Ctrl+click or right-click a photo and choose Batch Change, or choose Photos ➪ Batch Change to open the Batch Change sheet.**

3. **In the Set menu, choose the item you want to change: Title, Date, or Description.** The Batch Change sheet changes to show controls for changing the item. Figure 3.16 shows the Batch Change sheet for changing the date; if you choose Title or Description, you'll see different controls.

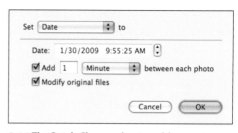

3.16 The Batch Change sheet enables you to change the date, time, or description on multiple photos at once.

4. **Choose the settings you want:**

   - **Title.** Choose Empty to remove the current title. Choose Text to apply the text you type, and select the Append a number to each photo check box if you want to add a number (giving you titles such as Vacation - 1, Vacation - 2, and so on). Choose Event Name to apply the Event's name, or Filename to apply the file's name. Choose Date/Time to apply the date, time, or both in the format you choose.

   - **Date.** Select the date and time to apply. Choose whether to add one or more seconds, minutes, hours, or days between each pair of photos. Select the Modify original files check box if you want to apply the date change to the original files rather than to iPhoto's copies.

   - **Description.** Type the text you want to use. Select the Append to existing Description check box if you want to add the new description to the existing description rather than replace it.

5. **Click OK to close the Batch Change sheet.** iPhoto applies the changes to the photos.

Creating your Quick Group list of keywords

Keywords are a great way of identifying photos because you can apply them in moments.

Your first move should be to set up a Quick Group list of keywords. Follow these steps:

1. **Choose Window ⇨ Show Keywords to display the Keywords window.**

2. **If the Keywords area contains keywords or symbols (such as the check box) you want to use frequently, drag them to the Quick Group area (see figure 3.17).**

3. **To add keywords of your own to the list, click Edit Keywords.** iPhoto displays the Edit Keywords dialog box.

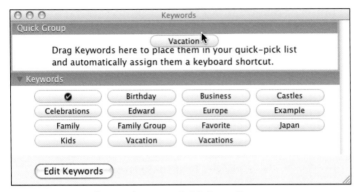

3.17 Drag existing keywords to your Quick Group list.

4. **Click the + button, type a keyword (see figure 3.18), and then press Return.**

3.18 You can add your own keywords and set up shortcuts in the Edit Keywords dialog box.

5. **iPhoto automatically suggests a shortcut letter for the keyword.** If the keyword's first letter hasn't yet been used for a shortcut, iPhoto suggests that letter. If the letter is already in use, iPhoto suggests the keyword's next letter if that letter is free.

6. **To change a shortcut, click the keyword, and then click in the Shortcut column.** Type the letter you want. If it's already in use, iPhoto warns you and lets you decide whether to use it.

Note

To remove an existing keyword, click it, and then click the – button. iPhoto warns you if you've applied the keyword to any photos and checks that you want to remove it. To rename an existing keyword, click it, click Rename, type the new name, and press Return.

7. **Click OK when you've finished editing keywords.** iPhoto returns you to the Keywords window.

8. **Drag your new keywords to the Quick Group area as needed, and then close the Keywords window.**

Adding keywords to your photos

1. **Select the photo to which you want to assign keywords.**

2. **If the keyword has a shortcut, type that letter.** If not, click the "add keywords" placeholder or an existing keyword to display the Keywords box, and then start typing the keyword. iPhoto automatically completes the keyword as soon as it recognizes it.

3. **To remove a keyword, click it, and then press Delete.**

Searching for photos via dates, keywords, or ratings

To find your photos, you can search using dates, keywords, ratings, file names, or descriptions. Here's how to search:

1. **In the Source list, choose the item through which you want to search.** For example, click Photos in the Source list to search through all your photos, or click a particular album to search only in that album.

2. **Press ⌘+F to jump to the Search box on the status bar, or simply click in the Search box.**

3. **If you want to search by only Date, Keyword, or Rating, click the Search pop-up menu and choose the item you want.** Otherwise, choose All in the Search pop-up menu (All may already be selected).

4. **Enter your search criteria:**

   ● **All.** Type the text you're searching for.

   ● **Keywords.** In the panel that appears, click each keyword you want to use (see figure 3.19).

3.19 You can quickly search by one or more keywords using the Search box.

- **Date.** In the panel that appears, choose the year and month.

- **Rating.** Click the number of stars.

5. **Work with the photos the search returns, or click the X button at the right side of the Search field to clear the search.**

Editing and Improving Your Photos

No matter how good you are at taking photos, you'll most likely need to edit some of your photos to bring out their best features and reduce any deficiencies. iPhoto packs a powerful set of editing tools that handle everything from rotating and cropping a picture to comprehensively changing its color balance.

Opening a photo for editing

For most editing moves, you must first open the photo for editing. iPhoto lets you edit photos either in the main iPhoto window or full-screen. Either way, you get the same editing tools, except that full-screen editing also lets you view photo information and compare two photos side by side.

You can also open a photo for editing in an external graphics application, such as Adobe Photoshop, if you have one installed on your Mac.

Note If you've selected the Edits photo option button in the Double-click photo area in iPhoto's General preferences, you can open a photo for editing by simply double-clicking it.

Two Ways to Avoid Photo Disasters

iPhoto lets you undo edits you've made to a photo, or even revert to the original version, but even so, it's often a good idea to duplicate a photo before editing it. Having an extra copy of the photo gives you the freedom to make more extensive edits — and then trash the photo if you ruin it. Or you may want to edit the same photo in different ways.

To duplicate a photo, Ctrl+click or right-click it and choose Duplicate. Alternatively, click the photo and choose Photos ⇨ Duplicate or press ⌘+D.

If you do manage to delete a valuable photo, you should be able to recover the file from backup if you're using Leopard's Time Machine feature. From iPhoto, choose File ⇨ Browse Backups to launch Time Machine.

To open a photo for editing, you click the Edit button on the toolbar. Clicking this button opens the selected photo for editing in the way set in the Edit photo pop-up menu in iPhoto's General preferences, so try both ways, decide which suits you best, and then choose the appropriate setting in the Edit photo pop-up menu.

You can override your default way of editing by Ctrl+clicking or right-clicking a photo and choosing the means of editing you want: Edit (to edit in the main window), Edit Using Full Screen, or Edit in External Editor.

When you've finished editing a photo, you can click the Done button to close it, or simply click the Next button or the Previous button to start editing another photo.

Genius When editing a photo, you can press either the right-arrow key or the down-arrow key to move to the next photo or the left-arrow key or up-arrow key to move to the previous photo.

Zooming in on the photo

When you open a photo for editing, iPhoto displays it at the biggest size at which the whole photo will fit in the iPhoto window or on the whole screen (depending on which view you're using). You can zoom in further if needed by dragging the Zoom slider on the toolbar.

Genius Press 1 to zoom to 100 percent, 2 to zoom to 200 percent, and 0 (zero) to zoom to fit the picture in the window or to the screen. Press Option+1 to zoom to 100 percent on the center of the photo, or Option+2 to zoom to 200 percent on the center of the photo.

Rotating and straightening a photo

If you've turned your camera vertically to take a photo, you'll need to rotate the photo after importing it into iPhoto.

The easiest way to rotate a photo is to click the Rotate button (to rotate the photo in the direction shown on the button) or to Option+click the Rotate button (to rotate the photo in the opposite direction).

After you've fixed the rotation, you can apply any straightening needed. To straighten a photo, click the Straighten button, and then drag the slider to the left or right. Use the gridlines that iPhoto displays to align horizontal or vertical features in the photo. Click the X button when you want to hide the slider.

Genius Press ⌘+R to rotate a photo in the direction set in General preferences. Press ⌘+Option+R to rotate the photo in the opposite direction.

Cropping a photo

To make your photos look their best, you'll often need to crop them. iPhoto lets you crop either to a specific size or size ratio — for example, so that a photo is the right size for your desktop, a book page, or a frame — or to whatever custom dimensions the photo's subject needs.

Here's how to crop a photo:

1. **Open the photo for editing.**

2. **Click the Crop button on the toolbar.** iPhoto displays the cropping tools, as shown in figure 3.20.

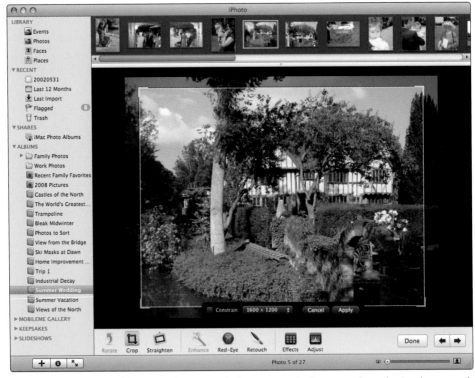

3.20 iPhoto lets you quickly crop a photo to exclude parts you don't want and emphasize those you do want.

3. **If you want to constrain the crop area to a particular size, open the Constrain pop-up menu and choose the size.** For example, choose the size marked "(Display)" — it'll have a name such as 1680 × 1050 (Display) — to constrain the crop area to the size of your Mac's desktop.

4. **Set the size of the crop area.** Drag one of the corner handles to change the cropping area in two dimensions, or drag an edge of the crop area to change the area in only one dimension (if you're not using a constraint). To temporarily override the constraint without turning it off, Shift-drag a corner handle or an edge.

5. **Reposition the crop area as needed by clicking in it and dragging it to where you want it.**

6. **Click Apply to apply the cropping to the photo.**

7. **If you've finished editing the photo, click Done.** Otherwise, leave the photo open for further editing.

Adjusting the colors in a photo

To quickly pump up the colors in a photo, click the Enhance button on the toolbar. This is well worth trying as a quick fix for any photo that looks anemic; if you don't like the effect, simply press ⌘+Z or choose Edit ➪ Undo Enhance Photo. You can click the Enhance button more than once if you want to intensify the effect.

For more subtle changes, click the Adjust button to open the Adjust window (see figure 3.21), and then use the controls in it to change the color balance. Table 3.1 explains what the tools in the Adjust window do.

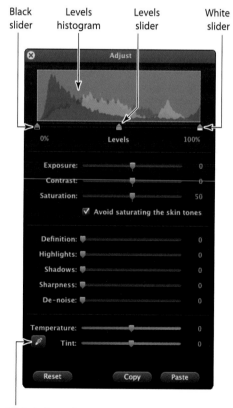

Black slider   Levels histogram   Levels slider   White slider

White balance dropper

3.21 The Adjust window provides powerful tools for changing the color balance of a photo.

93

Table 3.1 Tools in the Adjust Window

Tool	Effect
Levels histogram	The histogram shows how the colors in your picture are distributed between pure black (at the left end, 0 percent) and pure white (at the right end, 100 percent). The red, green, and blue show the individual red, green, and blue color channels in the image.
Black slider	Add black tones to the photo (drag the slider to the right).
White slider	Adds white tones to the photo (drag the slider to the left).
Levels slider	Adjusts the gray balance (drag to the left or right).
Exposure slider	Adjusts the brightness of the photo.
Contrast slider	Adjusts the contrast of the photo.
Saturation slider	Changes the intensity of the color.
Avoid saturating the skin tones check box	Lets you tell iPhoto not to saturate skin tones in the photos. Selecting this check box helps your subjects avoid getting rosacea.
Definition slider	Increases the clarity in the photo, letting you make details easier to see.
Highlights slider	Recovers contrast in highlights that have become too bright.
Shadows slider	Recovers contrast in shadows that have become too dark.
De-noise	Reduces the graininess of the photo, giving it a smoother look.
Temperature slider	Changes the color temperature. The left end of the slider gives a "cool" blue effect, and the right end gives a "warm" golden effect.
Tint slider	Changes the amount of green and red tones in the photo. Drag to the left to add red and reduce green; drag to the right to reduce the red and add green.
White Balance dropper	Lets you correct the photo's white balance by clicking a neutral white area in the photo.
Reset button	Resets all the sliders to how they were when you started editing. Hold down Option to change this button's name to Revert, and then click it to restore your last edit settings.
Copy button	Copies the settings you've made to this photo so that you can apply them to another photo.
Paste button	Pastes onto this photo the settings you've copied from another photo.

Genius The tools in the Adjust window affect the whole of the photo — you can't select part of the photo to work on. If you need to apply different adjustments to different parts of a photo, use an application such as Apple Aperture or Adobe Photoshop.

Applying effects to photos

To make a photo look different, you can apply any of eight different effects to it like this:

1. **Open the photo for editing.**

2. **Click the Effects button on the tool-bar to open the Effects window (see figure 3.22).**

3. **Click the effect you want and adjust it as needed:**

   - The B&W and Sepia effects can only be On or Off.

   - The Antique, Fade Color, Boost Color, Matte, Vignette, and Edge Blur effects have various settings. Click the effect to apply level 1, then click the right arrow to increase the effect or the left arrow to reduce it.

   - Click the Original "effect" to restore the original look.

4. **Close the Effects window when you're satisfied with the result.**

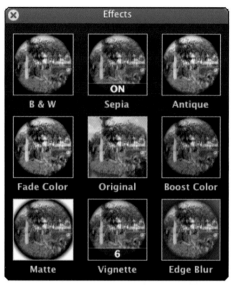

3.22 Applying one or more effects quickly changes a photo's look and feel.

Retouching a photo

If a photo has a blemish or embarrassing detail you want to remove, use the Retouch tool like this:

1. **Open the photo for editing.**

2. **Click the Retouch button on the toolbar to display the Retouch control.** The mouse pointer becomes a circle that you use for retouching.

3. **Drag the Size slider to adjust the size of the circle.**

4. **Click on the blemish, or drag over it.** iPhoto covers it using the surrounding color or colors.

5. **When you've finished retouching, click the X button to close the Retouch tool.**

Removing red-eye from a photo

iPhoto is great for removing red-eye, the red pupils you get when flash light goes through your subject's eye and reflects off the blood-rich retina just in time for the camera to capture it. Here's what to do:

1. **Open the photo for editing.**

2. **Zoom in on the eyes.**

3. **Click the Red-Eye button on the toolbar to display the Red-Eye control (see figure 3.23).**

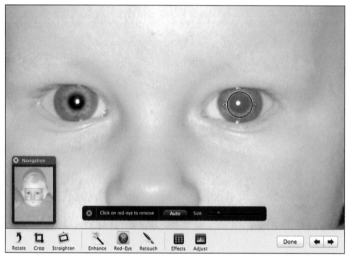

3.23 iPhoto's Red-Eye tool can quickly restore normality to wild youth.

4. **Drag the Size slider to adjust the size of the mouse pointer's circle to match the red-eye spot.** While you can simply click the Auto button, choosing exactly the right size of red-eye spot gives you greater control and takes only a moment longer.

5. **Position the mouse pointer over one of the red spots, and then click.** Repeat for any other feral eyes.

Reverting to the original photo

If you mess up with your edits, don't worry — you can revert to the original photo by Ctrl+clicking or right-clicking it in the Viewing area and choosing Revert to Original. When iPhoto warns you that you're about to lose all the changes you've made, click OK.

Keeping Multiple iPhoto Libraries

Normally, iPhoto puts all your photos into a single library, which it loads every time you open the application. But if you take so many photos that your library is slow to load, or if some of your photos are suitable for some audiences but not for others, you may prefer to separate your photos into different libraries. iPhoto lets you do this too with minimal effort.

Creating a new iPhoto library

First, create a new library. Here's how to create one:

1. **Quit iPhoto if it's running. Press ⌘+Q or choose iPhoto ➪ Quit iPhoto.**

2. **Hold down Option and click the iPhoto icon on the Dock to display the What photo library do you want iPhoto to use? dialog box (see figure 3.24).** Keep holding down Option until the dialog box appears — a quick Option+click doesn't usually do the trick.

3.24 The What photo library do you want iPhoto to use? dialog box lets you create a new iPhoto library or select one of your existing libraries.

3. **Click the Create New button to display a dialog box for creating a new library.**

4. **Type a descriptive name for the library (for example, Family Photos) in place of iPhoto's suggestion (iPhoto Library, 1iPhoto Library, and so on).** Choose the folder in which to store the library, and then click Save.

Note

iPhoto suggests saving each library in the Pictures folder in your user account (~/Pictures). If you've got plenty of hard disk space and will share the photos via iPhoto's sharing features, this folder is a good choice. But if you want to put the new library in another folder (for example, so that you can share the photos with other people through a network), click the disclosure triangle to the right of the Save As box to expand the dialog box, and then navigate to that folder

5. **iPhoto opens using the library you just created, so it is empty.** You can now add photos to the library as discussed earlier in this chapter. For example, drag photo files from a Finder window, or choose File ⇨ Import to Library.

After you've added photos to the library, you can use the library as normal. For example, you can edit the photos, organize them into Events, use Faces and Places, or create slideshows from them.

Selecting the library you want to load

To switch from one library to another, you use the What photo library do you want iPhoto to use? dialog box you saw a moment ago.

1. **Quit iPhoto if it's running.** Press ⌘+Q or choose iPhoto ⇨ Quit iPhoto.

2. **Hold down Option and click the iPhoto icon on the Dock to display the What photo library do you want iPhoto to use? dialog box.** Keep holding down Option until the dialog box appears.

3. **Select the library you want, and then click Choose.** If the library doesn't appear in the dialog box, click Other Library, locate the library manually, and then click Open.

Caution

The What photo library do you want iPhoto to use? dialog box may show backups of your iPhoto libraries — for example, ones on external hard disks. If you see multiple entries for the same library, make sure you open the right one. Click the library in the list, and then look at the folder path shown below the list.

When you want to switch to another library, simply quit iPhoto, and then hold down Option as you restart it. If you open iPhoto without holding down Option, iPhoto opens the last library you used.

Creating Powerful Slideshows

iPhoto lets you create attractive slideshows in moments, complete with music and transition effects if you like.

Running a quick slideshow

Here's how to run a quick slideshow without saving it:

1. **In iPhoto, select the photos you'll use in the slideshow.** If you want to quickly review your most recent photos, click the Last Import item in the Source list.

2. **Click the Slideshow button on the toolbar.** iPhoto displays the first photo full screen and opens the Slideshow dialog box with the Themes tab at the front.

3. **Click the Classic box or the Ken Burns box.** The Ken Burns Effect — zooming and panning over the photos — adds visual interest, but you'll want to turn it off when you're just checking out your latest photos.

4. **Click the Music tab to bring it to the front of the dialog box (see figure 3.25).**

5. **Select the Play music during slideshow check box if you want music with the slideshow.** If you prefer peace, clear the check box and skip the next step.

6. **Choose the song you want to play from the Sample Music folder, your GarageBand compositions, or your iTunes library.** You can search by using the Search box, and preview music by clicking Play.

7. **Click the Settings tab to bring it to the front of the dialog box (see figure 3.26)**

8. **In the Play each slide for a minimum of box, choose how many seconds to dwell on each slide.** If you prefer to use music, you can select the Fit slideshow to music option button instead.

3.25 You can accompany your slideshow with music from GarageBand or iTunes, or stick with the sample music that iPhoto offers.

3.26 Choosing settings for a slideshow

9. **If you want to use transitions between slides, follow these steps:**

    - Select the Transition check box.

    - In the Transition pop-up menu, choose the transition. None is a good choice when you're simply reviewing your photos and don't need extra pizzazz. For consistent changes, choose a transition such as Dissolve, Flip, or Twirl. If you're feeling more adventurous, choose Random to have iPhoto pick a different transition for each change.

    - Look to see whether the four direction buttons are available (the arrows are black) or not available (the arrows are gray). If two or more are available, click the direction you want to use for the transition.

    - Drag the Speed slider to set the speed of the transition.

10. **Choose other options to suit your preferences:**

    - If you want to include captions, select the Show Caption check box. In the pop-up menu, choose the text: Titles, Descriptions, Titles and Descriptions, Places, or Dates.

    - Select the Show title slide check box if you want to have a title slide at the beginning of the show.

    - Choose whether to shuffle the slides, repeat the slideshow at the end, and scale the photos to fill the screen.

    - Select the Use settings as default check box if you want to make these settings the default for future slideshows.

11. **Click Play.** iPhoto closes the Slideshow dialog box and starts the slideshow full screen.

Use the slideshow controls and navigation miniatures (see figure 3.27) toward the bottom of the screen to navigate the slideshow or to adjust the slideshow settings. You can summon up these controls at any point by moving the mouse pointer. To end the slideshow, click anywhere outside the controls or press Esc.

3.27 Move the mouse to display the slideshow controls and navigation miniatures.

Creating and saving a slideshow

If you want to create a slideshow and save it for future use, follow these steps:

1. **Click the album on which you want to base the slideshow, or select the photos you want to use.**

2. **Click the New button (the + button) in the lower left corner of the iPhoto window to open the New sheet, and then click the Slideshow button.**

3. **Type the name for the slideshow in the Name box.**

4. **If you selected photos for the slideshow, make sure the Use selected items in new slideshow check box is selected.**

5. **Click Create.** iPhoto adds the slideshow to the Slideshows category in the Source list and displays the Slideshow toolbar (see figure 3.28).

3.28 Creating a slideshow with custom settings

6. **Choose the theme for the slideshow.** Click the Themes button; choose Classic, Ken Burns, or another theme in the Choose a Slideshow Theme dialog box; and then click Choose.

7. **Choose the music — or lack of it — for the slideshow:**

    - Click the Music button to display the Music dialog box, which closely resembles the Music tab of the Slideshow dialog box (shown earlier in this chapter).

    - If you want music, select the Play music during slideshow check box, and then select the song.

    - Click Apply to close the dialog box.

8. **Choose default settings for the whole slideshow:**

    - Click the Settings button to display the Slideshow Settings dialog box (see figure 3.29). Make sure the All Slides tab is at the front.

101

- Choose how long to display each slide for, or select the Fit slideshow to music option button if you want the slideshow to play for the same length of time as the music you chose.

- To use transitions, select the Transition check box. Choose the transition in the pop-up menu, and pick a direction if the direction buttons are available. Drag the Speed slider to set the default speed.

- Choose whether to show captions (and if so, select the text) and a title slide.

- Choose whether to repeat the slideshow and scale the photos to fill the screen.

- In the Aspect Ratio pop-up menu, choose This Screen if you want to display the slideshow on your Mac's screen. Otherwise, choose the HDTV (16:9) format for HDTV or widescreen displays, the TV (4:3) format for a TV, or the iPhone (3:2) format for the iPhone and iPod touch.

- Leave the Slideshow Settings dialog open for the moment.

9. **In the filmstrip at the top, drag the pictures into the order in which you want them to play.** Put the first slide on the left.

10. **Click the first picture, click the This Slide tab in the Slideshow Settings dialog box (see figure 3.30), and then choose settings for the slide:**

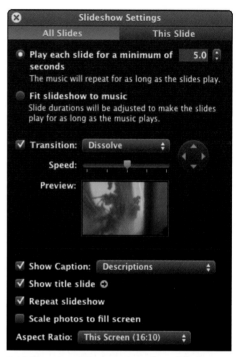

3.29 Choosing default settings for a slideshow

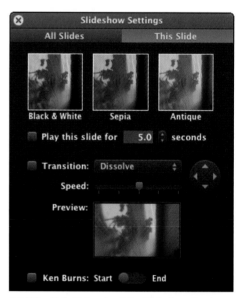

3.30 The This Slide tab of the Slideshow Settings dialog box lets you apply an effect to the slide, control how long it appears for, add a transition, and apply the Ken Burns effect.

- **Effect.** To apply an effect, click Black and White, Sepia, or Antique.

- **Duration.** Select the Play this slide for check box, and then set the number of seconds. This setting overrides the setting you've applied to the slideshow as a whole.

- **Transition.** Choose the transition from this slide to the next. To change the direction or speed, click the Adjust button, and then use the Transition and Speed controls. Again, you're overriding the setting applied to the slideshow as a whole.

- **Ken Burns Effect.** Select the check box if you want to use the panning and zooming effect. If necessary, zoom in by dragging the Size slider in the main iPhoto window, and then drag the picture to where you want its starting position. Move the Start/End switch to the End position, and then zoom and drag to set the end position.

- Close the Slideshow Settings dialog box and click the Preview button to preview the effect. If needed, reopen the dialog box and change the settings.

11. **Reopen the Slideshow Settings dialog box and repeat step 9 for each of the other slides in the slideshow.**

12. **Click Play when you're ready to view your slideshow.**

13. **To create a version of the slideshow you can use on an iPod, iPhone Apple TV, computer, or a MobileMe gallery, click Export, and then follow through the export process.**

Note

iPhoto automatically saves the changes you make to your slideshow, so you don't need to save them manually.

Sharing Your Photos with Others

To get the most enjoyment out of your photos, I bet you'll want to share them with other people. iPhoto lets you share photos in several ways: Directly with other iPhoto users on your local network, via your Gallery on Apple's MobileMe service, on Facebook or Flickr, through your Web site or your applications, or even via video chat. You can also go old-school and order hard-copy prints of your photos.

Sharing your photos with other iPhoto users

iPhoto makes it easy to share your photos with other Macs on your local network. After you set up sharing as described in Chapter 2, your iPhoto library (or the albums you've chosen to share) appears under the shared name you chose in the Shares category in the Source list in iPhoto running on other Macs on the network.

iPhoto doesn't give you any indication when someone connects to your shared library or albums. The only way to find out is by quitting iPhoto, which warns you that you're about to disconnect all sharing users (it doesn't tell you how many). Click Disconnect Sharing Users if you want to quit iPhoto anyway.

Viewing and copying other people's shared photos

If you selected the Look for shared photos check box in iPhoto's Sharing preferences, iPhoto shows other people's shared photo libraries in the Shared category in your Source list. To view the contents of a library, click it. If iPhoto displays the Photo Library Password dialog box prompting you for the password, type the password, and then click OK.

After you connect to someone else's library, you can browse through it much as you can your Mac's own library. Click the library's gray disclosure triangle to display the list of shared albums, and then click the album you want to display.

Because the photos are on someone else's Mac, you can't change them. You can open a photo for "editing," but when you do, you can do no more than zoom in and out. In full-screen view, you can also compare photos side by side.

However, you can copy photos to your library by dragging them from the shared library to your Photos library or an album in the Source list. You can also drag an album from the shared library to your library.

When you've finished using the shared library, click the Eject button to the right of the shared library's name in the Source list to disconnect from the shared library. You can also disconnect by quitting iPhoto.

Exporting your photos to your MobileMe Gallery

If you have a MobileMe subscription, you can share your photos with a wider audience by publishing an album to your MobileMe Gallery. You can make an album public so that anybody can access it, limit access to only the people you choose, or keep it to yourself.

Follow these steps to export an album to your MobileMe Gallery:

1. **Get the album ready for publishing.** Edit the photos so that they look just the way you want them to, and add any names and descriptions needed.

2. **Click the album in the Source list to display its photos.**

3. **Click the Web Gallery button on the toolbar or choose Share ➪ MobileMe.** The sheet shown in figure 3.31 appears.

Would you like to publish "A Trick of the Light" to your MobileMe Gallery?

This will create an album in Guy Hart-Davis's MobileMe Gallery. The album can be viewed with Safari or any modern web browser. The title of this album will be visible to everyone viewing your Gallery.

Album Viewable by: [Everyone   ▲▼]

Allow: ☐ Downloading of photos or entire album
☐ Uploading of photos via web browser
☑ Adding of photos via email

Show: ☑ Photo titles
☐ Email address for uploading photos

(Show Advanced)   (Cancel) (Publish)

3.31 Publishing an album to your MobileMe Gallery

4. **In the Album Viewable by pop-up menu, choose who may view the album:**

   - **Everyone.** Anyone on the Web can view the album.

   - **Only me.** You keep the album to yourself — good for personal or work photos.

   - **Public.** Anyone who knows your MobileMe public password can view the album.

   - **Edit Names and Passwords.** To add the name of a person or group and assign a password, click this item, and work on the sheet that appears. Click OK when you've finished.

5. **Choose options in the Allow area:**

   - Select the Downloading of photos or entire album check box if you want visitors to be able to download high-quality versions of the photos. Click the Show Advanced button to display the hidden section at the bottom of the sheet and choose the quality you want in the Download quality pop-up menu. Choose Optimized if you want to provide high-quality images with reasonably small file sizes. Choose Actual Size when you need to provide the full-quality photos, which will take longer to upload to your Gallery (and longer for visitors to download).

Caution

Clearing the Downloading of photos or entire album check box doesn't prevent visitors from downloading the photos in your album: Users can still right-click a photo in their Web browser and save it to a file on their computer. The difference is that they get only the photo displayed on their screen, not the higher-resolution version that your MobileMe Gallery enables you to provide.

- Select the Uploading of photos via web browser check box if you want visitors to be able to add photos to the album using a Web browser.

- Select the Adding of photos via e-mail check box if you want to be able to add photos by e-mail from any computer or from an iPhone or iPod touch.

6. **Choose options in the Show area:**

- Select the Photo titles check box if you want to include titles in the Gallery. Usually, having the titles is helpful.

- If you chose to allow uploading via e-mail and want to let visitors to the Gallery see the address, select the Email address for uploading photos check box. A visitor can then click the Send to Album icon in the Gallery to display the address.

7. **If you want to hide the album on your Gallery page, click the Show Advanced button, and then select the Hide album on my Gallery page check box.**

Genius

Hiding an album so that it doesn't appear on your MobileMe Gallery page is good for when you need to share different albums with different people. Instead of needing to password-protect a gallery to keep out people you don't want to see it, you can simply prevent the album from appearing, and give the album's URL to the people who need to be able to access it.

8. **Click Publish.** iPhoto publishes the album to your MobileMe Gallery and displays an icon to the right of the album's name in the Source list. After making changes online or in iPhoto, you can synchronize the album by clicking this icon.

Adding photos to a Gallery from an iPhone or iPod touch

If you have an iPhone or iPod touch, you can add photos to a MobileMe Gallery directly from the device. This is great both for when you take a photo on the iPhone that you need to share immediately and for when you want to share one of the other photos you're carrying on the device.

Here's how to add a photo to a MobileMe Gallery from the iPhone or iPod touch:

1. **On the iPhone or iPod touch, open the photo.** For example, open the Camera Roll on the iPhone and touch the picture.

2. **Touch the leftmost button on the toolbar (the button with the curving arrow).**

3. **Touch the Send to MobileMe button on the panel that appears.**

4. **On the MobileMe Albums page, touch the album you want to place the photo in.** The iPhone or iPod starts a mail message, addresses it to your MobileMe account, and adds the photo.

5. **Touch the Send button.** The iPhone or iPod sends the photo, which appears in the Gallery almost immediately.

Adding photos to a gallery from your Web browser

If you selected the Uploading of photos via web browser check box when exporting an album to your Gallery, any visitor can upload photos to the album by clicking the Upload button and using the form that appears.

Even if you cleared this check box, you can add photos and edit your albums from a browser by logging into MobileMe, clicking the Gallery button on the toolbar, and then working with the Gallery tools.

Sharing your photos on Facebook

If you have an account on the Facebook social networking site, you can use the iPhoto Uploader to upload photos directly from iPhoto. Follow these steps to set up the iPhoto Uploader:

1. **Click the Facebook icon on the toolbar or choose Share ⇨ Facebook.** iPhoto displays the Do you want to set up iPhoto to publish to Facebook? dialog box.

2. **Click the Set Up button to display the iPhoto Uploader dialog box (see figure 3.32).**

3. **Type the email address associated with your Facebook account and the account's password.**

4. **Select the Keep me logged in to iPhoto Uploader check box if you want to stay logged in so that you can upload photos at any time.**

5. **Click Login.** iPhoto displays the Allow Access? screen to confirm access.

6. **Click Allow, and then click Close.**

3.32 Enter your Facebook details in the iPhoto Uploader dialog box to set up iPhoto to publish photos directly to your Facebook account.

You can now upload photos in moments like this:

1. **Select the photos or album you want to upload.**

2. **Click the Facebook button.** iPhoto display a confirmation dialog box (see figure 3.33).

3. **In the Photos Viewable by pop-up menu, choose who may view the photos: Everyone, Friends of Friends, or Only Friends.**

4. **Click Publish.** iPhoto publishes the photos on Facebook and adds the album to the Facebook category in the Source list.

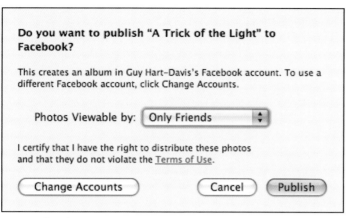

Do you want to publish "A Trick of the Light" to Facebook?

This creates an album in Guy Hart-Davis's Facebook account. To use a different Facebook account, click Change Accounts.

Photos Viewable by: [Only Friends ▲▼]

I certify that I have the right to distribute these photos and that they do not violate the Terms of Use.

[Change Accounts]   [Cancel] [Publish]

3.33 Confirm that you want to publish your photos to Facebook, and decide who's allowed to see them.

Sharing your photos on Flickr

If you have an account on the Flickr photo-sharing site, you can configure iPhoto to publish photos directly to it. Follow these steps:

1. **Click the Flickr icon on the toolbar or choose Share ➪ Flickr.** iPhoto displays the Do you want to set up iPhoto to publish to Flickr? dialog box.

2. **Click the Set Up button.** iPhoto cranks up your default Web browser (for example, Safari) and prompts you to log into Flickr.

3. **Log in, and then click the OK, I'll Allow It button on the Flickr: Authorize iPhoto Uploader page.**

4. **Close the browser window.** iPhoto automatically closes the Do you want to set up iPhoto to publish to Flickr? dialog box.

You can now upload photos to Flickr quickly like this:

1. **Select the photos or album you want to upload.**

2. **Click the Flickr button.** iPhoto display a confirmation dialog box (see figure 3.34).

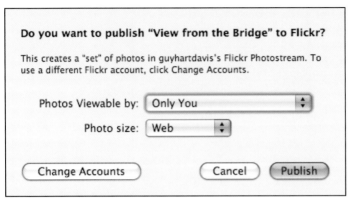

Do you want to publish "View from the Bridge" to Flickr?

This creates a "set" of photos in guyhartdavis's Flickr Photostream. To use a different Flickr account, click Change Accounts.

Photos Viewable by: [Only You ⇕]

Photo size: [Web ⇕]

[Change Accounts]   [Cancel] [Publish]

3.34 Confirm that you want to publish your photos to Flickr, decide who may view them, and choose the size.

3. **In the Photos Viewable by pop-up menu, choose who may view the photos: Only You, Your Friends, Your Family, Your Friends and Family, or Anyone.**

4. **In the Photo size pop-up menu, choose the size at which to publish the photos: Web (for viewing on screen), Optimized (for printing up to medium sizes), or Actual Size (for providing full-quality photos).** Depending on which type of Flickr account you have, you may be limited to using the Web size.

5. **Click Publish.** iPhoto publishes the photos on Flickr and adds the album to the Flickr category in the Source list.

Exporting your photos to a local Web site

If you have your own Web site on your Mac, you can quickly create Web pages containing photos from your iPhoto library. iPhoto creates an index page containing a thumbnail version of each picture, and a detail page containing the full photo.

To export photos to Web pages, follow these steps:

1. **Select the photos you want to export.**

2. **Choose File ⇨ Export to open the Export Photos dialog box, then click the Web Page button to display the Web Page tab (see figure 3.35).**

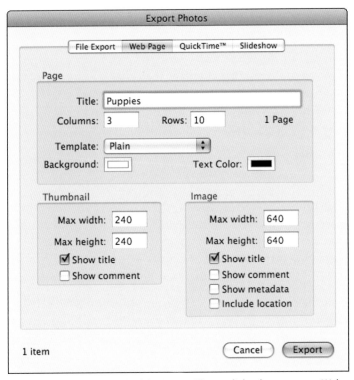

3.35 Use the Web Page tab of the Export Photos dialog box to create Web pages containing your photos.

3. **In the Page box, choose the details for the index page:**

   - **Title.** Type the title you want to give the page. This appears at the top of the page and in the browser's title bar.

   - **Columns and Rows.** Choose how many rows and columns to create. Watch the readout that shows the number of pages.

   - **Template.** Choose Plain for unadorned photos. Choose Framed to include a frame around each photo.

   - **Background and Text Color.** Pick the colors you want for the page background and the text.

4. **In the Thumbnail box, set the size and text for the thumbnails on the index page.** Set the maximum height and width, and choose whether to include the photos' titles and comments.

5. **In the Image box, set the size and text for the photos on their individual pages.** Set the maximum height and width, and choose whether to include the photos' titles, comments, metadata, and location. Titles are usually helpful; comments are sometimes helpful; metadata is usually overkill; and locations can be fascinating, an invasion of your privacy, or both.

6. **Click Export, choose the folder in which to store the pages, and then click OK.** iPhoto suggests storing the pages in the Sites folder in your Home folder.

To view the pages you've created, open a Finder window to your Sites folder or the folder you chose, open the site's subfolder, and then double-click the index.html file. Mac OS X opens the index page in your Web browser.

Exporting your photos for use in other applications

If you need to use your photos in other applications, you can export them from iPhoto like this:

1. **Select the photo or photos you want to export.**

2. **Choose File ⇨ Export to open the Export Photos dialog box, then click the File Export tab (see figure 3.36) if it's not displayed.**

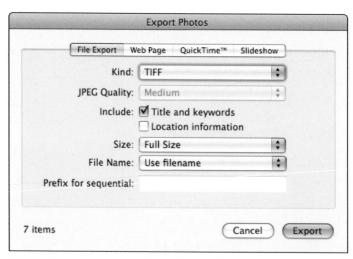

3.36 The File Export tab of the Export Photos dialog box lets you choose the format, size, and naming convention for the photo files you export.

3. **In the Kind pop-up menu, choose the format to use for the exported files:**

   - **Original.** The format in which you imported the files (typically JPEG or RAW).

   - **Current.** The format in which iPhoto is storing the photo (JPEG unless you've set iPhoto to store RAW files in TIFF format to preserve quality).

   - **JPEG.** The best choice for general use, although you lose quality. Choose the quality in the JPEG Quality pop-up menu: Low, Medium, High, or Maximum.

   - **TIFF.** A good choice for use in publishing.

   - **PNG.** The high-quality choice for general computer use.

4. **Select the Titles and keywords check box and the Location information check box if you want to include these details in the files.** These options aren't available for PNG files.

5. **In the Size pop-up menu, choose the size: Small, Medium, Large, Full Size, or Custom.** For Custom, an extra section of the dialog box appears that lets you choose the maximum dimension and the orientation.

6. **In the File Name pop-up menu, choose how to name the files: Use title, Use filename, Sequential, or Use Album.** If you choose Sequential, type the text in the Prefix for sequential box. For example, type **House** to get files named House 01, House 02, and so on.

7. **Click Export, choose the folder in which to save the photos, and then click OK.** iPhoto exports the files and then closes the Export Photos dialog box.

Sharing your photos via video chat

When you need to discuss your photos with someone across the Internet, you have several options, such as sending photos via e-mail or creating an album on your MobileMe Gallery. But here's another great option: to share the photos via iChat Theater with another Mac user, so you can both view the photos at the same time and talk them over.

To use iChat Theater to share photos, follow these steps:

1. **Launch iChat from the Dock or from the Applications folder.**

2. **Choose File ⇨ Share iPhoto With iChat Theater to open the iPhoto dialog box.**

3. **Choose the album or Event you want to share, and then click Share.** iChat displays a dialog box telling you that iChat Theater is ready to begin and prompting you to invite a buddy to a video chat.

4. **Click your buddy in the main iChat window, and then click the Start a Video Chat button on the toolbar at the bottom of the window.** iChat establishes the connection and starts displaying the photos.

Getting high-quality prints of your photos

iPhoto has a built-in connection to the Kodak Print Service that makes it easy to order prints online and pay via your Apple account. Select the photos, and then choose File ➪ Order Prints to open the Order Prints dialog box, which makes the ordering process simple.

When you're ordering large prints, double-check that the Order Prints dialog box isn't showing a yellow exclamation icon next to the size. This means that one or more of your photos' resolution is too low for getting good results at the size you've chosen.

Given that the resolution of digital cameras keeps increasing, resolution is usually a problem these days only if you've cropped your photos heavily.

Genius When you need to get prints made more quickly than the Kodak Print Service can deliver, use the File ➪ Export command to export the photos to a memory card that you can take to your local photographic specialist.

Using Your Photos Within Mac OS X

To get the greatest enjoyment from your photos, you'll probably want to use them as widely as possible within Mac OS X. For a quick and easy use of a photo, you can put a single photo on your desktop; for a more entertaining background, you can use a sequence of photos. Better yet, you can create custom screen savers, make a personal icon for your user account, and display a photo as the background in a Finder window for that custom touch.

Put a sequence of photos on your desktop

Instead of having a single, unchanging photo on your desktop, you may prefer to display a sequence of photos. You can do this easily too:

1. **In iPhoto, select the photos you want to use.** You have several options:

   - Select the photos by clicking the first and then ⌘-clicking each of the others.

   - Select an existing album. Alternatively, create a new album.

   - Flag the photos you want. This is a handy way of picking desktop photos from more than one Event or album.

2. **Click the Set Desktop button on the toolbar at the bottom of the iPhoto window.** iPhoto applies the first photo to the desktop and opens the Desktop tab of Desktop & Screen Saver preferences (see figure 3.37).

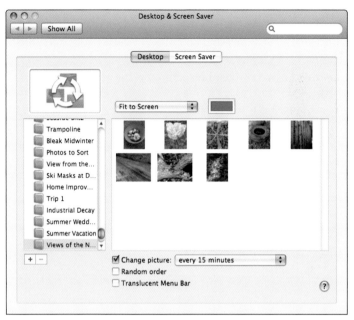

3.37 Use the Desktop & Screen Saver preferences to put a sequence of photos on your desktop.

3. **If you're using flagged photos, expand the iPhoto Albums list, and then click the Flagged item.** If you're using photos you selected, expand the Folders item and then click the iPhoto Selection item. Your photos appear in the box on the right.

4. **In the pop-up menu, choose how to display the photos:**

    ● **Fit to Screen.** Displays the photo at the largest size where the whole photo fits on the screen. You can choose a background color for the uncovered parts of the screen by clicking the color swatch and working in the Colors window that appears.

    ● **Fill Screen.** Fills the screen with the picture, hiding any parts that are too large to fit.

    ● **Stretch to Fill Screen.** Changes one of the photo's dimensions as needed to make the photo fit the screen exactly.

    ● **Center.** Displays the photo centered in the screen. You can choose a background color for the uncovered parts of the screen by clicking the color swatch and working in the Colors window that appears.

    ● **Tile.** Uses multiple instances of the photo to cover the screen. This setting is good for small photos or patterns.

5. **Select the Change picture check box and choose the frequency of change in the pop-up menu.** You can choose intervals from every 5 seconds to every day, or have the photo change when you log in or when you wake your Mac from sleep.

6. **Select the Random order check box if you want to go through the photos in random order rather than in sequence.**

7. **Select the Translucent Menu Bar check box if you want the desktop background to show through the menu bar.**

8. **Press ⌘+Q or choose System Preferences ➪ Quit System Preferences to quit System Preferences.**

Now the show will take place in the background as you work or play on your Mac!

Making screen savers from your photos

A great way to enjoy your photos full screen on your Mac is to make a screen saver from them. Here's what to do:

1. **In iPhoto, create an album or Smart Album containing the photos you want to use.** If you've already got a suitable album, you're all set. Alternatively, you can use an existing category (for example, Last Import or Flagged) or even your whole library if you want.

2. **Ctrl+click or right-click the desktop and choose Change Desktop Background to jump right to the Desktop & Screen Saver preferences.**

3. **Click the Screen Saver tab to display its contents.**

4. **In the Screen Savers box on the left, expand the Pictures section if it's collapsed.** Then click the album or item that contains the photos. The Preview box displays the first of the photos (see figure 3.38), showing the effect of the screen saver with its current settings.

5. **Choose the display style for the screen saver by clicking one of the three Display Style buttons:**

   • **Slideshow.** The screen saver shows each photo for a few seconds. You can choose whether to use cross-fading transitions and panning across the photos (the Ken Burns Effect).

   • **Collage.** The screen saver spins in each photo in turn, adding it to those already there to make a collage. You can display the titles and comments on the photos if you want.

● **Mosaic.** The screen saver slowly zooms out to form a mosaic that shows all the photos in miniature. It repeats the photos as necessary to fill the whole screen.

Genius

The Mosaic screen saver is visually entertaining, but you don't get much of a view of the photos. The Collage screen saver, on the other hand, is good for getting an overview of the photos in the album or collection — and seeing their titles and comments if you choose.

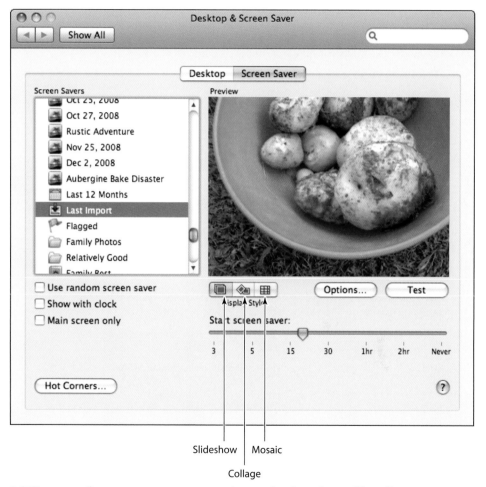

Slideshow | Mosaic
Collage

3.38 You can easily create custom screen savers that use the photos in your iPhoto library.

117

6. **Click the Options button and choose options on the sheet that appears.** Apart from an option for presenting the slides in random order, the options are different for the Slideshow (see figure 3.39), Collage, and Mosaic screen savers:

- **Slideshow.** Choose whether to cross-fade between slides, zoom back and forth, crop the slides to fit the screen, and keep the slides centered.

- **Collage.** Choose between a Classic-style (unadorned) slideshow or one annotated with the filenames and dates.

- **Mosaic.** Choose the number of rows to include in the mosaic and the speed at which to generate it.

7. **Click Test to test the screen saver.** Move the mouse to end the test. Change your settings as needed, and test again until satisfied.

8. **Drag the Start screen saver slider to tell Mac OS X how soon to start the screen saver when you leave your Mac inactive.**

9. **Select the Show with clock check box if you want to include a clock on the display.**

10. **Select the Main screen only check box if your Mac has multiple screens but you want to use only the main one.**

11. **Press ⌘+Q or choose System Preferences ➪ Quit System Preferences to quit System Preferences.**

The options for the Slideshow screen saver:
- Present slides in random order ☑
- Cross-fade between slides ☑
- Zoom back and forth ☑
- Crop slides to fit on screen ☑
- Keep slides centered ☐

Cancel   OK

3.39 The options for the Slideshow screen saver include cross-fades, zooming, and cropping.

Creating an account icon from a photo

Another fun use of a photo is to create a custom icon for your user account in Mac OS X. This is a great way of personalizing the Mac OS X login screen, either with portraits of the users — flattering or distorted, whichever you like — or simply with photos you and the other users like.

Here's how to create a custom icon for your user account:

1. **Click the System Preferences icon on the Dock or choose Apple menu ➪ System Preferences to open the System Preferences window.**

2. **Click Accounts (in the System section) to open the Accounts preferences.**

3. **Click your existing account picture (to the left of the Change Password button), and then click Edit Picture on the pop-up panel that appears (see figure 3.40).**

3.40 Click Edit Picture on the pop-up panel to start creating a custom icon for your user account.

4. **On the Edit Picture sheet that appears (see figure 3.41), add a picture in one of these three ways:**

   ● Click the Take a video snapshot button to take a picture using your Mac's iSight or another webcam you've plugged in. If no camera is connected, the Edit Picture sheet displays a prompt to plug in a camera instead of the Take a video snapshot button.

   ● Click the Open button, select the picture in the Open dialog box that appears, and then click the dialog box's Open button to close the dialog box and apply the picture.

   ● Drag a photo from iPhoto or from Photo Booth. Open iPhoto or Photo Booth, position the application so that you can see the System Properties window as well, and then drag the photo you want to the Edit Picture sheet.

Genius   If you've changed your user account icon before, you can quickly return to a picture you've used before by opening the Recent Pictures pop-up menu at the top of the Edit Picture sheet and choosing the picture you want from the panel.

5. **If you want to use only part of the picture, click and drag the Size slider to
zoom in.**

6. **After zooming, or if the photo is bigger than the icon area, you can click in
the preview and drag to change the
part of the photo that appears.**

7. **Click Set to close the Edit Picture
sheet and apply your new icon to the
Accounts window.**

8. **Press ⌘+Q or choose System
Preferences ⇨ Quit System
Preferences to quit System
Preferences.**

3.41 The Edit Picture sheet lets you take a video
snapshot of yourself or choose a photo either from
a folder or directly from iPhoto or Photo Booth.

Displaying a photo as the background in a Finder window

Icon view in the Finder is a great way of getting an overview of your files — and you can
make it even better by adding one of your
own photos as the background in the Finder
window.

You can set a different photo as the background in any folder. This is a handy way of making your
key Finder windows easier to recognize, especially when they're displayed in miniature on the
Dock. For example, if you give the Documents folder a background photo with a predominantly
blue color, and the Macintosh HD folder a background with a predominantly green color, you'll be
able to distinguish the miniature icons even at a glance.

Note   Folder background pictures appear only in Icon view, not in List view, Columns view,
or Cover Flow view.

Here's how to set a photo as the background for a folder:

1. **Click the Finder icon on the Dock to open a Finder window.** Navigate to the folder in which you want to display the photo.

2. **Make sure the folder is displayed using Icon view.** If it's not, choose View ⇨ As Icons or click the Icons button on the toolbar (the leftmost of the four View buttons).

3. **Choose View ⇨ Show View Options to open the View Options window.**

4. **Select the Always open in icon view check box to make the folder use Icon view every time you open it (so that you can see the background picture).**

5. **Select the Picture option button in the Background area, and then click Select to open the Select a Picture dialog box.**

6. **Select the picture you want to use.**

   ● To go straight to your iPhoto library, expand the Media category in the Sidebar, and then click Photos. You can then choose a photo much as you would in iPhoto itself — for example, from an Event, an album, or your Last Import.

   ● To choose a picture from a folder, simply navigate to the folder.

7. **Click Select to close the Select a Picture dialog box.** The Finder window displays the photo as its background.

8. **Close the View Options dialog box by clicking the red button (the Close button) on the window or choosing View ⇨ Hide View Options.**

How Do I Import Video into iMovie?

iMovie '09 not only packs a huge amount of power but it also includes lots of cool, new features that make it even better than before. If you've wanted to get started with iMovie but felt daunted by its complexity, start at the beginning of this chapter. If you're ready to go ahead and start importing your video from your DV camcorder or another source, jump in at the middle of the chapter. And if you've already imported video and want to review and sort it, go directly to the end of the chapter.

Navigating the iMovie Interface

Start iMovie by clicking the iMovie icon on the Dock. The first time you start iMovie, you'll see an introductory screen that highlights the application's new features. From here, you can click the Video Tutorials button to see walkthroughs of iMovie's main features, or simply click OK to close the introductory screen and get right to iMovie itself.

Note If the iMovie icon doesn't appear on the Dock, click the Desktop, choose Go ⇨ Applications, and then double-click the iMovie icon. Once iMovie is running, Control-click or right-click the iMovie icon on the Dock and choose Keep in Dock to make it stay there.

When you open iMovie, it automatically creates a new movie project called My First Project for you. The iMovie window should look like figure 4.1.

Open camera import window   Project frames   New project   Viewer

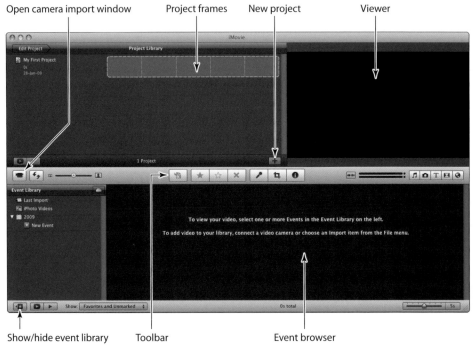

Show/hide event library   Toolbar   Event browser

4.1 The main parts of the iMovie window as it appears when you first open the application.

Here's what the main components of the iMovie interface are and what they do:

- **Project Library.** This pane lists all your movie projects, along with a few frames from each project to help you identify them, so you can easily move from one project to another. When you're ready to work on a project, click it and then click Edit Project to hide the Project Library pane.

- **Project Storyboard.** This area (not shown in figure 4.1) is where you put your movie projects together. iMovie displays the current project on the Project Storyboard as a series of *filmstrips*, sequences of frames from the clips you're using. To return to the Project Library, click the Project Library button.

- **Toolbar.** This strip across the middle of the iMovie window contains most of the controls you use for manipulating content and for displaying other parts of the iMovie interface, such as the Music & Sound Effects Browser or the Title Browser.

- **Event Library.** This pane lets you browse the Events that contain all the movie footage you import into iMovie. If you don't need to keep the Event Library open, click the Show/Hide Event Library button to hide it and give yourself more space for the Event browser.

Genius

Events in iMovie work in a similar way to Events in iPhoto (see Chapter 2). An Event is a tool for organizing your movie footage into categories that suit you. iMovie creates Events for you automatically when you import video, but you can also rearrange iMovie's Events and create your own Events as needed.

- **Event browser.** This pane displays the clips of movie footage contained in the Event you've selected in the Event Library. You use the Event browser to pick the footage you want to add to the Project Storyboard.

Note

When you restart iMovie, it automatically opens the last movie project you worked with. You can switch quickly to another movie project by clicking it in the Project Library.

Choosing Preferences to Make iMovie Work Your Way

Before you start importing video and building a movie project, take a couple of minutes to make sure iMovie's preferences are set to suit you. Choose iMovie ➪ Preferences to open the Preferences window (see figure 4.2), and then choose settings as described next. When you've finished choosing preferences, click the close button (the red button) to close the Preferences window.

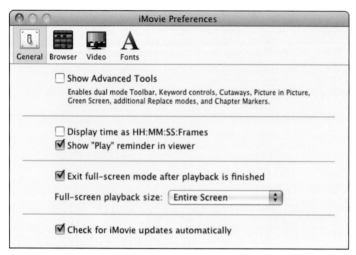

4.2 Use the iMovie Preferences window to set up iMovie to suit your movie-editing style.

Choosing general preferences

The General tab of the iMovie Preferences window displays the following assorted preferences:

- **Show Advanced Tools.** If you select this check box (which is cleared by default), iMovie displays several additional tools. You'll meet these tools later in this chapter and in the next two chapters.

- **Display time as HH:MM:SS:Frames.** Select this check box if you want iMovie to display clip lengths using professional-style timecodes in hours, minutes, seconds, and frames (such as 01:45:22:10 – 1 hour, 45 minutes, 22 seconds, and 10 frames) instead of seconds (such as 22.3 s – 22.3 seconds).

- **Show "Play" reminder in viewer.** Select this check box if you want to suppress the "Press the space bar or double-click to Play" message that appears when you move the mouse pointer over a filmstrip in the viewer window.

Exit full-screen mode after playback is finished. iMovie comes with this check box selected, so when it finishes playing back a movie in full-screen mode, it displays the iMovie window again. Normally, this behavior is handy, but if you want iMovie to stay in full-screen mode until you switch it back manually, clear this check box.

Full-screen playback size. In this pop-up menu, choose the size at which you want iMovie to play back movies when you use full-screen view. Normally, iMovie uses the Entire Screen setting, which stretches or squeezes the movie as needed to fill the screen. Choose Actual Size if you want to see the movie at its "real" size, Half Size for a smaller view, or Double Size for a larger view.

Check for iMovie updates automatically. Select this check box if you want iMovie to automatically check for updates when your Mac is online. Usually, installing the latest updates is a good idea because they may fix bugs in iMovie.

Choosing Event browser preferences

The Browser tab of the iMovie Preferences window lets you tell iMovie what to do when you click a filmstrip in the Event browser:

Show date ranges in Event list. Select this check box if you want iMovie to display the beginning and end date of each Event in the Event Library. Showing the date ranges is helpful when you're working by date as well as by content, but it can make the Event Library appear cluttered.

Use large font for project and Event lists. Select this check box if you want the Project Library and Event Library to use a larger font that's easier to read.

Always show active clip badges.

Clips in Event Browser use project crop setting. Select this check box if you want the Event browser to show clips using the cropping that you've applied to the project as a whole.

Show Fine Tuning controls. If you select this check box, when you point to a clip that you've already shortened, iMovie displays a button that you can use to change the clip's length. You'll learn how to do this in the next chapter. If you clear this check box, you can pop up the Fine Tuning buttons by pressing ⌘+Option while pointing to a clip.

Double-click to. Choose the action you prefer to occur when you double-click an event: Edit or Play.

Clicking in Events browser deselects all. Select this option button if you find it easier to select by clicking and dragging than by merely clicking.

- **Clicking in Events browser selects entire clip.** Select this option button to make a click select an entire clip rather than just the first part of it.

- **Clicking in Events browser selects.** Select this option button, then click and drag the slider to choose how many seconds you want to select at the beginning of a clip you click in the Event browser. Select the Add automatic transition duration check box if you want iMovie to include the length of any transitions you've decided to apply automatically.

Choosing video settings

The Video tab of the iMovie Preferences offers a couple of video-related options:

- **Video Standard.** In this pop-up menu, choose NTSC – 30 fps or PAL – 25 fps to tell iMovie which video standard you're using. NTSC (National Television Standards Committee) is the format used in North America, South America, and Japan, and PAL (Phase Alternating Line) is used in Europe, Australia, China, Africa, and the Middle East. Unless you've bought your DV camcorder or TV in another country, choose your local standard.

- **Import 1080i video as.** In this pop-up menu, choose whether to import high-definition video at full size (Full – 1920(1080)) or at the smaller size (counterintuitively called Large – 960(540), which takes up around a quarter as much space.

Genius

Unless you have a professional-quality HD camcorder or you must keep your high-definition video full quality, choosing Large in the Import 1080i video as pop-up menu is usually a good idea. Consumer HD camcorders typically record less data than the 1920(1080 format technically requires, which means the image is not full quality — so if you reduce the image to 960(540, the drop in actual image quality is so small few people notice it.

Choosing fonts settings

The Fonts tab of the iMovie Preferences window displays the list of fonts that comprise iMovie's Font Panel, which is a subset of your Mac's complete list of system fonts. For each of the nine listed fonts, you can choose a typeface and a color.

Starting a Movie Project

If you've just opened iMovie, and iMovie has created a project called My First Project for you, you're ready to start. First, though, you may want to rename the movie project and check that its properties are set the way you need them.

If you've already added material to My First Project, you may prefer to create a new project. To do so, follow these steps:

1. **Click the New Project button in the lower right corner of the Project Library, or choose File ⇨ New Project from the menu bar, or simply press ⌘+N.** iMovie displays the sheet shown in figure 4.3.

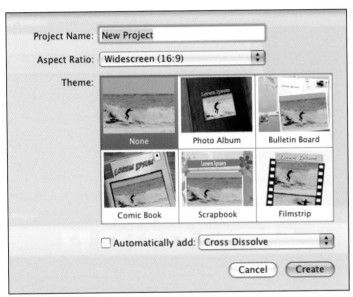

4.3 When you create a new project, you give it a name and choose its aspect ratio.

2. **In the Project Name box, type the name you want to give the project.** You can change this at any point, so go ahead and assign a working title if you haven't chosen a killer name yet.

3. **In the Aspect Ratio pop-up menu, choose the aspect ratio you want — the proportion of the frame's width to its height.** These are your choices:

   ● **Widescreen (16:9).** Choose this aspect ratio (16 units wide by 9 units high) for playing back on a high-definition TV or a widescreen monitor. If you play the project back on a standard TV or monitor, the video appears letter-boxed, with black bands above and below it.

   ● **Standard (4:3).** Choose this aspect ratio (four units wide by three units high) for playing back on a standard-shaped TV or monitor.

   ● **iPhone (3:2).** Choose this aspect ratio (three units wide by two units high) for playing back on an iPhone or another device with a screen that's one-and-a-half times as wide as it is high.

129

Note You can change a project's aspect ratio later if necessary by working on its Properties sheet, as described shortly.

4. **In the Theme section, click the predefined iMovie theme you want to use (or click None if you don't want to use a theme).** Each theme comes with a predefined set of scene transitions, as well as titles and other effects. Digital video editing doesn't get any easier than this!

5. **Tell iMovie whether you want it to add scene transitions automatically.** How you do this depends on whether you selected a theme in step 4:

   • **If you selected None:** In this case, select the Automatically add check box and then use the pop-up menu to click the type of transition you want iMovie to apply throughout your project. You'll meet the various transitions in Chapter 6, but the best transition for automatic use is Cross Dissolve.

   • **If you selected a theme:** In this case, iMovie selects the Automatically add transitions and titles check box for you. Clear this check box if you don't want the automatic transitions and titles.

6. **Click Create.** iMovie creates the movie project for you and adds it to the Project Library.

Genius Notice that unlike most applications (and unlike previous versions of iMovie itself), iMovie '09 doesn't let you choose the folder in which to store your project. Instead, iMovie automatically stores the project in the ~/Movies/iMovie Projects folder (where the tilde, ~, represents your home folder). iMovie also automatically saves the changes you make to your projects, so you don't need to save them yourself.

Renaming a movie project

My First Project isn't the greatest of names, so you may want to change it to something more suitable. To do so, double-click the existing name to display an edit box, type the new name, and then press Return to apply the change.

Setting properties for a movie project

Before you start working on a project, make sure its properties are set the way you need them. Follow these steps:

1. **Control-click or right-click the project in the Project Library and choose Project Properties.** iMovie displays the Project Properties sheet (see figure 4.4).

2. **Use the General tab to change the aspect ratio, choose a theme, or add automatic transitions.** See the discussion of these controls earlier in this chapter for details.

3. **If you select the Add automatically check box to add automatic transitions and your project already contains clips, iMovie expands the dialog box as shown in figure 4.4, and you use the following options to decide how to handle the ends of the project's current clips:**

   ● **Overlap ends and shorten clip.** iMovie moves each clip after the first to overlap its predecessor, and then applies the transitions. This is usually the best choice because you use only the footage in the clips. The one problem is when you've already set up your project with a carefully timed soundtrack: iMovie's shifting of the clips throws off the timing.

   ● **Extend ends and keep duration the same (where possible).** iMovie extends the end of each clip to provide enough time for the transitions. To get this extra time, iMovie reveals extra frames you've hidden in the clip. If the clip doesn't contain any hidden frames at the end, iMovie can't extend the clip.

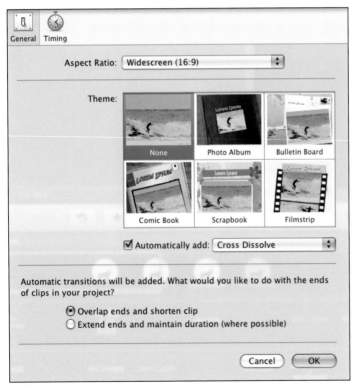

4.4 If you tell iMovie to add automatic transitions to a movie project, you need to decide whether to overlap the ends of the clips or extend the ends.

3. In the Timing tab (see figure 4.5) choose transitions settings like this:

- **Transition Duration.** Click and drag the slider to set the length of the transition, from 0.5 seconds up to 4 seconds.

- **Theme Transition Duration.** Click and drag this slider to set the length of the theme transitions, from 0.5 seconds up to 4 seconds. Note that this slider is disabled if you haven't selected a theme.

- **Applies to.** These option buttons are available only if you clear the Add automatically check box. Select the Applies to all transitions option button if you want iMovie to use these settings for all transitions — those you've placed so far (if any) and those you add from now on. Otherwise, select the Applies when added to project option button to apply automatic transitions only to clips you add from now on.

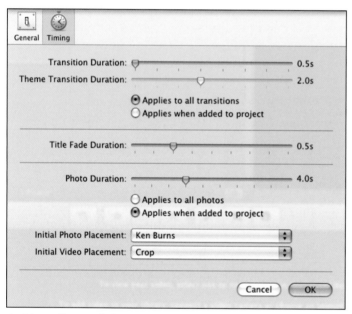

4.5 It's usually a good idea to set properties on the Project Properties sheet before working on a project.

4. Click and drag the Title Fade Duration slider to tell iMovie how long to fade the titles in and out. You can set from 0 seconds to 2 seconds.

5. Choose settings for still photos you add to the project:

- **Photo Duration.** Click and drag the slider to tell iMovie how long to play a photo for by default (from 1 second to 9 seconds).

● **Applies To.** Select the Applies to all photos option button if you want to apply this duration to all photos you've already placed as well as to any you place from now on. Select
the Applies when added to project option button if you want to apply the duration only
to photos you place from now on.

● **Initial Photo Placement.** In this pop-up menu, choose the standard placement for photos: Fit in Frame, Crop, or Ken Burns. You're just setting your default placement here; you
can always change the placement for a photo after you place it.

Genius

The Fit in Frame placement makes iMovie add letterboxing to photos and videos
that are the wrong aspect ratio for the project. The Crop placement makes iMovie
enlarge the photo or video so that it occupies the full aspect ratio, cropping off parts
of the dimension that was already fitting. For example, if a photo's aspect ratio makes
it too wide and short for the frame, Crop increases the photo's height to match the
frame, and then crops off the extra parts of the width.

6. **In the Initial Video Placement pop-up menu, choose the initial video placement: Fit in
Frame, or Crop.**

7. **Click OK to close the Project Properties sheet.** iMovie applies your preferences to the
project.

Genius

If you create stacks of movie projects, the Project Library can get crowded. To ease
the congestion, you can use folders within the Project Library to organize your movie
projects. To create a folder, Control-click or right-click in the Project Library window,
choose New Folder, type the name, and then press Return.

Importing Video

You can bring your video content into iMovie in several ways:

● **Import video directly from your digital video camera.** The process is different for a DV
camcorder that uses tape than for one that doesn't.

● **Copy video from your digital video camera or digital camera to your iPhoto Library,
and then access the files from iMovie.**

● **Import existing video files you have on your Mac.** You can also import video from iMovie HD projects.

● **Record live video directly into iMovie using an iSight or a DV camcorder.**

Importing video from a DV tape camcorder

To import video from a DV camcorder that records onto tape:

1. **Connect the DV camcorder to your Mac.** Most DV camcorders connect via a FireWire cable, usually with a four-pin (small) plug at the camcorder end and a regular, six-pin plug at the Mac's end.

Caution　Connecting a DV camcorder via FireWire can disconnect an external FireWire drive you're using. This shouldn't happen — but it does. So before you connect your DV camcorder for the first time, close any files that you've opened from any external FireWire drive you're using, just in case the DV camcorder knocks the drive off your Mac's FireWire chain.

2. **Switch the DV camcorder to play mode or VCR mode.** When iMovie recognizes the DV camcorder, it automatically displays the Import From window (see figure 4.6). If you don't see the window, click the Open Camera Import Window button (you can also choose File ➪ Import from Camera or press ⌘+I).

4.6 iMovie displays the Import From window when it recognizes a DV camcorder connected and switched on. This is a tape camcorder.

Importing all the video on the tape automatically

If you want to import all the video on the tape, follow these steps:

1. **Make sure the mode slider in the lower left corner of the Import From window is set to Automatic.**

2. **Click the Import button.** iMovie displays the sheet shown in figure 4.7.

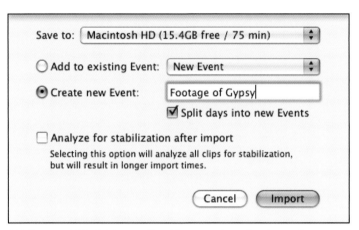

4.7 Choose which disk to save the video on and whether to create a new Event or add it to an existing Event.

3. **In the Save to pop-up menu, choose the hard disk on which you want to save the video.** Your Mac's internal hard disk is usually the best bet unless you've attached an external hard drive to give yourself extra space for working with video.

4. **Tell iMovie which Event to make the video part of:**

   - To add the video to an existing event, select the Add to existing Event option button, and then choose the Event in the pop-up menu.

   - To create a new Event, select the Create new Event option button. Type the name for the new Event in the text box; iMovie suggests *New Event* and the date, but you'll find that more descriptive names are more helpful. Select the Split days into new events check box if you want iMovie to create a separate event for each day on the imported video.

5. **If you want iMovie to apply stabilization to your clips, select the Analyze for stabilization after import check box.** This feature (new in iMovie '09) adjusts your clips to compensate for the telltale signs of shakiness that are the hallmark of handheld video footage. Note, however, that it can take quite a while for iMovie to apply stabilization, so your import will take longer than normal.

6. **Click OK.** iMovie rewinds the tape to the beginning, and then imports the video, displaying it in the Import From window as it does so (see figure 4.8).

135

4.8 Letting iMovie import all the video from a tape automatically

7. When iMovie displays the Camera Import Complete sheet (see figure 4.9), click OK. You can now turn off your DV camcorder and start working with the video you've imported.

4.9 iMovie tells you when it has finished importing the video.

Importing video from your DV camcorder manually

If you want to grab only some of the video from your DV camcorder, follow these steps:

1. Move the mode switch in the lower left corner of the Import From window to the Manual position. iMovie displays the transport controls for the DV camcorder (see figure 4.10).

2. Use the transport controls to reach the part of the tape you want to import. For example, fast-forward to approximately the right part of the tape, play the video until where you want to start importing, and then stop it.

3. Click the Import button. iMovie displays the sheet for choosing where and how to save the video.

4. In the Save to pop-up menu, choose the hard disk on which you want to save the video.

5. Choose whether to make the video part of an existing Event or to create a new Event for it, as discussed earlier in this chapter.

4.10 Move the mode switch to Manual to access iMovie's transport controls for your DV camcorder.

6. **If you want iMovie to apply stabilization to your clips, as described in the previous section, select the Analyze for stabilization after import check box.**

7. **Click OK.** iMovie starts importing the video from the point you chose.

8. **Click the Stop button when iMovie reaches the end of the video you want to import.** iMovie processes the clip you imported, and then displays the blue screen of the Import From window again.

9. **If you want to import more video from the DV camcorder, follow Steps 2 through 8 to select and import it.** When you've finished, click Done to close the Import From window.

Importing video from a DV tapeless camcorder

If your camcorder stores the video on a hard drive, memory card, or DVD, import the video files like this:

1. **Connect the camcorder to your Mac.** Most tapeless camcorders connect via USB rather than FireWire.

Genius

If possible, connect the tapeless camcorder to a USB jack on your Mac rather than on a USB hub connected to your Mac. Avoid using the low-power USB port on a desktop Mac's keyboard.

137

2. **Switch the camcorder on and put it into Playback mode.** Some camcorders call this mode PC mode or VCR mode.

Genius

If your Mac doesn't recognize the camcorder and launch iMovie, you may need to plug the camcorder into a power outlet to persuade the camcorder it has more than enough power to transfer all your video.

3. **Your Mac should open or activate iMovie automatically when it notices the camcorder in Playback mode.** If not, try quitting iMovie (if it's running) and then reopening it manually.

4. **iMovie automatically generates thumbnail previews for the clips on the camcorder, and then displays the thumbnails in a panel at the bottom of the Import From screen.** Figure 4.11 shows an example.

4.11 When you connect a tapeless camcorder, iMovie shows you thumbnails of the clips it contains.

Note

If your camcorder takes Advanced Video Coding/High Definition (AVCHD) video, you need to have an Intel-based Mac to import the video. Even a powerful G5-based Mac can't handle AVCHD video.

5. **Choose which clips you want to import:**

   - If you want to import all the clips, simply click Import All, and go to the next step. Otherwise, click and drag the switch in the lower left corner of the Import From window from Automatic to Manual. iMovie adds a check box to each clip (see figure 4.12).

   - To play a clip, click its thumbnail, and then click the Play button. You can then click the Previous button or the Next button to play another clip.

4.12 Move the switch to Manual to reveal check boxes for selecting the clips you want to import.

   - Select the check box for each clip you want to import. If you want to import most of the clips, click Check All, and then clear the check boxes for those clips you don't want.

   - Click Import Selected.

6. **In the Save to pop-up menu, choose the hard disk on which you want to save the video.**

7. **Choose whether to make the video part of an existing Event or to create a new Event for it, as discussed earlier in this chapter.**

8. **If you want iMovie to apply stabilization to your clips, as described in the previous section, select the Analyze for stabilization after import check box.**

9. **Click OK.** iMovie starts importing the video, displaying a progress indicator so you can see how it's doing. iMovie displays an Import Complete dialog to let you know when it has finished.

10. **Click OK to close the Import Complete dialog.**

11. **Click Done to close the Import From window.**

Importing video from a digital camera

If your digital camera takes video clips, you may want to use these in iMovie. Depending on your digital camera, you can import the clips into iMovie in one or other of these ways:

● **Import the clips into iPhoto.** If iPhoto recognizes your digital camera, but iMovie does not, import the clips into iPhoto. You can then use the iPhoto Videos Event in iMovie's Events browser to browse the clips.

● **Click and drag the clips from the Finder.** Connect your digital camera to your Mac via the camera's USB cable, and Mac OS X mounts the camera's storage as a drive in the Finder. Open the drive, locate the video clips you want, and then click and drag them to the Event in which you want to place them in the Event Library.

Genius

If Mac OS X doesn't recognize your digital camera, remove the storage medium from the camera and insert it in a card reader connected to your Mac. For example, remove a CompactFlash card or an SD card from your camera and insert it in a card reader. Once Mac OS X mounts the volume and displays it in the Finder, you can click and drag the video clips from the Finder to an Event in the Event Library in iMovie.

Importing existing video files

If you already have video files on your Mac that iMovie doesn't know about, you can import them into iMovie by using either the Finder or the Import Movies command.

The simplest way to import existing video files is by clicking and dragging them from the Finder.

If you want to put the video files you're importing in a new event, use the Import Movies command instead. Follow these steps:

1. **In iMovie, choose File ⇨ Import ⇨ Movies.** iMovie displays the sheet shown in figure 4.13.

2. **Navigate to the video files and select them as usual.**

3. **In the Save to pop-up menu, choose the hard drive on which you want to store the imported video.**

4. **Choose whether to add the files to an existing Event or whether to create a new Event.**

5. **If you're importing 1080i video, make sure the correct setting (Large or Full) is chosen in the Import 1080i video as pop-up menu.**

6. **Select the Copy files option button or the Move files option button.** Copying the files lets you change the files in iMovie without worrying about the originals, but it takes twice as much disk space. If the files are large, you may want to move them rather than copy them.

Save to: [Macintosh HD (99.1GB free / 1478 min)]

○ Add to existing Event: [Garden Tour]

⦿ Create new Event: [Museum Visit]

Import 1080i video as: [Large – 960x540]

This setting has no effect for DV, MPEG-2 or MPEG-4 video.
Selecting Large significantly reduces file size with little image quality loss.

⦿ **Copy files**   1080i movies will be converted to Large (960x540) and
○ **Move files**   copied to the event. The original files will be left in place.

(Cancel) (Import)

4.13 This importing sheet lets you choose whether to create a new Event and whether to copy or move the files you're importing.

7. **Click Import.** iMovie imports the files and then generates thumbnails for them, keeping you informed of its progress (see figure 4.14).

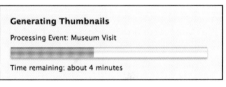

Generating Thumbnails

Processing Event: Museum Visit

Time remaining: about 4 minutes

4.14 iMovie generates thumbnails for the video files you import.

Importing an iMovie HD project

If you've used a previous version of iMovie, you've probably created projects in it — and you may want to bring them into iMovie '09. In most applications, using files created in earlier versions is easy; in fact, it's something that most people assume you'll be able to do without problems such as losing data. But because iMovie '09 and its predecessor iMovie '08 are actually new applications rather than an updated version of iMovie 6, opening earlier projects is more complicated than usual.

141

When you bring in a project from iMovie HD, iMovie '09 imports only the clips. You don't get the audio tracks, the titles, credits, or the special effects, and iMovie replaces each transition with a cross-dissolve.

If you're prepared to lose all these elements from your project, import the project like this:

1. **Choose File ⇨ Import ⇨ iMovie HD Project.** iMovie displays the sheet shown in figure 4.15.

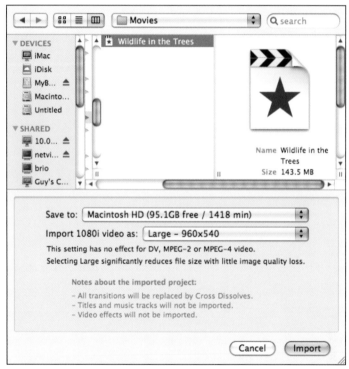

4.15 When you import an iMovie HD project, iMovie '09 warns you in small print that you will lose the audio, titles, transitions, and more.

2. **Navigate to the folder that contains the iMovie HD project file, and then click the file.**

3. **In the Save to pop-up menu, choose the hard drive on which you want to store the imported video.**

4. **If you're importing 1080i video, make sure the correct setting (Large or Full) is chosen in the Import 1080i video as pop-up menu.**

5. **Click Import.** iMovie imports the clips, generates the thumbnails, and then adds an Event containing the project to the Event Library.

Recording live video from an iSight or a camcorder

Another option is to record video directly from an iSight video camera or a DV camcorder connected to your Mac. The iSight can be either built into your Mac or connected via FireWire.

To record live video, follow these steps:

1. **If you're using an external iSight or another external DV camera, connect it to your Mac via FireWire.** For a camera other than an iSight, turn its control knob to the Record position or Camera position (depending on the model).

2. **Open the Import From window by clicking the Open Camera Import Window button or choosing File ⇨ Import from Camera.** If you're using an external camera other than an iSight, the Import From window may open automatically when you switch the camera to the Record position or Camera position. The illustration on the opening page of the chapter shows iMovie ready to record from an iSight.

3. **If you have two or more cameras connected, choose the camera you want from the Camera pop-up menu.**

4. **If the Video Size pop-up menu appears, choose the resolution you want (see figure 4.16).** Some iSight cameras can provide different resolutions (for example, 640(480 or 1024(576), while others can manage only a single resolution.

4.16 The Video Size menu appears if your iSight or external camera offers different resolutions.

5. **Aim the iSight or camera and any external microphone you're using.**

6. **Position your subject (for example, yourself) in the frame.**

143

7. **Click the Capture button (or the Import button) when you're ready to start recording.** iMovie displays the sheet shown in figure 4.17.

8. **In the Save to pop-up menu, choose the hard drive on which you want to store the imported video.**

9. **Choose whether to add the files to an existing Event or whether to create a new Event.** Select the Split days into new events check box if you want iMovie to create a new event for each day you film. Unless the clock is ticking toward midnight or you're planning a marathon filming session, you don't normally need to worry about this check box when recording live.

4.17 Choose where to store the footage, which Event to make it part of, and whether to split days into new Events.

10. **If you want iMovie to apply stabilization to your clips, as described in the previous section, select the Analyze for stabilization after import check box.**

11. **Click OK.** iMovie starts recording through the camera.

12. **Click the Stop button when you want to stop capturing video.**

13. **Click the Done button when you're ready to close the Import From window.** iMovie adds your new footage to the Event you chose.

Reviewing and Sorting Your Video Clips

After you import your video clips as described earlier in this chapter, review them to see what footage you've got and what parts of it you want to keep. iMovie lets you quickly mark clips you want to keep as favorites and ones that don't make the grade as rejects. To make your clips easy to sort and search, you can add keywords to them, and you can organize them into different Events so that you can easily find the footage you need.

Navigating through your Events

As you've seen in this chapter, when you import video clips, iMovie assigns them to Events. To work with Events, you use the Event Library in the lower left corner of the iMovie window. Figure 4.18 shows the Event Library with various events added.

Swap events and projects
Thumbnail size slider
View events by volume

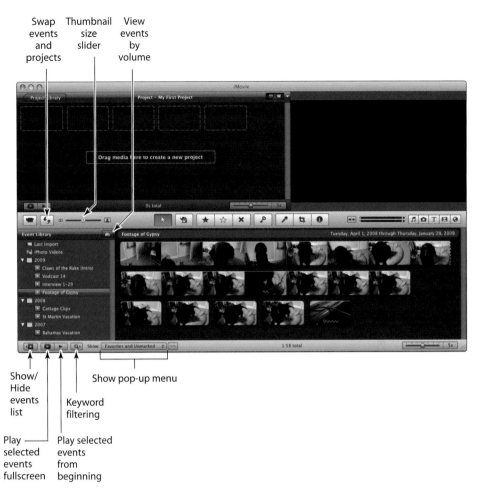

Show/ Hide events list
Keyword filtering
Show pop-up menu

Play selected events fullscreen
Play selected events from beginning

4.18 The Event Library with various events

The Event Library organizes your Events like this:

- **Last Import.** This Event contains the last batch of clips you brought in from your video camera. If you've just imported some video, this is the place to start.

- **iPhoto Videos.** This Event contains the videos you've imported into iPhoto from your digital camera.

- **Year folders (2009, 2008, and so on).** Each folder contains the Events for footage shot in that year. For example, if you dredge up a tape from 2005 and import it, iMovie puts it in the 2005 folder rather than the folder for the current year. (iMovie picks up the date from the timecode on the video.)

145

Depending on the video format your digital camera uses, you may find that iMovie displays the "No matching video" message when you select the iPhoto Videos Event in the Event Library — even though your iPhoto library contains videos that you can play in QuickTime Player by double-clicking them in iPhoto. If this happens, use QuickTime Player's Export command to export the videos in another format, such as MP4, which iMovie can play.

Changing the Event Library's sort order

Normally, the Event Library sorts the Events and folders in reverse date order, so the most recent items appear at the top of the list, where they're handiest. If you want to switch to conventional date order, choose View ➪ Most Recent Events at Top to remove the check mark by it.

Viewing Events by month or day

If you want to see the Events listed by month in the Event Library, choose View ➪ Group Events by Month. iMovie adds a separate category for each month that has footage. Choose the same command again if you want to hide the months again.

Viewing Events and folders by drives

If you want to see the Events and folders listed by the drives on which they're stored (see figure 4.19), click the Group Events by Disk button in the upper right corner of the Event Library (this button is labeled in figure 4.18). Alternatively, choose View ➪ Group Events By Disk to place a check mark by this item.

To return to the reverse date order, just click the Group Events by Disk button again. Alternatively, choose View ➪ Group Events by Disk again to remove the check mark.

4.19 Viewing Events by disk lets you tell easily which drive an Event's clips are stored on.

146

Viewing the clips in an Event

To view the clips in an Event, click the Event in the Event Library. iMovie displays the clips in the Event browser (see figure 4.20) as filmstrips, sequences of frames that show you the contents of the clips.

Filmstrip   Toggle audio skimming   Filmstrip continuation mark

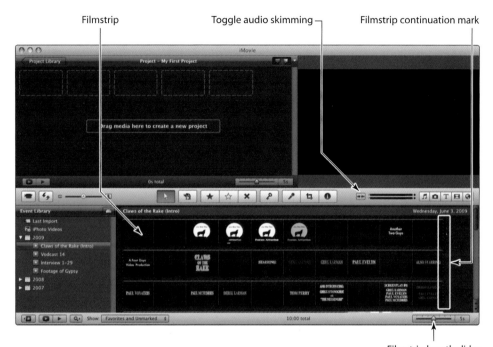

Filmstrip length slider

4.20 Viewing an Event's clips as filmstrips in the Event browser

To change the size of the video thumbnails, drag the Thumbnails Size slider to the left or to the right. (Figure 4.18 shows where this slider is.)

To change the number of frames iMovie displays for a filmstrip, drag the Filmstrip Length slider to the left or right. If you drag the slider all the way to the left, iMovie displays a single frame for each clip.

You can play clips in any of these ways:

- Double-click a clip to play it in the viewer.

- To play a clip full screen, Control-click or right-click it and choose Play Full Screen.

147

● Click the Play selected Events from beginning button to play all the clips in the selected Event (or Events) in the viewer.

● Click the Play selected Events full screen button to play all the clips in the selected Event (or Events) full screen. This way you can get the full impact of the clips.

Skimming through a clip

To move through a clip at your own pace, posi-tion the mouse pointer over the filmstrip in the Event browser so that iMovie displays a red line representing the Playhead (see figure 4.21), and then move the mouse to the left or right to move through the frames. iMovie shows the current frame both in the Event browser and in the viewer, so you can get a good view of what's happening. iMovie calls this technique *skimming*.

4.21 Drag the Playhead (the red line) to skim through a clip.

When you skim through a clip, iMovie plays the audio. If you don't want to hear the audio, click the Toggle Audio Skimming button on the toolbar to turn off audio skimming. (Figure 4.20 shows where the Toggle Audio Skimming button is.) Click the button again when you want to turn it on again.

Genius

When you've placed the Playhead in a clip, you can press the Left Arrow key or the Right Arrow key to move through the clip one frame at a time.

Switching the Event and Project areas

When you're reviewing your clips, you may want to switch the Event area and the Project area around so that the Event Library and Event browser appear at the top of the iMovie window along-side the viewer.

To switch the two areas, click the Swap Events and Projects button. iMovie swaps them over with a swirly animation. Figure 4.22 shows iMovie with the Event Library and Event browser at the top of the window. Click the button again when you want to switch the areas back.

4.22 You can swap the Event area and the Project area to make browsing your clips easier.

Selecting the footage to keep

To save space on your Mac's hard drive, you'll usually want to trim down your clips by selecting only the footage you want to use. Use these techniques to select the footage:

- **To select a standard-length chunk of video, click the clip.** iMovie displays a yellow outline around it, starting from the point where you clicked. By default, iMovie selects four seconds.

Note

To change the number of seconds of video that iMovie selects when you click a clip, choose iMovie ⇨ Preferences, click the Browser tab, and then click and drag the Clicking in Events Browser selects slider to the number of seconds you want.

- **To select as much video as you want, click and drag through a clip.** iMovie displays a yellow outline around the part you've selected (see figure 4.23).

4.23 Click and drag to select as much of a clip as you want.

149

- **To change the length of the selection, drag the handle at either side to the left or right.** Alternatively, Shift-click another point in the clip to make the nearest handle snap to where you click.

- **To move the selection without changing its length, drag its top or bottom border to the left or right.**

- **To select an entire filmstrip, Option-click it.** Alternatively, Control-click or right-click and choose Select Entire Clip.

- **To select multiple filmstrips, click the first, and then ⌘-click each of the others.** The first click gets you however many seconds iMovie is set to select, but as soon as you ⌘-click the second clip, iMovie selects the whole of the first clip as well.

Marking your video clips as favorites or rejects

Once you've selected the footage you want, you can quickly mark it as a favorite. Similarly, you select footage you don't want to keep and mark it as a reject:

- **Mark as a favorite.** Click the Mark Selection as Favorite button on the toolbar (see figure 4.24) or press F. iMovie puts a green bar across the top of the selected part of the clip.

4.24 Use these toolbar buttons to quickly mark favorites and rejects.

- **Mark as rejected.** Click the Reject Selection button or press R. iMovie puts a red bar across the top of the selected part of the clip.

- **Remove the marking.** Click the Unmark Selection button or press U. iMovie removes the green bar or red bar.

After marking favorites and rejects, you can narrow down the clips displayed by opening the Show menu and choosing Favorites Only, Favorites and Unmarked, or Rejected Only, as appropriate. When you want to see all the clips again, open the Show pop-up menu once more and choose All Clips from it.

Adding keywords to video clips

To make your video clips easier to sort and to find, you can add keywords to them. Follow these steps:

1. **Choose iMovie ➪ Preferences, click the General tab, select the Show Advanced Tools check box, and then click the close button (the red button on the title bar) to close the Preferences window.** iMovie displays the Advanced tools.

2. **Click the View Keywords for Selection button — the button with the key icon — that appears in the middle of the toolbar.** iMovie displays the Keywords window (see figure 4.25).

3. **Change the list of keywords to suit your needs:**

   ○ **To change an existing keyword, double-click it on either tab.** Type the replacement word, and then press Return.

   ○ **To remove a keyword, click it on either tab, and then click Remove.**

   ○ **To add a keyword, type it in the box in the lower left corner of the Auto-Apply tab, and then click Add.**

   ○ **To rearrange the list of keywords,**

4.25 Use the Keywords window to tag clips with keywords that make them easier to identify.

   drag them up and down the list. iMovie automatically assigns the numbers 1 to 9 to the first nine keywords so that you can apply them quickly.

4. **To apply keywords to a selected clip, click the Inspector tab, and then select the check box for each keyword you want to apply.** You can also press the 1 through 9 keys to apply the keywords currently assigned those numbers.

5. **To apply the same keywords quickly to several clips, use Auto Apply like this:**

   ○ **Click the Auto-Apply tab.**

   ○ **Select the check box for each keyword you want to apply.**

   ○ **Drag across each section in the filmstrip that you want to give the keywords.** To apply the keywords to a whole filmstrip, Option-click it.

6. **When you've finished working with keywords, close the Keywords window.** Either click the close button (the X button) in the upper left corner of the Keywords window, or simply click the Keywords button in the middle of the toolbar.

Filtering your clips by keywords

After you've applied keywords to your clips, you can use the keywords to filter the clips so that you see only the clips that have the keywords you choose. Here's how to do this:

1. **Click the Keyword Filtering button to display the Keyword Filter panel (see figure 4.26).** The panel appears between the Event Library (if it's displayed) and the Event browser.

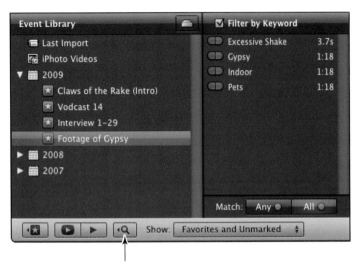

Keyword filtering button

4.26 Use the Keyword Filter panel to display only the clips that match the keywords you select.

2. **Select the check box for each keyword by which you want to filter.**

3. **Set the Any/All switch to Any if you want to see clips that have any of the keywords you've selected.** Set the switch to All if you want only clips that have all the keywords.

4. **When you've finished using the Keyword Filter panel, click the Keyword Filtering button to close the panel again.**

Organizing clips into Events

To make your clips more manageable, you'll often need to move a clip from one Event to another. You may also need to split, merge, or rename Events — or even delete Events and their contents.

Moving a clip from one Event to another

To move a clip from one Event to another, follow these steps:

1. **Control-click or right-click the clip and choose Select Entire Clip.** iMovie puts a yellow hoop around the clip.

2. **Click and drag the clip to the Event in which you want to place it.** iMovie displays the Move Clip to New Event dialog.

3. **Click OK.** iMovie moves the clip to the Event you chose.

Splitting an Event into two Events

Here's how to split an Event into two events:

1. **Click the Event in the Event Library to display its clips.**

2. **Control-click or right-click the clip before which you want to split the Event, and then choose Split Event Before Clip.** iMovie creates a new Event containing the clip you clicked and those clips that follow it.

3. **Double-click the default name for the new clip, type the new name, and then press Return.**

Merging two Events into one

If you find that iMovie has split clips that belong together into separate Events, you can easily merge the Events. Follow these steps:

1. **Click the Event whose name you want to lose and drag it on top of the Event whose name you want to keep.** iMovie displays the renaming sheet shown in figure 4.27.

4.27 You can merge two Events into a single Event to pool their clips.

2. **If necessary, type a new name for the merged Event.** If you simply want to use the name of the second Event you used, you're all set.

3. **Click OK.** iMovie merges the Events and puts the merged Event in the appropriate place in the Events list.

How Do I Turn My Content into a Movie?

As most directors will be quick to tell you, shooting the film is only the first part of the long process of creating a movie. Once you've shot your footage, brought it into iMovie, and chosen favorite clips as described in the previous chapter, you're ready to edit your clips and put your movie together on the Storyboard. You can also add still photos to your movies and create custom Ken Burns Effects to bring them to life. First, though, you need to know how iMovie applies edits to your clips because you can edit clips either in the Event browser or on the Storyboard — and the effects are different.

How Editing Affects Your Clips

For most editing maneuvers, iMovie gives you the choice of editing a clip either in the Event browser or after you place it on the Storyboard. This may seem puzzling at first, but it makes good sense when you get used to it.

As you saw in Chapter 4, the Event Library is where you store all the footage you may want to use in your projects. All the clips you import from your DV camcorder or digital camera go into the Event Library, and you can use the clips for any project. You narrow down the amount of footage available by creating favorites, by rejecting clips and footage you don't want to keep, and by organizing the clips into Events.

Changes you make to a clip in the Event browser apply to any project in which you use that clip. By contrast, changes you make to a clip after you place it on the Storyboard for a project apply only to that project.

This means you'll want to make general changes to clips in the Event browser and more specific changes to clips once you've placed them on the Storyboard. Here's a quick example using cropping:

- **Event browser.** If a clip has a cropping problem such as having a bystander's head and shoulders appear in the corner of the frame at a sporting event, you'll probably want to crop it in the Event browser. This obstruction will be a problem in any project you add the clip to.

- **Storyboard.** If you need to create a special effect by emphasizing the subject of the clip, crop the clip after placing it on the Storyboard. This way, you can use the clip as normal in other projects.

Either way, the edits you make to your clips in iMovie are still *nondestructive* — they don't actually change the video footage you've shot, just the way in which it appears. This means that you can undo any of your edits or redo the edits differently as needed, even when you make changes in the Event browser rather than in the Storyboard.

Arranging the Clips on the Storyboard

When you've chosen the footage you like, you can start creating your movie by arranging clips on the Storyboard, the area that appears when you hide the Project Library in the iMovie window.

If you're like me, you'll find the easiest way to start putting your movie together is by adding clips to the Storyboard in the order in which you want them to appear in the movie. Doing this lets you lay out the story of the movie in a natural and logical way.

Other times, though, you may need to add a clip to a different part of the Storyboard. This takes only a moment longer.

Adding a clip to the end of the Storyboard

iMovie gives you two easy ways to add a selected clip to the end of the Storyboard:

- **Keyboard.** Press E.
- **Mouse.** Click the Add Selection to Project button on the toolbar (see figure 5.1).

5.1 Click the Add Selection to Project button or press E to add the selected clip to the Storyboard.

When you add a clip to the Storyboard, iMovie places an orange bar across the bottom of the clip in the Event browser (see figure 5.2) to indicate that you've used the clip in the current project. (If you click another project in the Project Library, iMovie changes the bars to show the clips used in that project, so you can always see exactly what you've used.)

5.2 The orange bar on a clip in the Event browser indicates you've already used this clip in the current project.

Adding a clip elsewhere in the Storyboard

When you need to add a clip to another part of the Storyboard than the end, click the clip and drag it to where you want it.

You can drop the clip either between two clips that are already on the Storyboard or inside a clip. When you're dropping a clip inside another clip, move the mouse pointer over the destination clip to skim through the footage to the point at which you want the clip you're dragging to appear (see figure 5.3), and then drop the clip there.

5.3 You can also click and drag a clip to the point in the Storyboard where you want it to appear.

Adding multiple clips to the Storyboard

If you want, you can add two or more clips to the Storyboard at the same time like this:

1. **Select the first clip you want to add, and then Shift-click each of the other clips.**

157

2. **Press E or click the Add Selection to Project button on the toolbar.** iMovie pops up a bossy Editing Tip dialog box (see figure 5.4) suggesting that your movie will be optimal if you use only your best video segments. Little does it know that you've selected them already.

3. **Click Continue.** iMovie adds the clips to the end of the Storyboard.

5.4 iMovie objects to your adding two or more clips to the Storyboard at once. Click Continue to proceed.

Adding clips quickly with the Edit tool

Adding clips to the Storyboard using the techniques discussed so far in this chapter is quick enough for most people. But if you want to be able to add footage even faster, try the Edit Tool.

First, you need to display iMovie's advanced tools because iMovie hides the Edit Tool until you do this. Choose iMovie ➪ Preferences, click the General tab, select the Show Advanced Tools check box, and then click the close button (the red button) on the window frame.

Now, you can click the Edit Tool button on the toolbar (see figure 5.5) to turn on quick-add mode.

When you do this, the mouse pointer takes on a little sheet bearing a star. With this pointer, skim across a clip to where you want to start selecting, then click and drag. As you drag, iMovie turns the selected footage light orange (see figure 5.6). When you release the mouse button, iMovie adds the selected footage to the end of the Storyboard.

5.5 The Edit Tool button lets you quickly add footage to the Storyboard.

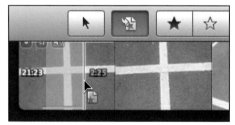

Keep selecting footage using this technique. When you've finished, click the Edit Tool button again to turn off the Edit Tool and restore normality.

5.6 After clicking the Edit Tool button, click and drag across clips in the Event browser to select the footage you want.

If you find yourself dragging across the wrong part of a clip, press Esc to cancel the selection without adding it to the end of the Storyboard, and then release the mouse button.

Playing back video on the Storyboard

To see how your movie looks with the clips you've added so far, you can play back the footage you've placed on the Storyboard. Without effects, transitions, titles, and added sound, the movie may seem pretty bald, but you'll be able to see how it's developing.

Playing back everything on the Storyboard

To play back in the viewer everything you've put on the Storyboard from the beginning, choose View ➪ Play from Beginning or press the \ (backslash) key. Press \ again to stop playback.

To play everything full screen, click the Play Project full screen button. Alternatively, Ctrl-click or right-click in the Storyboard and choose Play Full Screen.

When playing full screen, you can move the mouse to pop-up the navigation strip (see figure 5.7). Here's how it works:

- **Play/Pause.** Click the Play/Pause button at the left end of the navigation bar. You can also press the Spacebar.

- **Skim through clips.** Pause playback, and then move the mouse pointer through the clips on the navigation bar.

- **Change location.** Double-click another clip in the navigation bar to start playback there. Or else click another clip in the navigation bar to move there and pause playback.

- **Exit full screen.** Click the X button in the bottom left corner of the navigation bar or press the Esc key.

5.7 Use the navigation strip to move around a project you're playing full screen.

Playing back from a particular point

To start playback in the viewer, click at the point at which you want playback to start, and then click the Play button (or choose View ➪ Play.). You can also skim through the footage to the point where you want to start, and then press Spacebar to start playback. Click anywhere in the iMovie window or press Spacebar to stop playback.

To start playback full screen, skim to the point at which you want to start, and then press ⌘+G.

Genius

If you find your movie looks weird when playing full screen, it may be because it's stretched out of its aspect ratio. Choose iMovie ⇨ Preferences, click the General tab, and use the Full-screen playback size pop-up menu to choose Actual Size or Half Size instead of Full Screen. Try playing back again, and "full screen" playback will have black borders rather than actually filling your screen, but the project will appear at its correct aspect ratio.

Playing back just a short section

If you want to play back just part of what you've placed on the Storyboard, click and drag to select it, and then press the / (forward slash) key. Press the / key again if you want to stop playback before the end of your selection.

Genius

To play just a couple of seconds of video, point to the area of interest, and then press the [key (to play one second) or the] key (to play three seconds) around where you point.

Moving a clip to a different point

Here's how to move a clip to a different point on the Storyboard:

1. **Select the clip or the part of it you want to move.** You can move either an entire clip or just a selected part of one.

2. **Click the clip or selection and drag it to where you want to place it.** As when placing a clip initially, you can drop the clip either between two clips that are already on the Storyboard or inside a clip. When you're dropping a clip inside another clip, move the mouse pointer over the destination clip to skim through the footage to the point at which you want the clip you're dragging to appear.

Editing Your Clips

To get your clips looking just right, you'll almost certainly need to edit them, if only to trim them to exactly the length you need. iMovie provides easy-to-use editing tools that enable you to make good video look great and even salvage video that has problems with cropping, exposure, or color balance.

First, it's a good idea to set iMovie up to give you a better view of what you're doing.

Preparing to edit a clip

Normally, when you edit a clip, you'll want to see as much of it as possible. Use these five suggestions to improve your view:

- **Zoom the iMovie window as large as possible.** Unless you need to see other applications at the same time, give all your screen space to iMovie. Click the green zoom button in the upper left corner or choose Window ⇨ Zoom.

- **Increase the size of the viewer by choosing Window ⇨ Viewer ⇨ Large or pressing ⌘+0.** Alternatively, you can play your clips full screen.

Genius
You can quickly change the size of the viewer window by pressing ⌘+8 (Small size), ⌘+9 (Medium size), or ⌘+0 (Large size) instead of fiddling about with the Window ⇨ Viewer commands.

- **Show only the clips you're interested in.** When you're working in the Event Library, select the Event that contains the clips you want to work with. Then open the Show pop-up menu and choose Favorites Only or Favorites and Unmarked to make the Event browser hide clips you've rejected.

- **Make the thumbnails larger.** Click and drag the Thumbnail Size slider to the right to pump up the size of the thumbnails and make their contents easier to see.

- **Adjust the number of frames per filmstrip.** Either in the Event browser or in the Storyboard, click and drag the Filmstrip Length slider to increase or decrease the number of frames each filmstrip displays.

Genius
How many frames you need to have displayed in a filmstrip depends on how long the clip is and how much its contents change. For example, a long clip of a little-changing scene usually needs fewer frames displayed than a shorter take in which the camera pans or the subjects move. You may well need to change this setting as you move from clip to clip.

Adjusting the length of a clip

One of the most important edits you'll need to make is adjusting the length of a clip. You can do this by trimming off a selected part of the clip or cutting the clip down to only the part you selected, adjusting the clip's playing length using the Trim Clip pane, or making precise adjustments using the Fine Tuning buttons.

Trimming off the beginning or end of a clip

When you need to trim off the beginning or end of a clip, follow these steps:

1. **Click the clip to display a yellow selection rectangle around it.**

2. **Click and drag the left selection handle to the point at which you want to start delet-ing.** If you want to start deleting from the beginning of the clip, you don't need to move the selection handle.

3. **Click and drag the right selection handle to the point where you want to stop deleting.** If you want to stop deleting at the very end of the clip, you don't need to move the selection handle. Figure 5.8 shows an example of dragging the right selection handle.

Action button

5.8 Click and drag the yellow selection handle to select the part of the clip you want to delete. The yellow figures show the clip's length in seconds and frames.

4. **Press Delete or choose Edit ⇨ Delete Selection.**

Note

If you want to remove the selection and paste it into another part of the movie, Ctrl-click or right-click and choose Cut instead of deleting the selection. Move the mouse pointer to where you want to paste the selection, Ctrl-click or right-click, and then choose Paste.

Trimming a clip to only the part you want

The other way to approach the process of trimming a clip is to select the part you want and then dispose of the rest. Here's how to do that:

1. **Click the clip to display a yellow selection rectangle around it.**

2. **Click and drag the left selection handle to the beginning of the part you want to keep.**

3. **Click and drag the right selection handle to the end of the part you want to keep.**

4. **Ctrl-click or right-click in the selection and choose Trim to Selection.** iMovie gets rid of the parts you didn't select, leaving those you selected.

Adjusting a clip with the Clip Trimmer

When you need to dig deeper into a clip than you can on the Storyboard, open the clip in the Clip Trimmer.

Here's how to use the Clip Trimmer:

1. **Open the Clip Trimmer (see figure 5.9) by moving the mouse pointer over a clip, click- ing the Action button that springs up (pointed out in figure 5.8), and then clicking the Clip Trimmer.** You can also choose Window ⇨ Clip Trimmer, or press ⌘+R.

5.9 The Clip Trimmer appears in place of the Event Browser and gives you a full-length view of the clip you're editing. The selection rectangle shows the part of the clip you're using.

2. **Change the part of the clip you're using.** For example:

    ● Click and drag one of the selection handles to increase or reduce the amount of footage selected.

    ● Click and drag the bottom edge or top edge of the selection rectangle to move it along the clip without changing its length.

    ● Point at the end of the clip you want to move, and then press Option+Left Arrow or Option+Right Arrow to move it one frame at a time.

3. **When you've selected the part of the clip you want, click Done to close the Clip Trimmer and return to the Storyboard.**

Making a short adjustment with the Fine Tuning buttons

When you need to adjust the length of a clip by less than a second, use the Fine Tuning buttons. Note that the Fine Tuning controls are turned off by default in iMovie '09, so to turn them on choose iMovie ➪ Preferences, click the Browser tab, and then select the Show Fine Tuning controls check box.

You can now follow these steps to use the Fine Tuning controls:

1. **Move the mouse pointer over the clip so that the Fine Tuning control buttons spring out on it (see figure 5.10).**

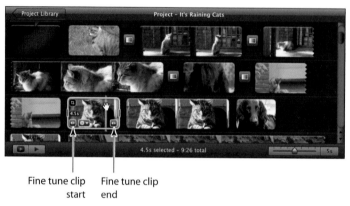

Fine tune clip   Fine tune clip
start   end

5.10 The Fine Tuning buttons and the Trim Clip button appear when you position the mouse pointer over a clip on the Storyboard.

2. **Click the Fine Tune Clip Start button or the Fine Tune Clip End button to display an orange handle for trimming the start or end of the clip.**

3. **Click and drag the handle to the left or right, as appropriate.**

Genius   To quickly change the beginning or end of a clip by only a few frames, move the mouse pointer toward the end you want to affect. Press Option+Left Arrow to move the end to the left or Option+Right Arrow to move the end to the right.

Figure 5.11 shows an example of trimming the end of a clip. The readout shows the number of frames you moved the clip end and the current length of the clip.

5.11 Click and drag the orange handle to fine-tune the start or end of a clip.

You can also display the orange handle for fine-tuning a clip by holding down ⌘+Option while you point to the clip's start or end. If you cleared the Show Fine Tuning buttons check box in iMovie's Preferences, you need to use this technique because the Fine Tuning buttons won't appear when you point to a clip.

Splitting a clip into two or three pieces

Often, you need to split a clip into two so that you can use different parts of it easily in different sections of your movie. Or you may want to insert another clip — for example, a cutaway — between the different parts of the clip to add visual interest.

From the Storyboard, you can split a clip into either two pieces (a beginning piece and an end piece) or three pieces (a beginning piece, a middle piece, and an end piece). Here's what to do:

1. **In the Storyboard, select the part of the clip that you want to split off from the rest.**
   You can split a clip into two parts by selecting either the beginning or the end, or split it into three parts by selecting a section in the middle.

2. **Choose Edit ⇨ Split Clip.** iMovie splits the clip into the required number of parts.

Cropping a video

To get the best effect in your video, you may need to crop a clip so that only part of it appears on the screen. Cropping applies to an entire clip rather than just part of it, but you can split off the part you want to crop into a separate clip by using the technique just described.

165

Genius You can crop a frame down to 50 percent of the original dimensions. As you'd imagine, quality suffers when you crop an image because the remaining data must appear at a larger size to occupy the whole frame. But you can usually get good results if you crop standard-definition video only a modest amount. And if you have high-definition video, you can crop up to that 50-percent limit and still retain good quality.

Here's how to crop a clip:

1. **Click the clip in the Event browser or on the Storyboard.** iMovie displays the clip in the viewer.

2. **Click the Crop button on the toolbar.** iMovie displays the cropping and rotation buttons in the viewer.

3. **Click the Crop button in the upper left corner of the viewer.** iMovie displays green cropping handles and a frame in the viewer (see figure 5.12) and adds a red dot to the Playhead on the clip.

Crop   Inspector

5.12 Click and drag the green cropping handles to select the part of the frame you want to keep. The green cross shows the middle of the cropping area.

4. **Click and drag a corner handle to resize the cropping area proportionally.** iMovie stops you at the 50-percent limit of size and height if you drag that far.

5. **If necessary, reposition the cropping area by clicking and dragging anywhere in the rectangle.** The mouse pointer turns to a hand when it's in the cropping area.

6. **Check the effect of the cropping in either of these ways:**
   - Click and drag the red dot on the Playhead to skim through the crop.
   - Click the Play button in the viewer to play the clip.

7. **Click Done to apply your cropping.**

Genius

Cropping is an effect that you apply to the clip rather than a change that you make to it, so you can change the cropping if you need to. Just open the clip for cropping again, and choose the cropping effect you want. If you want to get rid of the cropping, click the Fit button.

Adjusting color

One of the neatest things that iMovie can do is adjust the color of your video clips. So if you find that a precious clip is overexposed or underexposed, or if the color balance makes everyone's otherwise healthy face look green, you may be able to save the day.

To adjust the color of a clip, follow these steps:

1. **In the Event browser or the Storyboard, click the clip whose colors you want to adjust.** As usual, if you click the clip in the Event browser, the color adjustments apply to all projects that use the clip. If you click the clip on the Storyboard, the adjustments apply only to the current project.

2. **Click the Inspector button on the toolbar and then click the Video tab in the Inspector window (see figure 5.13).** iMovie also adds a Playhead with a red dot to the clip.

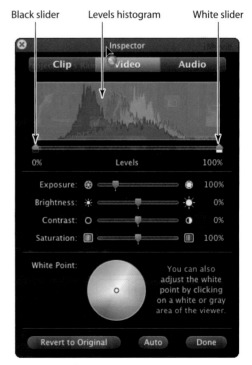

5.13 The Video Adjustments window lets you correct the exposure, brightness, contrast, saturation, and color balance of your video clips.

Note Like cropping, color adjustments apply to the whole of a clip rather than part of it, so if only a part of a clip needs adjustment, you will need to split it off into a separate clip, as described earlier in this chapter.

3. **Click and drag the Playhead dot to select a frame that gives you a good view of the colors you want to adjust.**

4. **If you want to use iMovie's automatic best guess at the color adjustments needed, click the Auto button.** If you don't like the effects, click the Revert to Original button to restore the previous color balance. If you do like them, either adjust them further as described next, or simply skip the remaining steps in this list.

5. **If necessary, use the histogram at the top of the Video Adjustments window to change the overall color balance:**

   • Click and drag the black slider to the right to add black tones to the clip.

   • Click and drag the white slider to the left to add white tones to the clip.

Genius The histogram shows how the colors in the selected video frame are distributed between pure black (at the left end, 0 percent) and pure white (at the right end, 100 percent). The red, green, and blue show the individual red, green, and blue color channels in the image.

6. **To adjust the exposure of the clip, click and drag the Exposure slider.** The scale goes from 0 percent to 100 percent, but generally you'll need to make only small changes to improve the clip's look considerably.

7. **To adjust the brightness of the clip, click and drag the Brightness slider.**

8. **To increase or decrease the contrast, click and drag the Contrast slider.**

9. **To boost or lower the intensity of the colors, click and drag the Saturation slider.**

10. **To alter the color balance of the clip, click and drag the Red Gain slider, the Green Gain slider, or the Blue Gain slider, as needed.**

11. **To correct the clip's white balance, set the white point by clicking the appropriate color on the color wheel or clicking a white or gray area of the frame in the viewer.** You may need to try several different colors to find one that gives the look you want.

12. When you're satisfied with the effect you produced, click Done to close the Video Adjustments window.

Getting color adjustments right can be a ticklish process you don't want to repeat unnecessarily. When you've applied color adjustments to one clip, you can apply the same adjustments to another clip by copying them and pasting them on. Ctrl-click or right-click the clip you fixed and choose Copy, then select the target clip and choose Edit ⇨ Paste Adjustments ⇨ Video. Repeat this trick for other clips as needed.

Rotating video

Another effect that iMovie lets you apply to a clip is rotation. Again, this applies to the whole clip rather than part of it, so you may need to split a clip into smaller clips to separate the footage you want to rotate.

Rotation is a dramatic effect best used for special occasions, such as when you want to make a clip play upside down for laughs. But rotation can also be useful if you (or your camera operator) has recorded a clip with the camera on its side, something that's easy to do with a digital camera you're used to turning vertically to take still photos in portrait orientation rather than landscape orientation.

To rotate a clip, follow these steps:

1. **Click the clip in the Event browser or on the Storyboard.** iMovie displays the clip in the viewer.

2. **Click the Crop button on the toolbar (or press C).** iMovie displays the cropping and rotation buttons in the viewer.

3. **Click the Rotate Counterclockwise button or the Rotate Clockwise button in the viewer.** Each click gives you a 90-degree rotation in that direction.

4. **If necessary, crop the video to make it the right aspect ratio in its new orientation.**

5. **Click Done to apply the rotation and any cropping.**

Restoring a clip to how it was before

Because iMovie's editing is nondestructive, you can always restore a clip to the way it was before. To restore a clip, open the tool you used to edit it, and then remove the change you made. For example:

- **Remove cropping.** Click the clip, click the Crop button to display the cropping and rotation buttons, and then click the Fit button to fit the video back to the frame.

- **Remove color adjustments.** Click the clip, click the Inspector button, click the Video tab, click the Revert to Original button, and then click Done.

- **Remove rotation.** Click the clip, click the Crop button to display the cropping and rotation buttons, and then click the rotation button needed to put the clip the right way around again. Change the cropping as well if necessary.

Genius

The reason iMovie doesn't automatically delete your rejected footage is that you may need it again. For example, you may need to lengthen a clip by using some of the rejected footage, or you may simply have rejected some valuable footage by accident when working quickly.

Deleting your rejected footage

Video tends to hog disk space, and even with today's ever-larger hard disks, creating and editing movies can run you out of space quickly. You can reclaim disk space by deleting your rejected footage, as described here, or use iMovie's Space Saver feature (described next) to attack the problem even more aggressively.

Here's how to delete your rejected footage:

1. **In the Event Library, click the Event from which you want to remove the footage.** You can select several Events if necessary. For example, select a month (or even a year) to work with all the Events it contains.

2. **Open the Show pop-up menu and choose Rejected Only to make iMovie display only the rejected clips (see figure 5.14).**

3. **Review the clips to make sure there's nothing valuable.** Depending on how many clips are involved, you may want to play them all or simply glance at the filmstrips and skim any clips you don't recognize.

5.14 Review your rejected clips before clicking the Move Rejected to Trash button.

4. **Click the Move Rejected to Trash button in the Event browser or choose File ⇨ Move Rejected Clips to Trash.** iMovie displays the Move Rejected Clips to Trash dialog box (see figure 5.15) to make sure you understand what's happening.

5.15 Confirm your decision to trash the rejected clips from the Event.

5. **Click the Move to Trash button to move the clips to the Trash.** iMovie changes the selection in the Show pop-up menu to Favorites and Unmarked.

6. **When you're ready to empty the Trash, click the Trash icon on the Dock, and then click the Empty Trash button.**

Reclaiming disk space with Space Saver

If you deleted your rejected footage (as just described), but you need to free up more space, try the Space Saver feature. Space Saver provides a way to grab all the frames that you haven't used or made into favorites — and then delete them.

Caution
Don't run Space Saver casually because it's important you understand what the command does before you use it to delete footage you'll later regret losing. The right time to run Space Saver is when you finish creating a project and need to get rid of all the extra space it consumes on your Mac's hard disks.

171

Here's how to run Space Saver:

1. **Select the Event you want to strip of unused video.** You can select several Events if you want.

2. **Choose File ⇨ Space Saver.** iMovie displays the Space Saver dialog box (see figure 5.16).

3. **In the Reject entire clips if any portion is area, make sure that only the check boxes you need are selected:**

   - **Not added to any project.** Select this check box if you want iMovie to get rid of any clips that you haven't made part of any project.

   - **Not marked as Favorite.** Select this check box if you want iMovie to dispose of any clips you haven't marked as favorites.

   - **Not marked with keyword.** Select this check box if you want iMovie to dispose of any clips you haven't marked with one or more keywords

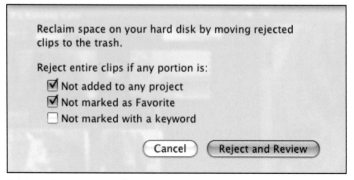

5.16 Use the Space Saver feature to reclaim valuable space on your Mac's hard disk by disposing of clips you're not using.

4. **Click Reject and Review.** iMovie closes the dialog box and switches the Show pop-up menu to Rejected Only, marking the clips with the red bar across the top that means they're rejected.

5. **Skim or play the clips to make sure there's nothing you want to keep.**

6. **Click the Move Rejected to Trash button at the right end of the Rejected Clips bar.** iMovie displays the Move Rejected Clips to Trash dialog box (shown earlier in this chapter) to confirm the decision.

7. **Click the Move to Trash button to move the clips to the Trash.** iMovie changes the selection in the Show pop-up menu to Favorites and Unmarked.

8. **When you're ready to empty the Trash, click the Trash icon on the Dock, and then click the Empty Trash button.**

Genius

If you realize you've rejected vital footage, choose Edit ⇨ Undo Move Rejected Clips to Trash immediately in iMovie. If it's too late for that, but you haven't yet emptied the Trash, open the Trash folder and go spelunking in the iMovie Temporary Items folders. You can click and drag the items named *clip* and the date and time (for example, *clip-2008-09-01 19;57;42.mov*) to the Event's folder in the ~/Movies/iMovie Events folder to restore the clips. Click and drag the contents of the iMovie Thumbnails folder in the iMovie Temporary Items folder in the Trash to the iMovie Thumbnails folder inside the Event. Restart iMovie.

Finding out where a clip lives

When you've placed many clips on the Storyboard, you may need to find out which Event a particular clip belongs to. To do so, Ctrl+click or right-click the clip on the Storyboard and choose Reveal in Event Browser.

iMovie can also show you a clip's file in the Finder, which is useful when you want to duplicate a clip or share it with someone else. Just Ctrl+click or right-click the clip on the Storyboard or in the Event browser and choose Reveal in Finder. iMovie opens a Finder window showing the folder containing the clip.

Adding Still Photos to a Movie

As its name suggests, iMovie is primarily designed for working with movie footage, but the application also makes it easy to use still photos in your movies. Now, *completely* still photos tend to lack visual excitement compared with moving pictures, but iMovie lets you easily apply the Ken Burns Effect to add life and movement to your still photos.

Preparing your photos for use in iMovie

To get your photos ready for use in iMovie, you'll normally want to import them into iPhoto as described in Chapter 2. Use iPhoto's tools for rotating your photos, editing them, cropping them, and adjusting the colors as necessary.

Bringing a photo into iMovie

To bring a photo into iMovie from iPhoto, you use the Photos browser pane. Click the Photos browser button (see figure 5.17) to open the Photos browser pane.

After you open the Photos browser pane (see figure 5.18), use its controls to navigate to the photo you want.

Photos browser   Transitions browser

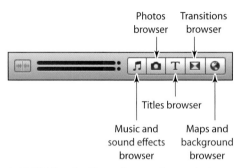

Titles browser

Music and sound effects browser   Maps and background browser

5.17 Clicking the Photos browser button is the easiest way to open the Photos browser pane for inserting a photo in your movie.

Album list

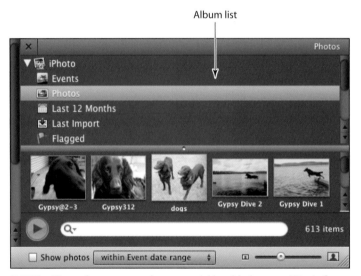

5.18 The Photos browser pane lets you quickly add photos to iMovie from your iPhoto albums.

Here's how to find the photo you want and insert it in your iMovie project:

1. **In the Albums list at the top of the Photos browser pane, choose the album that contains the photo you want.** For example, if the photo is in the last set of photos you imported, choose the Last Import item. If you want to see the last year's worth of photos, choose the Last 12 Months item.

Genius
Alternatively, click in the Search box and enter a search term. You can click the drop-down button at the left end of the Search box and choose Keywords from it to restrict the search to items you've tagged with a particular keyword in iPhoto. This is another good reason to tag your photos in iPhoto.

2. **Select the photo or photos you want.** If necessary, click and drag the Thumbnail Size slider in the lower right corner of the Photos Browser pane to zoom in on the thumbnails (or zoom out so that you can see more at once).

3. **Click and drag the photo or photos to the Storyboard.** iMovie displays a vertical green line to show where they'll land.

Genius
Instead of using iPhoto to bring photos into iMovie, you can click and drag a graphic file directly from a Finder window (or your desktop) to a project to place the graphic on the Storyboard. This technique can be handy sometimes for pictures you don't want to have in your iPhoto library. But usually you'll get better footage in iMovie by importing your photos into iPhoto, cropping and adjusting them there, and then using the Photos pane to place them in your iMovie projects.

Setting the duration for a photo

When you place a photo on the Storyboard, iMovie automatically assigns it a four-second duration. Try playing back the part of the movie that contains the photo and see if this is suitable. If not, set the duration like this:

1. **Click the photo to select it.**

2. **Click the Inspector button in the tool-bar (or press I).** The Inspector window appears.

3. **Click the Clip tab (see figure 5.19).**

4. **Type the duration in the Duration box.**

5. **If you want to set the duration for all your photos, select the Applies to all stills check box.**

5.19 Set the duration (in seconds and frames) for iMovie to display the photo.

6. **Click Done to close the Inspector window.** Try playing back the movie around the photo, and make sure the setting is suitable.

Setting cropping and Ken Burns Effect

When you place a still photo on the Storyboard, iMovie automatically applies a Ken Burns Effect to it with a modest amount of zoom — just enough to give that elusive soupcon of visual interest. For some photos, you may want to remove the Ken Burns Effect and simply show the full picture (or a cropped version of it) without panning and zooming. More likely, though, you'll want to set up a custom Ken Burns Effect to highlight the parts of the picture you want your audience to concentrate on.

Here's how to crop a picture or customize the Ken Burns Effect:

1. **Click the photo on the Storyboard to display it in the viewer.**

2. **Click the Crop button on the toolbar to display the cropping tools and Ken Burns Effect tools for still photos (see figure 5.20).**

3. **To crop the photo without adding the Ken Burns Effect, follow these steps:**

   - Click the Crop button.

   - Click and drag one or more corners of the green cropping frame to select the crop size you want.

   - If necessary, click and drag the cropping frame so that it contains the part of the photo you want to use.

   - Skip to Step 5 in this list.

5.20 The cropping tools and Ken Burns Effect tools for still photos.

176

4. **To customize the Ken Burns Effect, follow these steps:**

- Click the Ken Burns button if it's not already selected.

- Click and drag a corner or side of the green Start rectangle to select the photo size to display at the beginning of the pan and zoom. If necessary, click within the Start rectangle and drag it to select a different area of the picture. The green cross shows you where the middle of the Start rectangle is, and the yellow arrow shows you the direction and extent of the pan you'll get.

- Click and drag a corner or side of the red End rectangle to select the photo size to display at the end of the pan and zoom. As with the Start rectangle, click within the End rectangle and drag it to select a different area of the picture. The red cross shows you where the middle of the End rectangle is. Figure 5.21 shows an example.

- Click the Play button to view the effect and judge how well it works.

5. **Click Done to apply the cropping or Ken Burns Effect to the photo.**

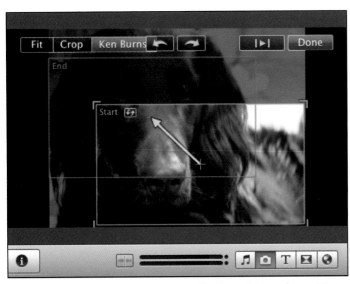

5.21 You can create a custom Ken Burns Effect by resizing and repositioning the green Start rectangle and the red End rectangle. The yellow arrow shows you the direction and extent of the movement.

177

Exporting a still picture from a video clip

One trick you'll probably want to use when working with still pictures is creating a still picture from a video clip. This trick is great when you've shot a brief amount of compelling movie footage and you want to make the most of it — for example, by using the Ken Burns Effect to zoom and pan over it.

Genius

You can also use your still pictures to create a freeze-frame scene, making the action stop for a moment — or as many moments as you choose — before restarting again. Or you can use a still picture with a Ken Burns Effect, followed by another still picture of the same frame, to create an effect of panning and zooming, then holding on the subject.

Here's how to export a still picture from a video clip:

1. **Either in the Event browser or on the Storyboard, skim through the clip to the frame you want.**

2. **Ctrl-click or right-click and choose Add Freeze Frame.** iMovie creates a still picture from the frame and adds it to the Storyboard.

Genius

When you create a still photo from a clip in the Event Library, iMovie automatically applies a small Ken Burns Effect to the still picture, so you'll probably want to customize the effect, as described next. When you create a still picture from a clip on the Storyboard, iMovie doesn't apply a Ken Burns Effect.

3. **Move the still picture to where you want it to appear in the project.**

Genius

If you want to use the still picture elsewhere in Mac OS X, Ctrl-click or right-click the picture's clip on the Storyboard and choose Reveal in Finder. iMovie opens a Finder window showing the contents of the Stills folder within the project. You can then copy the picture file to wherever you need it.

How Do I Finish My Movie and Share It?

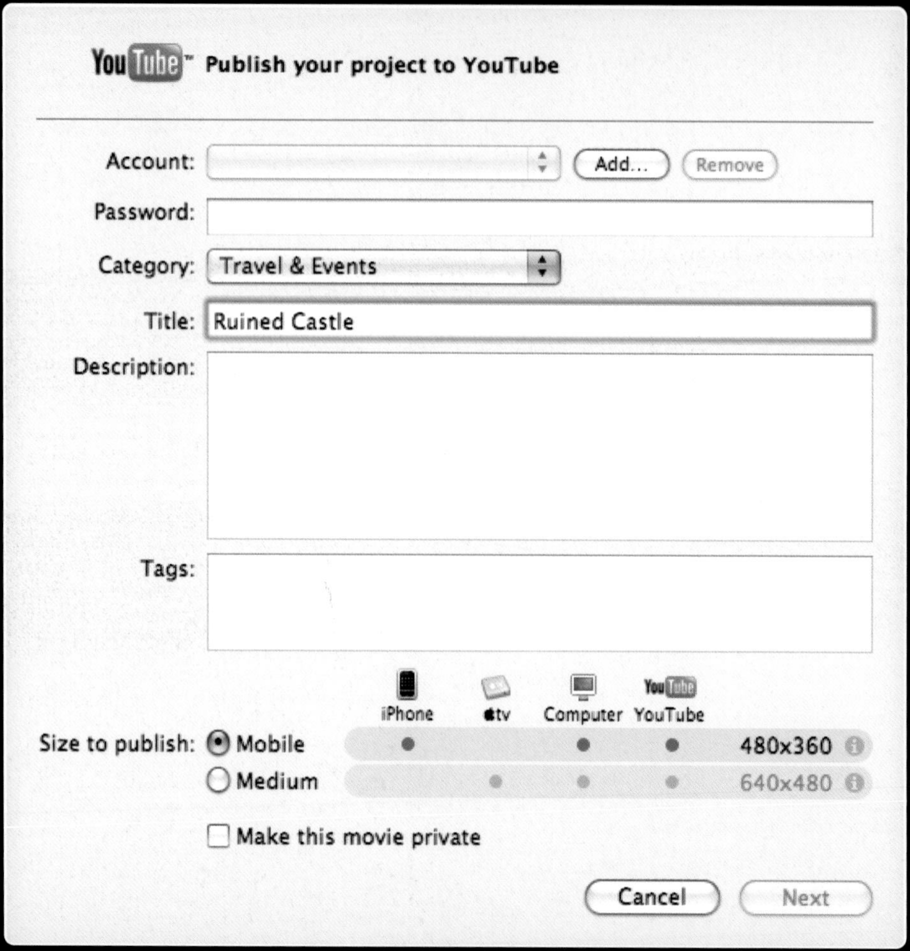

You Tube Publish your project to YouTube

Account: _____ ‹Add...› (Remove)

Password: _____

Category: Travel & Events ‹›

Title: Ruined Castle

Description:

Tags:

	iPhone	tv	Computer	YouTube

Size to publish: ● Mobile ● ● ● 480x360 ⓘ
○ Medium ● ● ● 640x480 ⓘ

☐ Make this movie private

(Cancel) (Next)

With your clips placed in the right order and edited to fit in with each other, your movie is starting to look like a finished product. Now you need to increase its impact by adding titles, transitions, and audio, and polish the movie until you're satisfied with it. It may then feel like time to rest on your laurels — but what you should do first is share your movie. iMovie makes it easy to share your movie with iTunes on your Mac or with the world by publishing it to YouTube or your MobileMe Gallery. When you need to use your movie elsewhere, you can export it either as an MPEG-4 movie file or a wide variety of other file formats — or even put it on your camcorder for easy transfer or safe storage.

Applying a Theme to a Movie

One of the goals of iMovie '09 is to make digital video editing as effortless as possible. To that end, iMovie '09 lets you apply a theme to a project, and that theme comes with its own set of titles and transitions that get added automatically, saving you lots of work. There are five themes in all — Photo Album, Bulletin Board, Comic Book, Scrapbook, and Filmstrip — and if one of them is suitable for your project, then applying it will cut down on your production time.

You saw in Chapter 4 that you can choose a theme when you first start your project. If you didn't choose a theme at the beginning, it's no problem to choose one later on. Here are the steps to follow:

1. **Choose File ➪ Project Properties, or press ⌘+J.** The project properties dialog box box appears.

2. **Click the General tab.**

3. **Click the theme you want to use.**

4. **Select the Automatically add transitions and titles check box.** If your project already contains clips, iMovie expands the dialog box box, and you use the following options to decide how to handle the ends of the project's current clips:

   ● **Overlap ends and shorten clip.** iMovie moves each clip after the first to overlap its predecessor, and then applies the transitions. This is usually the best choice because you use only the footage in the clips. The one problem is when you've already set up your project with a carefully timed soundtrack: iMovie's shifting of the clips throws off the timing.

   ● **Extend ends and keep duration the same (where possible).** iMovie extends the end of each clip to provide enough time for the transitions. To get this extra time, iMovie reveals extra frames you've hidden in the clip. If the clip doesn't contain any hidden frames at the end, iMovie can't extend the clip.

4. **Click OK.** iMovie adds the theme's titles and transitions.

Adding Titles to a Movie

Most movies need one or more title screens at the beginning and credits at the end — and many require other text screens strategically placed within the movie.

To start working with titles, open the Titles Browser by clicking the Titles Browser button on the toolbar, choosing Window ➪ Titles, or pressing ⌘+3. Figure 6.1 shows the Titles Browser.

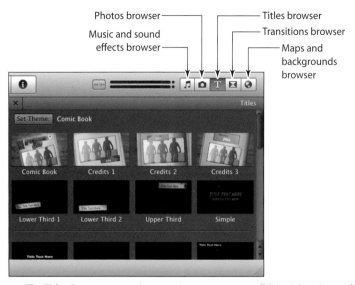

Photos browser
Music and sound effects browser
Titles browser
Transitions browser
Maps and backgrounds browser

6.1 The Titles Browser pane gives you instant access to all iMovie's various titles.

iMovie provides over 30 different styles of titles (plus four extra styles if you have a theme applied; see figure 6.1), far more than in previous versions. Many of the titles are animated, which can be very effective if used in moderation. (To see a preview of a title's animation effect, hover the mouse pointer over the title thumbnail in the Title Browser.) In most cases, you'll use the animated titles on their own, such as the Scrolling Credits title style shown in figure 6.2.

6.2 Some title styles, such as Scrolling Credits shown here, are best applied on their own.

You can use the static title styles on their own or superimpose them over a clip. For example, the Gradient – Black title style is a classy way to identify what's onscreen or provide a name for an upcoming video segment.

6.3 You can superimpose titles on existing video clips. This style, Gradient – Black, gives a discreet effect.

Applying the title

To apply a title, simply click it in the Titles Browser and drag it to where you want to place it on the Storyboard.

Applying a title on its own

To place the title on its own, follow these steps:

1. **Click and drag the title to the Storyboard so that iMovie displays a vertical green bar between clips where you want to place it (see figure 6.4).**

2. **Drop the title in the Storyboard.** iMovie displays the Choose Background window.

3. **Click the background color or pattern you want to use for the title.** iMovie extends the movie by adding enough frames to cover the duration of the title (four seconds, by default) and displays a title box over the new frames.

4. **Type the title text, as described later in this chapter.**

5. **Change the duration of the title, as described later in this chapter.**

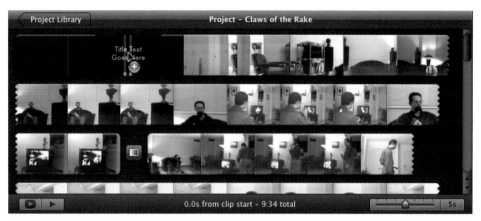

6.4 Placing a title between two clips adds to the length of the movie.

Superimposing a title on a clip

To superimpose the title on a clip, click and drag it to the clip on which you want to place it. You can drag it to the middle of the clip to use the title for the entire clip, to the beginning to use it for the first part of the clip, or to the end to use it for the last part.

As you drag the title, iMovie displays shading on the clip and a time readout so you can see what's covered (see figure 6.5). The title appears above the clip in a little balloon, and you can drag the sides of the balloon to extend or shorten the time the title appears. You can fine-tune these settings later as needed. Superimposing a title on a clip works well for any title style.

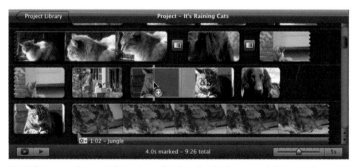

6.5 When you drag a title onto a clip, the shaded area and time readout show you where and how long the title will play.

Genius

If you put a title in the wrong place, you can remove it by Ctrl+clicking or right-clicking it on the Storyboard and then choosing Delete Selection.

Applying theme titles

You saw earlier that if you apply a theme to your project, iMovie adds some titles and transitions automatically. As far as titles go (I talk about transitions later in this chapter), applying a theme adds two titles to your project automatically:

- An opening title, which is the name of your project superimposed on the first few seconds of the movie.

- A closing title, which displays "Directed By" followed by your user account name, that is superimposed over the last few seconds of the movie.

iMovie also adds four theme-related title styles to the top of the Titles browser (refer to figure 6.1), so you can also add your own theme titles.

Adding the text to the title

When you've put the title on the Storyboard, you can edit its text by clicking the title's box on the Storyboard and then working in the viewer. Click to select a line of the placeholder text and then type the text you want.

Most of the title styles include a subtitle. Select that line too and type a subtitle if you want one; if not, just press Delete to delete the subtitle.

To change the font used, select the part of the title you want to affect, and then click Show Fonts to display the Fonts window (see figure 6.6). These are the essential moves you'll need:

- **Font.** Choose a font collection in the Collections box (or simply choose All Fonts), then choose the font family in the Family box. In the Typeface box, choose the typeface — for example, Regular, Italic, Bold, or Bold Italic. Then choose the Size size in the Size list, or drag the Size slider beside the Size list.

- **Underline and Strikethrough.** Use the Text Underline pop-up menu and the Text Strikethrough menu if you need to apply these effects.

- **Text Color.** Click the Text Color button to open the Colors window, pick the color, and then click the close button (the red button) to return to the Fonts window.

Note

In iMovie the Document Background control does not change the background color of the black slide you get with freestanding titles.

- **Text Shadow.** Click the Text Shadow button to toggle text shadow on. You can then use the Shadow Opacity slider, Shadow Blur slider, Shadow Offset slider, and Shadow Angle knob to adjust the shadow.

- **Style.** Click the Bold, Italic, Underline, or Outline button, as needed.

- **Alignment.** Click the Left, Center, Justify, or Align button to align the title's paragraph with the margins.

- **Line Spacing.** Drag the slider to increase the line spacing. This is especially useful for spacing out scrolling credits.

- **Kerning.** Click the left button to move the selected letters closer together, or click the right button to move them farther apart.

- **Baseline.** Click the left button to move the baseline of the selected letters down, or click the right button to move the baseline up.

- **Outline.** Drag the slider to change the strength of the outline.

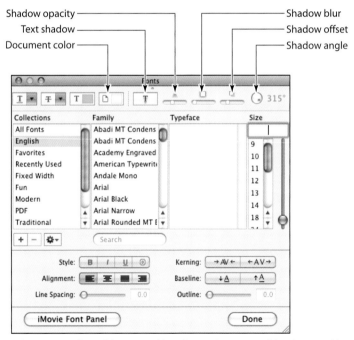

6.6 You can apply a wide range of font formatting to any titles that need it.

The Fonts window is certainly loaded with options, but if you want a friendlier font interface, click the iMovie Font Panel button to switch to the Choose Font window shown in figure 6.7. The main part of the window is divided into three columns: The left column is the font family; the middle column is the font color; and the right column is the font size. Click the item you want in each column to set the basic font. You can also click the Style and Alignment options to fine-time the font.

6.7 iMovie '09 comes with the Choose Font window for easier font formatting.

Note

Remember that you can cutomize the layout of the Choose Font panel. Choose iMovie ➪ Preferences, click the Fonts tab, and then customize each of the nine font family choices and the nine font color choices.

To see the effect of the titles you create, you have two choices:

- In the Fonts window, click Play in the viewer.

- In the Choose Font window, place the mouse pointer near the beginning of the font family box you chose, then move the pointer to the right. As you move the pointer, a playback bar appears inside the box, and the viewer displays the title effect. You can use the same technique in any font family box, any font color box, and any font size box.

When you finish working on the text of the titles, click Done.

Changing the duration and timing of the title

As you saw, when you drop a title on a clip, you can set the title's approximate duration by dragging it to the middle, beginning, or end of the clip on which you're placing it. Here's how you can fine-tune the duration and timing of a title:

1. **To change the duration of the title, position the mouse pointer over the beginning or end of the title so that the pointer changes to a two-headed arrow, and then drag to the left or right.** As you drag, iMovie displays the new duration on the left side of the title box.

Genius

You can also use the Inspector dialog box to change the duration of a title. Click the title box and the click the Inspector button in the toolbar. In the Inspector dialog box, use the Duration text box to type the duration. If you want to override the default fade and fade out times, click the Manual option and then drag the slider to set the fade time you want to use. Click OK to put the new settings into effect.

2. **To change the timing of the title, click the title box on the Storyboard and drag it to where you want it.** The Playhead on the clip shows where the title will start, and iMovie tells you how far from the beginning of the clip the title will start (see figure 6.8). Watch the viewer to get a close-up on the frame that the Playhead is over.

Timing from clip start

6.8 Click and drag the title to where you want it to start.

Adding Transitions to a Movie

When one clip of your movie ends, the next clip begins. The changeover between the two is called the *transition*. If you don't apply one of iMovie's transition effects, you get what's called a *straight cut* — iMovie blips straight from the last frame of the first clip to the first frame of the second clip.

If those last and first frames are similar in contents, a straight cut can work well. If the contents are substantially different, a straight cut can produce a jarring effect. Sometimes, you may want to give the audience that jar, but often, you will want to treat the audience more gently. To reduce the disjunction of the change between two clips, you can apply one of iMovie's transition effects to the transition between those clips.

189

To start working with transitions, open the Transitions browser by clicking the Transitions browser button on the toolbar, choosing Window ⇨ Transitions, or pressing ⌘+4. Figure 6.9 shows the Transitions browser.

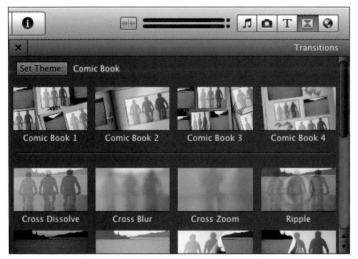

6.9 The Transitions browser pane lets you apply iMovie's 20 transitions to your clips in moments. Point to a transition to preview its effect.

Choosing a suitable transition to apply to a clip

The key to using transitions successfully in your movies is to use the right transition at the right time. Table 6.1 explains the various types of transitions that iMovie provides.

Note

iMovie '09 comes with 20 transitions, and marked improvement over the 12 transitions in iMovie '08. If you apply a theme to your project, iMovie '09 adds an extra four transitions to the top of the Transitions browser (see figure 6.9). You can apply a theme right from the Transitions browser, too: click Set Theme, click the theme you want, and then click OK.

Table 6.1 iMovie's Transitions and When to Use Them

Transition Name	Explanation
Circle Open	Displays a small circle on the first clip that gradually opens to reveal the contents of the second clip. This is a dramatic effect that suggests the second clip is springing from the first.
Circle Close	Draws the first clip gradually into a circle that shrinks down, revealing the second clip, and then disappears. This is a dramatic effect that suggests the first clip is vanishing into the distance.

Transition Name	Explanation
Cross Blur	Gradually cross-fades from the first clip to the second clip, where the second clip starts off blur and gradually comes into focus. This is useful if you want to obscure the second clip briefly to add tension to the transition.
Cross Dissolve	Gradually cross-fades from the first clip to the second clip. This transition is widely useful, and you can make it almost imperceptible by shortening it to 10 frames or so.
Cross Zoom	Gradually cross-fades from the first clip to the second clip, where the second clip zooms in quickly and then zooms back to its normal size. Use this transition to emphasize speed or the rapid passing of time.
Cube	Uses Apple's widely used rotating-cube effect to switch from the first clip to another. This transition suggests a complete change of focus to something happening separately in parallel. Use Cube with care because it's not subtle.
Doorway	The first clip splits vertically as though opening a double-doorway. The second clip zooms in as though entering the doorway. This is an occasionally useful transition when you need to introduce someone or something.
Fade Through Black	Fades out the end of the first clip to a black screen and then fades in the second clip. This transition is good for suggesting that whatever was happening in the first clip has ended and that the movie's subject is changing.
Fade Through White	Fades out the end of the first clip to a white screen and then fades in the second clip. This transition tends to give a ghostly feeling; use it in moderation if at all.
Mosaic	Divides the first clip into a series of small squares, each of which turns randomly to reveal parts of the second clip, which is them consolidated into the actual scene. This transition is useful for indicating that the second clip is a different aspect of, or the opposite of, the first clip in some way.
Page Curl Left	Curls down the upper right corner of the frame of the first clip and pulls it down and across to the left, revealing the second clip underneath. This is a dramatic transition that can easily bother the audience, but it can be effective at suggesting a major change if you use it in moderation.
Page Curl Right	This is the same as Page Curl Left, except that it curls down the upper left corner of the frame of the first clip and pulls it down and across to the right.
Ripple	Creates a ripple in the middle of the first clip as through you dropped a stone in a still pool. As the ripple spreads outward, it reveals the second clip. Use this transition with care.
Spin In	The second clip starts off in a small rectangle set at an angle. The clip gradually grows larger and rotates into place. This is a trick transition that can be effective if you use it in moderation.
Spin Out	This is the same as Spin In, except the first clip transitions out of the scene by shrinking into a small rectangle set at an angle.
Swap	This transition reduces the first clip to a thumbnail and displays it beside a thumbnail of the second clip in a distinctly Cover Flow-like arrangement. The second clip then turns and zooms into the scene. Use this transition if you want the audience to briefly compare the two scenes.

continued

191

Table 6.1 continued

Transition Name	Explanation
Wipe Down	Gradually wipes down across the first clip from the top, revealing the second clip.
Wipe Left	Gradually wipes left across the first clip from the right, revealing the second clip.
Wipe Right	Gradually wipes right across the first clip from the left, revealing the second clip.
Wipe Up	Gradually wipes up across the first clip from the bottom, revealing the second clip.

Caution

iMovie makes it easy to use transitions, but don't use transitions just because they're there. Before you apply a transition, always ask yourself whether the clips need the transition. If a straight cut works fine, don't embellish it. When you do apply a transition, check that it works as you intended; if not, replace it with another transition, or simply remove it.

Applying a transition between clips

To apply a transition between clips, click the transition type in the Transitions browser, drag it to the Storyboard, and then drop it between the clips you want to affect. iMovie displays a green bar to show where the transition will land, and then displays an icon representing the transition. Each transition type has a different icon, but some of the icons are hard to decipher at first.

Genius

If possible, stick with just one transition type to give your movie a consistent look, or use cross-dissolves and one other type of transition. Using many different types of transitions tends to grate on the audience.

To delete a transition, Ctrl+click or right-click it, and then choose Delete Selection. To replace a transition with another transition, click and drag the replacement transition on top of the existing transition.

Note

If you didn't apply a theme for your project, but you did select the Add automatically check box for transitions in the Properties sheet for the movie project, iMovie automatically adds transitions of the type you choose. If you want to prevent iMovie from doing this, Ctrl+click or right-click the movie project in the Project Library, choose Project Properties, clear the Add automatically check box, and then click OK.

Changing the transition duration

iMovie automatically makes each transition you add to your movie project the length you set in the project's Properties sheet. You can change the duration of a transition like this:

1. **Click the transition on the Storyboard.**

2. **Click the Inspector button in the toolbar.** iMovie displays the Inspector dailog box for transitions.

3. **In the Duration box, type the length you want to use for the transition.**

4. **If you want iMovie to use this duration for all your transitions, select the Applies to all transitions check box.**

5. **Click Done.** iMovie applies the change.

Caution

iMovie limits any transition to occupying only up to half of a clip (so that you can also put another transition at the other end of the clip). You may find this limiting with short clips because even if you set the exact transition length you want, you won't get it if the clips aren't long enough.

Adjusting the transition with the Precision Editor

When you add a transition between two clips, the increased visual appeal is sometimes offset by having a bit of your footage obscured in some way. For example, if you're using a Fade to Black transition, iMovie increasingly darkens the last few frames of the first clip, and increasingly lightens the first few frames of the second clip. Similarly, if you're using a Cross Blur transition, iMovie slowly blurs the last few frames of the first clip, and slowly focuses the first few frames of the second clip.

This is all normal, of course, but what if there's something significant in those darkened or blurred frames that you don't want the audience to miss? In previous versions of iMovie there wasn't anything you could do. In iMovie '09, however, you can use the new Precision Editor tool to adjust exactly where the transition occurs. So, for example, if want fewer frames at the end of the first clip to be darkened or blurred (or whatever) during the transition, you can shift the transition towards the second clip.

Here's how it works:

1. **Move the mouse pointer over the clip that comes after the transition you want to adjust.** The Action button pops up.

2. **Click the Action button and then click Precision Editor.** iMovie '09 displays the Precision Editor in the bottom half of the window, as shown in figure 6.10. This window has the following features:

   - The top filmstrip shows the frames from the first clip.

   - The bottom filmstrip shows the frames from the second clip.

   - The bar in the middle represents the transition.

   - The brightened frames in both filmstrips represent clip footage that appears in the movie.

   - The darkened frames in both filmstrips represent clip footage that doesn't appear in the movie.

   - In both filmstrips, the diagonal separation of bright and dark within the transition zone represent the progress of the transition. In the top filmstrip, for example, the decreasing brightness indicates the increase of the transition effect (such as darkening or blurring).

   - You can use the Playhead to play the filmstrips (move the mouse pointer across filmstrip) or the transition (move the mouse pointer across the transition bar).

6.10 iMovie '09 comes with the Precision Editor tool for frame-by-frame transition adjustments.

3. **Use any of the following techniques to adjust the transition:**

  ● To adjust the position of the transition relative to both clips, move the mouse pointer over the transition bar and then click and drag the bar left or right,

  ● To include a particular frame in the transition, click the frame in its corresponding filmstrip.

  ● To change just the start point of the transition, click and drag the left edge of the transition bar.

  ● To change just the end point of the transition, click and drag the right edge of the transition bar.

4. **Click Done.**

Adding Audio to a Movie

If you've ever seen a silent movie, you'll know what a huge difference a soundtrack makes. And though most video footage you shoot includes sound, you'll usually want to work on your movie's audio to make it sound right and give it the impact you need.

Understanding how iMovie handles audio

iMovie '09 lets you add music and sound effects to your movie:

  ● **Music plays from the start of the movie and continues to the end.** Music can either be a single song or a playlist of songs that you assemble in iTunes.

  ● **A sound effect or song plays at the point of the clip to which you attach it.** If you move the clip, the sound effect goes along.

That sounds a bit limiting, but you can also use a song as a sound effect by attaching it to a clip rather than adding it to the movie as a whole. You can find more about this in the next section.

To add either music or sound effects, open the Music and Sound Effects browser by clicking the Music and Sound Effects browser button on the toolbar, choosing Window ➪ Music and Sound Effects, or pressing ⌘+1. Figure 6.11 shows the Music and Sound Effects browser.

6.11 The Music and Sound Effects browser lets you quickly place sound effects from iMovie and iLife and songs from GarageBand and iTunes in your movie.

Adding music and sound effects to a movie

Here's how to add music and sound effects to a movie:

1. **In the Music and Sound Effects browser, choose the item that contains the music or sound effect you want:**

   - **GarageBand.** Choose GarageBand to see the songs you've composed in GarageBand.

   - **iTunes.** Choose iTunes to see all the songs in iTunes.

   - **A playlist or playlist folder.** Choose a particular playlist or playlist folder in iTunes to see only the songs in that playlist or the playlists in the folder.

   - **iMovie Sound Effects.** Choose this item to see iMovie's wide range of sound effects — everything from an alarm and a dog barking to a walrus roar and whale sounds.

   - **iLife Sound Effects.** Choose this item to see the hundreds of sound effects available to the iLife applications. Choose one of the folders — Ambience, Animals, Booms, Foley (extra sound effects usually added after a movie has been shot), Jingles, Machines, People, Sci-Fi, Sports, Stingers, Textures, Transportation, and Work – Home — to see only the effects that folder contains.

2. **Find the song or sound effect you want.** If necessary, click in the Search box and start typing a word to find matching items.

3. **To play a song or sound effect, click it, then click the Play button in the lower left corner of the Music and Sound Effects Browser.** Alternatively, double-click the song or sound effect. Click the Play button or press Spacebar to stop playback.

4. **Click the song or sound effect and drag it to the Storyboard:**

   ● **Music.** To apply the song or sound effect as background music, drop it in open space on the Storyboard. You can easily see when it's in the right place, as iMovie displays a green border around the area in the Storyboard that will be affected and applies green shading to everything within the border (see figure 6.12).

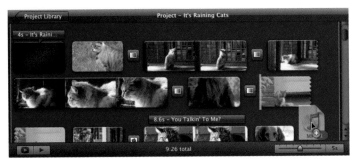

6.12 The green border and shading indicates that iMovie will apply the sound effect or song as music to the whole movie.

   ● **Sound effect.** To apply the song or sound effect as a sound effect attached to a clip, drag it over the clip, move the Playhead to where you want the sound to start, and then drop the song or sound effect.

Note

If you want to remove music or a sound effect, Ctrl+click or right-click it and choose Delete Selection.

Changing when the music starts

Once you've added music to a project, iMovie keeps it in place even if you edit the movie. This is handy if you're editing the movie to suit the music, but if you want the music to suit the movie, you may need to change when the music starts. To do so, follow these steps:

1. **Make sure the music isn't selected on the Storyboard.** If it is selected, click outside its left border or right to deselect it.

2. **Click the name of the music at the top of the Storyboard (scroll up if necessary) and then drag to the right.** iMovie changes the green shading to purple and lets you move the beginning of the music (see figure 6.13).

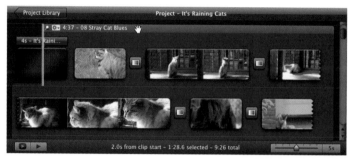

6.13 Click and drag the name of the music to the right to change the music's starting point.

3. **When the mouse pointer reaches the frame at which you want the music to start, release the mouse button.**

To change when a sound effect plays, simply click its box on the Storyboard and drag it till its pointer and the Playhead reach the frame where you want the effect to start.

Trimming a song or sound effect

When you need to trim a song or sound effect quickly, you can do so like this:

1. **Click the sound effect's box to select it.**

2. **Move the mouse pointer over the left end or right end of the box so that the mouse pointer turns to a double-headed arrow.**

3. **Click and drag to shorten the sound effect from the end you drag.**

For greater control, or when you need to trim a music track rather than a sound effect, use the Clip Trimmer pane like this:

1. **Click the Action button that appears on the left side of the music track or sound effect and then click Clip Trimmer.** iMovie displays the Clip Trimmer pane (see figure 6.14).

2. **Click and drag the left handle or right handle to trim the beginning or end.** Click the Play button to check your trimming.

3. **Click Done to close the Clip Trimmer pane.**

6.14 Use the Clip Trimmer pane to trim a music track down to the right length.

Adding a voiceover

Many movies need a voiceover — spoken words that help set the scene, explain what's happening, or bridge show-stopping gaps in the plot that you can no longer patch with footage. Here's how to add a voiceover to your movie:

1. **Click the Voiceover button on the toolbar (the microphone button) or press O to open the Voiceover window (see figure 6.15).**

2. **In the Record From drop-down list, choose the microphone or sound source you want to use.** For example, choose Built-in Microphone if you're recording through your Mac's microphone.

6.15 Choose the recording source and set the input volume in the Voiceover window.

3. **Speak into the microphone at the volume you'll use.** Drag the Input Volume slider as needed to put the volume bars about three-quarters of the way across to the right, but not so that you're getting the red LEDs at the right end all the time.

4. **If you're recording in a noisy environment, you may need to adjust the Noise Reduction slider to get good results.** This slider allows you to tell the microphone to try to filter out background noises so that it picks up your voice clearly.

199

5. **Select the Voice Enhancement check box if you want iMovie to try to improve the sound of your voice.** You should experiment with this feature and see if you like the effect; if not, turn it off by clearing the check box.

6. **Select the Play project audio while recording check box if you need to hear the project's audio as you speak your narration.** You'll need to wear headphones to prevent your microphone from picking up the audio and recording it into the voiceover.

7. **In the Storyboard, skim to the point at which you want to start recording the voiceover.**

8. **When you're ready to begin, click where you want to start.** The viewer prompts you to get ready and then counts down from 3 to 1, showing you the three seconds of footage before you clicked.

9. **Speak the voiceover, and then press Spacebar to stop.** iMovie displays a purple bar called Voiceover Recording under the clips (see figure 6.16).

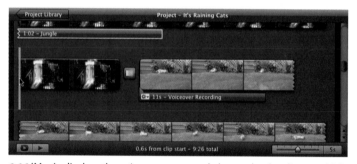

6.16 iMovie displays the voiceover as a purple bar under the clips to which it's attached.

10. **Repeat Steps 7 to 9 if you need to record more voiceovers.**

11. **When you finish recording, click the Close button (the (button) to close the Voiceover window.**

Genius

You can make voiceovers overlap if need be. And you can trim a voiceover either by clicking it and dragging one of its end handles or by Ctrl+clicking or right-clicking it, clicking Trim, and working in the Trim Clip pane.

Adjusting audio volume and fading

When you add music, sound effects, or a voiceover to your movie, you usually need to adjust one or more of the audio clips to make sure the parts you want to hear are audible. You can also adjust the audio that's part of the video clip, which is useful when you need to boost it, reduce it, or suppress it altogether.

To adjust an audio clip's volume, fading, and normalization, follow these steps:

1. **Click the audio clip you want to adjust.** For example, click a Voiceover Recording clip or the music clip. To work with the audio in the video track, click the video clip.

2. **Click the Inspector button on the toolbar or press I to display the Inspector dialog box box with the Audio tag displayed (see figure 6.17).**

3. **Drag the Volume slider to increase or decrease the volume.** You can mute the track altogether by dragging the slider all the way to the left.

4. **Apply ducking if the track needs it.** *Ducking* means reducing the volume of the other tracks while this track plays, and then restoring their volume. To set ducking:

   • **Drag the Reduce volume of other tracks slider to the left or right.** iMovie automatically selects the Ducking check box for you. (You can select it first manually if you prefer.)

   • **Listen to the effect to see if your track is audible over its competition.** Increase or decrease the ducking as needed.

6.17 Use the Audio tab in the Inspector dialog box to change the volume on an audio clip.

5. **If you want to create a gradual fade-in instead of using iMovie's automatic rapid fade-in, select the Manual option button in the Fade In area.** Drag the slider to the right to set the number of seconds and frames the fade-in occupies. The maximum setting is 2 seconds.

6. **If you want to create a gradual fade-out instead of using iMovie's automatic rapid fade-out, select the Manual option button in the Fade Out area.** Drag the slider to the right to set the number of seconds and frames the fade-out occupies. As with the fade-in, the maximum setting is 2 seconds.

7. **If your audio was recorded at different volumes, try clicking the Normalize Clip Volume button to even it out.** If you don't like the result, click the Remove Normalization button.

8. **To work with another clip, click it, and then repeat Steps 3 to 7.**

9. **When you finish working with audio, click Done to close the Inspector dialog box.**

Genius

If you mess up a clip's audio by working with the Inspector dialog box, click the Revert to Original button to restore the clip to its original state.

Sharing and Exporting a Movie

Watching your movie on your Mac is great with your family, but you'll probably want to share it with other people too.

iMovie lets you share your movies quickly and easily in five different ways:

- **iTunes.** You can add a movie to iTunes so that you can watch it in iTunes, on an iPod or iPhone, or on an Apple TV.

- **iDVD.** You can burn your movie to a DVD using the iDVD application.

- **Media Browser.** You can publish a movie to iLife's Media Browser so that you can use it in iDVD or iWeb.

- **YouTube.** You can publish a movie straight from iMovie to the YouTube video-sharing site on the Web.

- **MobileMe Gallery.** If you have a MobileMe subscription, you can publish a movie straight from iMovie to your Gallery on MobileMe so that visitors to your MobileMe site can view it.

If you want to turn your movie into a file you can use on other sites, you can export your movie in three different ways:

● **Export Movie.** This command lets you quickly save the movie as an MPEG-4 file using standard settings.

● **Export using QuickTime.** This command gives you more control over the exported movie. You can choose exactly the settings you need, and you can save it in any of various file formats. For example, you can create a movie file in the AVI format to share with Windows users.

● **Export Final Cut XML.** This command lets you create a version of the movie that you can bring into Final Cut Express or Final Cut Pro, Apple's more powerful video-editing applications.

Understanding the essentials of sharing

When you share a movie, you decide which size or sizes to use for it. iMovie offers four sizes; for some types of sharing, you choose a single size, but for others, you can use multiple sizes. Table 6.2 explains the four sizes iMovie offers, their resolutions, and the devices on which they work.

Table 6.2 iMovie's Sizes and Resolutions for Exporting Movies

Name	Resolution	iPod	iPhone	Apple TV	Computer
Tiny	176(144 pixels		✓		
Mobile	480(360 pixels		✓		✓
Medium	640(480 pixels	✓		✓	✓
Large	720(540 pixels			✓	✓

Seeing where you exported a movie

Given these various ways of exporting a movie, it can become difficult to keep track of which copies of the movie you put where. Luckily, iMovie automatically tracks the various copies you export and keeps you up to date with a clear readout at the top of the Storyboard.

Figure 6.18 shows the Storyboard for a video that has been shared to iTunes and published to both MobileMe and YouTube. You can click a View button to view the movie in iTunes or on the site, or click a Tell a friend button to start an e-mail giving a friend the URL of a movie on MobileMe or YouTube.

6.18 The Storyboard shows you where you published a movie and provides buttons for viewing it.

iMovie also places icons to the right of the movie project's name in the Project Library, showing that you've shared the movie (the beam icon) and which sizes you've created for it (the four rounded rectangles). Figure 6.19 shows an example. A white rectangle indicates a size you've created, and a gray rectangle indicates a size you haven't created yet.

6.19 The Project Library shows you which projects you've shared and which sizes you've created for them.

Updating a movie you already published

If you change a movie project after publishing it to iTunes, MobileMe, or YouTube, iMovie warns you that the published project is now out of date (. Click OK to continue making the edit, or click Undo if the warning has made you change your mind.

iMovie then displays a yellow triangle with an exclamation point and an *out of date* notice at the top of the Storyboard (see figure 6.20). The yellow triangle icon also appears on the project's sharing icon in the Project Library.

6.20 These yellow exclamation icons remind you that the published version of the movie is out of date.

When you finish updating the movie, Ctrl+click or right-click the project and choose the appropriate command: Re-publish to iTunes, Re-publish to MobileMe Gallery, or Publish to YouTube. iMovie displays the dialog box for publishing the movie (you'll see these dialog boxs shortly) but reapplies the settings you chose the first time. Make any changes, and then click the button to publish the movie.

Publishing a movie to iTunes, iPod, or Apple TV

If you want to be able to watch your movie in iTunes, on your iPod or iPhone, or on an Apple TV, export it to iTunes like this:

1. **Choose Share ➪ iTunes.** iMovie displays the Publish your project to iTunes dialog box (see figure 6.21).

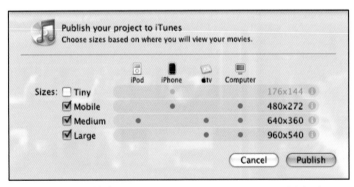

6.21 When you publish a project to iTunes, you can create multiple sizes to ensure the movie looks good on different devices.

2. **Choose the sizes you want to create.**
   - Usually you'll want to select the Mobile check box, the Medium check box, and the Large check box so that you can watch the movie on an iPhone, an Apple TV, or your Mac.

- iMovie creates a separate movie file for each, adding the size to the project's name — for example, *Our New Arrival – Mobile* and *Our New Arrival – Medium* — so that you can distinguish the files.

3. **Click Publish.**

The more sizes you choose, the longer the publishing takes. When iMovie has finished creating the files, it automatically launches or activates iTunes so that you can check out the movies. Click the Movies item in the Sidebar to see the list of movies.

Publishing a movie to YouTube

iMovie makes it easy to publish a movie to YouTube. Here are the essentials:

- **Set up a YouTube account.** If you don't already have a YouTube account, go to the YouTube Web site (www.youtube.com), click the Sign Up link, and follow the instructions.

- **Publish a movie to YouTube.** Click the project in the Project Library, and then choose Share ⇨ YouTube. Choose the account you want to use, and then follow the prompts.

- **Remove a movie from YouTube.** Click the project in the Project Library, and then choose Share ⇨ Remove from YouTube. iMovie opens your Web browser on the page for managing your videos. Select the check box for the movie you want to delete, click Delete, and then click OK.

Publishing a movie to your MobileMe Gallery

If you have a MobileMe subscription, you can easily publish a movie to your MobileMe Gallery.

First, if you're not currently signed in to your MobileMe account, you should sign in before publishing your movie. Click System Preferences in the Dock, click MobileMe, click Sign In, and then enter your MobileMe credentials.

Now follow these steps in iMovie:

1. **Select the movie project in the Project Library.**

2. **Choose Share ⇨ MobileMe Gallery.** iMovie displays the Publish your project to your MobileMe Gallery dialog box (see figure 6.22).

3. **Improve the title in the Title box if necessary.**

4. **Type a description of the movie in the Description box.**

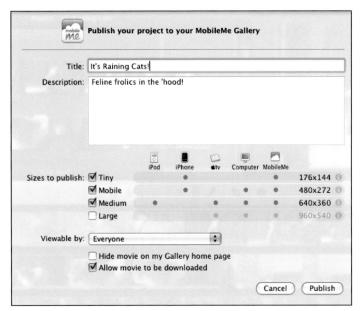

6.22 You can put up to four different sizes of movie on your MobileMe Gallery. This allows visitors to download the size they want.

5. **In the Sizes to publish area, select the check box for each size you want to publish.**

6. **In the Viewable by pop-up menu, choose who may view the movie:**

   ● **Everyone.** Anyone on the Web can view the album.

   ● **Only me.** You keep the album to yourself — good for personal or work photos.

   ● **Edit Names and Passwords.** To add the name of a person or group and assign a password, click this item, and work on the sheet that appears. Click OK when you finish.

7. **If you want to hide the movie on your Gallery page, select the Hide movie on my Gallery home page check box.**

8. **Select the Allow movie to be downloaded check box if you want people to be able to download the movie rather than just watch it online.**

Genius

Hiding a movie so that it doesn't appear on your MobileMe Gallery page is good for when you need to share different movies with different people. Instead of needing to password-protect a movie to keep out people you don't want to see it, you can simply prevent the movie from appearing, and give the movie's URL to the people you want to watch it.

9. **Click Publish.** iMovie prepares the movie sizes you chose and publishes them to your Gallery, then displays a dialog box telling you it has done so.

10. **Click Tell a Friend to start an e-mail message announcing your movie, click View to view your Gallery, or click OK to close the dialog box.**

Putting a movie on a DVD

iMovie '09 gives you two ways to publish a movie to a DVD: you can publish straight to the iDVD application, or you can share the movie with iLife's Media Browser, from which iDVD can pull in the movie.

See Chapter 12 for the details on using iDVD to create a DVD.

Exporting a movie quickly to an MPEG-4 file

If you want to export a movie quickly to a Tiny, Mobile, Medium, or Large size MPEG-4 file using iMovie's preset settings, creating a file that will play on almost any type of computer, follow these steps:

1. **Select the movie project in the Project Library.**

2. **Choose Share ⇨ Export Movie or press ⌘+E.** iMovie displays the Export As dialog box shown in figure 6.23.

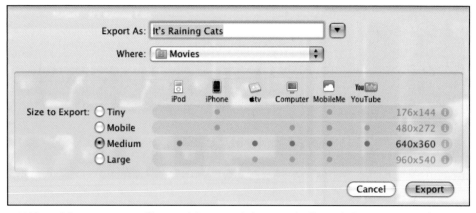

6.23 The quick way to create a file containing a movie is to use the Share ⇨ Export command.

3. **In the Export As box, iMovie enters the project's name.** Edit this name or type a new name as necessary.

4. **In the Where pop-up menu, choose the folder in which to store the exported file.** If necessary, expand the dialog box so that you can see the Sidebar.

5. **In the Size to Export area, select an option button — Tiny, Mobile, Medium, or Large — as appropriate.** Table 6.2 (earlier in this chapter) explains the sizes.

6. **Click Export.** iMovie exports the movie to the file and saves it in the folder you chose.

Exporting to another file format

When you need a file format other than MPEG-4, or when you need to control exactly how iMovie exports the file, you can export to a QuickTime file instead. Here's what to do:

1. **Select the movie project in the Project Library.**

2. **Choose Share ⇨ Export using QuickTime.** iMovie displays the Save exported file as dialog box shown in figure 6.24.

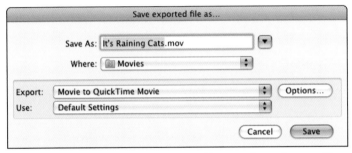

6.24 The Export using QuickTime command lets you choose from a wide variety of export formats.

Genius

You can also export a movie to a QuickTime file when you need to bring it into iMovie HD — for example, so that you can export it to your DV camcorder, as described later in this chapter.

3. **In the Save As box, iMovie enters the project's name.** Edit this name or type a new name as necessary.

4. **In the Where pop-up menu, choose the folder in which to store the exported file.** If necessary, expand the dialog box so that you can see the Sidebar.

5. **In the Export pop-up menu, choose the format you want.** Table 6.3 explains your options.

Table 6.3 Export Options Using QuickTime

Export Format	Explanation
Movie to 3G mobile phones.	Creates a movie in the 3gp format, streaming the movie to 3G
Movie to Apple TV	Creates a movie in the MPEG-4 format. This gives you the same result as choosing Share ⇨ Export Movie and choosing the Medium size (which is easier). The movie's resolution is 640(480 pixels.
Movie to AVI	Creates a movie in the AVI format, which is widely used on Windows. You can choose the quality and compression (if any).
Movie to DV Stream	Creates a movie in a DV format. You can choose whether the movie is formatted for NTSC or for PAL.
Movie to FLC	Creates a movie in the FLIC animation format. You can choose the frame rate and whether the movie uses Windows Colors or Mac Colors.
Movie to Image Sequence	Creates an image file for each frame of the movie. You can choose from various image formats (such as JPEG).
Movie to iPhone	Creates a movie in the MPEG-4 format suitable for viewing on the iPhone or iPod touch. This gives you the same result as choosing Share ⇨ Export Movie and choosing the Small size. The movie's resolution is 480(360 pixels.
Movie to iPhone (Cellular)	Creates a movie in the 3GP format suitable for watching as a stream on the iPhone. The movie's resolution is 176(132 pixels.
Movie to iPod	Creates a movie in the MPEG-4 format suitable for viewing on any iPod or on a TV to which it's connected. The movie's resolution is 640(480 pixels, the same as the Movie to Apple TV export format, but it uses a lower bitrate and so has a smaller file size.
Movie to MPEG-4	Creates a movie in the MPEG-4 format. This is the same as choosing Share ⇨ Export Movie, except you can click the Options buttons to set a wide variety of movie options, including the image size, frame rate, and audio format.
Movie to QuickTime Movie	Creates a movie in the QuickTime format. You can choose from a wide variety of settings to get the resolution and quality you need.
Sound to AIFF	Exports the sound track from the movie to a file in the AIFF format, an uncompressed, full-quality format used widely on the Mac.
Sound to AU	Exports the sound track from the movie to a file in the AU format. This file format is less widely used than AIFF or WAV.
Sound to WAV	Exports the sound track from the movie to a file in the WAV format, an uncompressed, full-quality format used widely on Windows.

Genius

QuickTime's *Sound To* export formats are great for grabbing the audio from a movie so that you can use it elsewhere.

6. **If the Options button is available instead of being dimmed, you can click it to choose options for the export format.** For example, if you choose the Movie to QuickTime Movie export format, you can choose options like this:

● **Click the Options button to display the Movie Settings dialog box.**

● **To change the video settings, click the Settings button in the Video box, and then choose compression, motion, data rate, and encoding settings in the Video Compression Settings dialog box.**

● **To apply a special effect such as Lens Flare, click the Filtering button, and then choose settings in the Filtering dialog box.**

● **To change the resolution of the video, click the Video Size button, and then choose settings in the Export Size Settings dialog box.**

● **To use a different sound format or quality, click the Settings button in the Sound box, and then choose settings in the Sound Settings dialog box.**

● **If you want to be able to stream the movie across the Internet, select the Prepare for Internet Streaming check box, and then choose Fast Start, Fast Start – Compressed Header, or Hinted Streaming.** Fast Start is usually the best choice for general use. Hinted Streaming is for use with QuickTime Streaming Server.

● **Click OK to close the Movie Settings dialog box and return to the Save exported file as dialog box.**

7. **Click Save.** iMovie exports the file in the format you chose.

Exporting to a Final Cut XML file

If you have Final Cut Express or Final Cut Pro, Apple's more powerful video-editing applications, you may want to bring into it movies that you've created in iMovie so that you can develop them further.

To do this, you can use the Export Final Cut XML command. But before you do, it's vital that you're clear on what you get and what you don't get:

- **Video.** You get the video footage, but iMovie removes any color adjustments you made.

- **Audio.** You get the audio tracks, but iMovie removes any voiceovers, sound effects, and music tracks.

- **Transitions.** iMovie replaces all your custom transitions with Cross Dissolves.

- **Titles.** You lose all the titles.

- **Cropping and Ken Burns Effects.** iMovie removes these as well.

That may sound as though there's not much left. But if what you're looking to do is get your edited video into one of the Final Cut applications so that you can re-edit it there, you get just about enough.

Here's how to export your movie project to a Final Cut XML file:

1. **Click the movie project in the Project Library.**

2. **Choose Share ⇨ Export Final Cut XML.** iMovie displays the Export FCP XML dialog box (see figure 6.25).

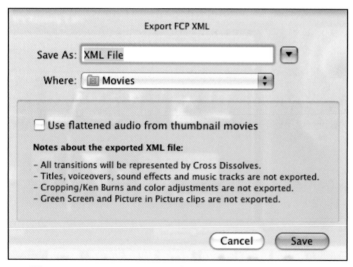

6.25 When you export a movie to Final Cut XML, you lose transitions, voiceovers, cropping, and more — but you do transfer the footage.

3. **In the Save As box, type the name you want to give the file.** iMovie suggests XML File, which isn't helpful.

4. **In the Where pop-up menu, choose the folder in which to store the exported file.** If necessary, expand the dialog box so that you can see the Sidebar.

5. **Select the Use flattened audio from thumbnail movies check box if you want to include the rendered audio.** Clear this check box if you plan to render the audio in Final Cut (which gives you more control over how it sounds).

6. **Click Save.** iMovie exports the file. You can then import it into Final Cut.

Exporting a movie to your camcorder

iMovie '09 doesn't give you a way of exporting a movie to a camcorder, but there is a workaround if you have iMovie HD on an older Mac: You can export the movie to iMovie HD and then export it from there. Follow these steps:

1. **In iMovie '09, select the movie project in the Project Library.**

2. **Choose Share ⇨ Export using QuickTime.** iMovie displays the Save exported file as dialog box.

3. **In the Save As box, change the movie name if necessary.** iMovie suggests the movie project's title.

4. **In the Where pop-up menu, choose the folder in which to store the exported file.** If necessary, expand the dialog box so that you can see the Sidebar.

5. **In the Export pop-up menu, choose Movie to QuickTime Movie.**

6. **Click the Options button to display the Movie Settings dialog box.**

7. **Click the Settings button in the Video box to display the Video Compression Settings dialog box.**

8. **Choose Apple intermediate Codec in the Compression Type pop-up menu, and then click OK to close the Video Compression Settings dialog box.** This codec gives you full video quality.

9. **Click OK to close the Movie Settings dialog box.**

10. **Click Save in the Save exported file as dialog box.** iMovie saves the file.

You now have a file that you can open in iMovie HD. From there you can choose File ⇨ Share, click the Videocamera tab, and follow through the process of exporting the movie to your camcorder.

213

How Do I Set Up a Virtual Studio in GarageBand?

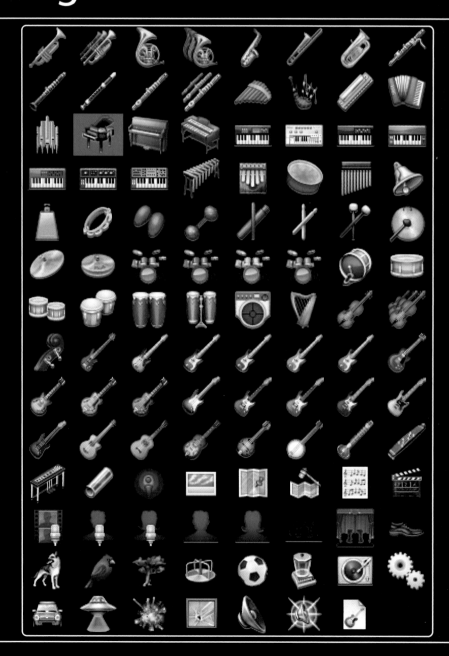

GarageBand gives you all the tools you need to create professional-quality music on your Mac. But because of its power and complexity, GarageBand has a steep learning curve and takes some getting used to. This chapter shows you how to come to grips with GarageBand, assemble and configure your computerized music studio, use GarageBand's "magic" feature to quickly create a customized backing track containing exactly the type of music you want to play along to, and even have GarageBand teach you how to play songs.

Understanding What You Can Do with GarageBand

GarageBand lets you create original music quickly and easily by using your Mac on its own or with musical instruments.

GarageBand comes with a library of prerecorded audio loops for many different instruments, from rock music standards such as drums, bass, and guitars (lead and rhythm) to instruments such as woodwind, brass, and organs. You can arrange these loops to play back in the order you want, repeat them as needed, and even change their tempo and pitch. You can use the Magic GarageBand feature to quickly whip together a backing track from loops that work with each other.

You can connect a MIDI keyboard to your Mac and use its keys to play either keyboard-based Software Instruments (such as pianos or synthesizers) or instruments such as guitars or drum kits. You can play along to tracks you've built out of prerecorded loops, record your performances, and choose the best of them.

You can connect a physical musical instrument such as a guitar or bass to your Mac (usually through an external audio interface) and play along with a backing track. You can record what you play, and manipulate it to make it sound better.

You can connect one or more microphones to your Mac (again, usually through an external audio interface) so that you can add vocals or other instruments you cannot connect directly to your Mac. For example, you can record an acoustic guitar, a flute, or a drum kit through one or more microphones. You can record these tracks too, and improve them in GarageBand.

You can mix your loop-based tracks and your recorded tracks, adding effects as needed, to give you a professional-quality result. You can then export the resulting song to iTunes or to a disk.

If you want to improve your playing, you can use the Learn to Play feature to take lessons in instruments such as piano and guitar. You can download both basic lessons to get you started and lessons from individual artists who teach you how to play particular songs of theirs.

Last but not least, you can unleash the full power of GarageBand on the tiny task of creating a ringtone for the iPhone.

Understanding Real and Software Instruments

GarageBand uses two kinds of instruments: Software Instruments and Real Instruments.

Software Instruments are synthesized instruments whose sounds GarageBand creates on the fly as needed. You play Software Instruments using one of GarageBand's onscreen keyboards (discussed later in this chapter) or an external MIDI keyboard connected to your Mac.

Real Instruments are physical instruments that you connect to your Mac — for example, a guitar or bass that you connect via an audio interface, or a microphone you connect to record vocals, drums, or another acoustic instrument.

Where things get confusing is that GarageBand contains Real Instrument loops as well as Software Instrument loops. Real Instrument loops are recordings of real instruments playing, whereas Software Instrument loops are sounds generated by software — as it were, recipes that tell your Mac how to put together the right sounds.

Real Instrument loops appear in blue in the GarageBand interface, and Software Instrument loops appear in green. You can edit Software Instrument loops much more extensively than you can edit Real Instrument loops.

Note GarageBand also lets you create podcasts. Chapter 11 covers this topic.

Creating and Saving a Song Project

The first time you launch GarageBand by clicking the GarageBand icon in the Dock or (if the icon doesn't appear there) double-clicking the icon in the Applications folder, GarageBand displays the opening screen shown in figure 7.1.

Note The next time you open GarageBand, it automatically loads the project you were working on the last time you quit the application. If you closed the project before quitting GarageBand, the application displays the opening screen so that you can decide between opening an existing project and starting a new project.

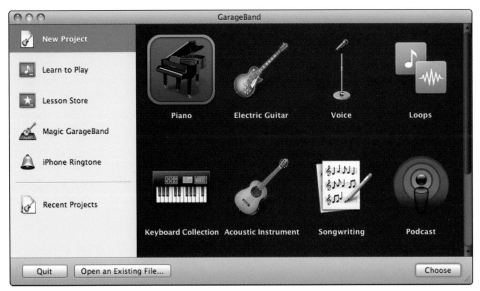

7.1 When you open GarageBand, the application displays this screen to let you choose which feature to use.

Create and save your song project like this:

1. **If the New Project button in the left panel isn't selected, click it so that you see the available instruments (such as Piano, Electric Guitar, and Voice) and features (such as Songwriting and Podcast).**

2. **Click the instrument you want to use — for example, Keyboard Collection — and then click the Choose button.** GarageBand displays the New Project from Template dialog (see figure 7.2).

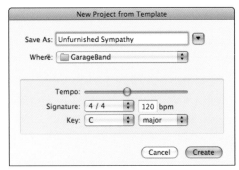

3. **In the upper part of the dialog, name your song, and choose where to save it.** As usual, you can click the drop-down arrow to the right of the Save As box to reveal the dialog's navigation area.

7.2 In the New Project from Template dialog, name your song, choose where to save it, and set the tempo, signature, and key.

Note

Chapter 11 discusses how to use GarageBand to create podcast episodes and distribute them via iWeb.

4. **Set the tempo for the song by dragging the Tempo slider to adjust the number in the bpm box.** See the nearby sidebar for advice on choosing the tempo, signature, and key.

5. **Choose the time signature for the song in the Signature pop-up menu.**

Genius

GarageBand wraps up each song into a package file that contains all the track information and any audio files that you record into the song. The result is that GarageBand song files that include recorded audio can be large, so don't try to save them on any disk that's short of space.

6. **Choose the key in the Key pop-up menu, and then choose major or minor in the pop-up menu to the right of it.**

7. **Click Create.** GarageBand closes the New Project from Template dialog and displays your project.

Choosing the Tempo, Signature, and Key for Your Song

If (like most people) you haven't composed music before, you may not be familiar with tempos, signatures, and keys:

- **Tempo.** The *tempo* is the number of beats per minute. You can set from an ultra-slow 40 bpm to a super-high-energy 240 bpm. GarageBand suggests 120 bpm to start you off.

- **Signature.** The *signature* or time signature sets the relationship between beats and measures in the song. Your choices are 2 / 2, 2 / 4, 3 / 4, 4 / 4, 5 / 4, 7/ 4, 6 / 8, 7 / 8, 9 / 8, or 12 / 8. The number to the left of the slash is the number of beats in each measure; the number to the right of the slash is the length of the note that gets one beat. For example, in the widely used 4 / 4 time signature, there are four beats per measure, and each quarter note receives one beat.

continued

continued

● **Key.** The key is the central note in the musical scale for the song. Your choices are C, Db (D flat), D, Eb, E, F, F# (F sharp), G, Ab, A, Bb, or B. You can also choose between major and minor keys.

Unless you already have a firm idea of the song you're composing, it's hard to know which tempo, signature, and key will work best. In this case, try accepting GarageBand's default values: a tempo of 120 beats per minute, the 4 / 4 time signature, and the C major key.

You can change the tempo, time signature, and key easily when you're working with GarageBand's Real Instruments and Software Instruments in the project, so you don't have to magically get them exactly right when creating the song. What's important is to fix these settings before you start recording your own audio because GarageBand can't change the tempo and key on these.

Getting Up To Speed with the GarageBand Interface

After you create your first project, the GarageBand window should look something like figure 7.3. GarageBand starts the project with a track for the instrument you chose or a sample selection of tracks, but you can delete any track — or change it to another instrument — as needed.

These are the main elements of the GarageBand window:

● **Tracks column.** You place a track in this column for each Software Instrument or Real Instrument you want to play or record. The track header shows the instrument type and contains controls for recording the track, listening to it, changing its volume, and panning it.

● **Playhead.** The triangle in the Timeline and the red line down across the tracks indicate the current play position. The playhead moves as you play back the tracks. You can also move it by dragging or by using the Transport controls.

● **Timeline.** This is the area where you arrange loops, tracks, and sounds so that they start when you want them to and play for the required length.

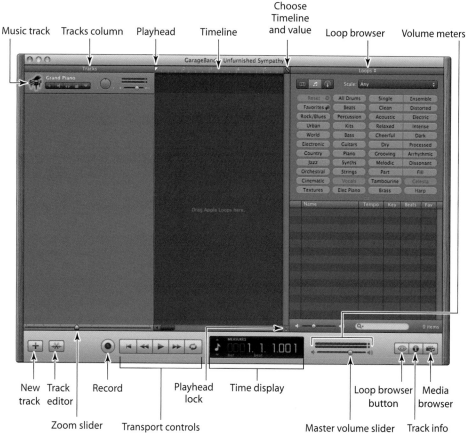

7.3 When you create a song project, GarageBand looks something like this. The track or tracks depends on the instrument or feature you chose in the New Project from Template dialog box.

- **Zoom slider.** Drag this slider to zoom in on the timeline so you can see it in more detail, or to zoom out to see more of your project at once.

- **New Track button.** Click this track to open the dialog for adding a new Software Instrument track or Real Instrument track.

- **Loop Browser.** This pane lets you pick prerecorded audio loops to place in the sog.

- **Loop Browser button.** Click this button to display or hide the Loop Browser, which you use to pick prerecorded audio loops.

Note The Loop Browser, Track Info pane, and Media Browser share the same area on the right side of the screen, so you can display only one of these items at once. To give yourself more space for the timeline, you can also hide whichever of these three is currently displayed.

- **Track Info button.** Click this button to display or hide the Track Info pane, which you use for working with Software Instruments and Real Instruments.

- **Media Browser button.** Click this button to display or hide the Media Browser, which you use to select audio clips, photos, and movies, just like in most of the other iLife applications. You use the Media Browser when creating podcasts rather than when creating songs; see Chapter 11 for details.

- **Track Editor button.** Click this button to display the Track Editor, which you use to edit the audio in a track.

- **Record button.** Click this button to start or stop recording.

- **Transport controls.** Use these buttons to move the playhead to where you want it.

- **Time display.** This readout displays details of the time, measures, chord, or project. To switch among the four available sets of information, either click the up and down arrows, or click the icon on the left and choose from the pop-up menu.

- **Master Volume slider.** Drag this slider to control the master volume of the song. (Use the controls in the Mixer column to set the volume level for an individual track.)

- **Volume meters.** These meters display the output level for the song as a whole.

- **Playhead Lock button.** Click this button to lock or unlock the playhead in the timeline from the playhead in the Track Editor. By unlocking the two playheads, you can work with a different part of the song in the timeline than in the Track Editor, which can be handy.

- **Choose Timeline Grid Value button.** Click this button to change the note value shown in the timeline grid. For many projects, it's best to use the default setting, Automatic, which lets GarageBand change the note value automatically as you zoom in and out.

Using the onscreen keyboard and Musical Typing

To play Software Instruments on your Mac, you'll most likely want to connect an external musical keyboard, as discussed later in this chapter. This gives you the greatest flexibility and lets you play almost as if you were using a full-size instrument.

If you don't have a musical keyboard, or for times when you can't take a musical keyboard with you (for example, when you travel), GarageBand provides an onscreen keyboard that you can play either with the mouse or by pressing the keys on your Mac's keyboard.

Using the onscreen keyboard

To display or hide the onscreen keyboard, choose Window ➪ Keyboard or pressing ⌘+K. Figure 7.4 shows the onscreen keyboard.

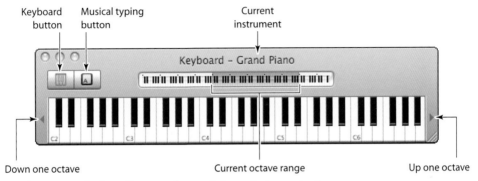

7.4 The onscreen keyboard lets you play any Software Instrument using your mouse.

The onscreen keyboard is easy to use, but it has a couple of hidden features:

- **Choose the instrument.** Click the Software Instrument track you want to play. The Keyboard window's title bar shows the instrument.

- **Play a note.** As you'd guess, you click the key. But the farther down the key you click, the harder you strike it. So if you want to play a note gently, click near the top of the key.

- **Change the octave range.** Click the gray button at the left end to move down an octave, or click the gray button at the right end to move up an octave. Or simply drag the blue-shaded area on the miniature keyboard at the top.

- **Resize the keyboard.** Drag the sizing handle in the lower right corner of the Keyboard window to stretch out the keyboard or to shrink it back down. Drag the handle all the way to the right to display the entire keyboard so that you don't need to use the octave arrows.

Using Musical Typing

If you're handy with the mouse, you can play the onscreen keyboard pretty well in a pinch — one note at a time. But what you may find easier is to play using your Mac's keyboard. GarageBand calls this feature Musical Typing.

To use Musical Typing, click the Software Instrument track you want to play with the keyboard, and then choose Window ⇨ Musical Typing or press ⌘+Shift+K. GarageBand displays the Musical Typing window (see figure 7.5).

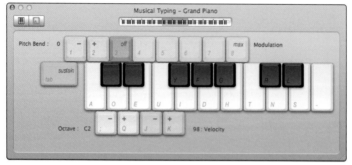

7.5 The Musical Typing keyboard lets you play piano — or any other Software Instrument — using your Mac's keyboard instead of an external keyboard.

Note If you already have the Keyboard window open, you can switch to Musical Typing by clicking the Musical Typing button, the right-hand button of the two on the upper left side of the toolbar. Click the Keyboard button (the left button) when you want to switch back to the keyboard.

The title bar shows the instrument you're currently playing. You can switch the keyboard to play another Software Instrument by clicking that instrument's track header in the main GarageBand window.

The Musical Typing keyboard is easy to use:

- **Playing a note.** Press the note shown on the key.

- **Changing octave.** Click the piano keyboard at the top of the window to pick an octave, or drag the blue shaded area to the left or right. You can also press Z to move down an octave or X to move up an octave.

- **Sustain a note.** Hold down Tab to sustain the note you're playing.

- **Change velocity.** Press C to reduce the velocity or V to increase it.

- **Add pitch bend.** Press 1 to lower the pitch or 2 to raise it. Keep holding down the key for as long as you want to bend the pitch.

- **Add modulation.** Press the number keys 4 through 8 to add modulation (the higher the number, the more modulation). To turn modulation off, press 3.

If you prefer, you can click the buttons on the Musical Typing keyboard instead of (or as well as) pressing the keys.

Meeting the loop browser

To make the best use of the space available in the window, GarageBand makes the loop browser, the Track Info pane, and the Media Browser share the some area. That means you can display only one of them at a time.

To add audio loops to your projects, you use the loop browser. Click the Loop Browser button to display the loop browser on the right side of the window. You can then click one of the category buttons in the top part of the loop browser to display the matching loops in the list at the bottom. For example, figure 7.6 shows the loop browser open with the All Drums button clicked, so the list at the bottom displays all drum loops.

7.6 Open the loop browser and then click a category button to see a list of matching loops. Click a loop to listen to it; click again to stop, or click another loop to start it.

Click the loop you want to hear, or drag it to the Track list to create a new track that uses that loop. GarageBand adds the loop to the track as a *region*, a section of the track.

You can increase the depth of the loop browser so that it shows more category buttons by clicking the two-bar handle above the Tempo column and dragging downward.

Meeting the Track Editor

To display the Track Editor across the bottom of the GarageBand window, click the Track Editor button. You can then click a region to open it for editing in the Track Editor (see figure 7.7) or double-click a region to bring it to the leftmost position in the Track Editor.

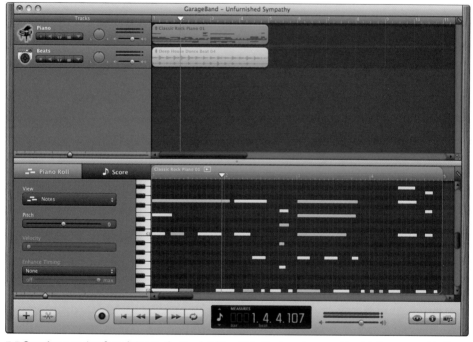

7.7 Opening a region for editing in the Track Editor. Hide the loop browser, Track Info pane, or Media Browser to give the Track Editor more space.

You can increase the depth of the Track Editor so that it shows a wider range of notes by dragging upward the bar that divides it from the upper part of the window.

Meeting the Track Info pane

You use the Track Info pane to check and change the settings for a selected instrument track or for the master track (which controls the song as a whole). To display or hide the Track Info pane, click the Track Info button or press ⌘+I. Figure 7.8 shows the Track Info pane as it initially appears for a Real Instrument track, Male Rock Vocals. The Browse tab lets you choose among the different instruments that GarageBand provides, and select the input source and recording level for Real Instrument tracks.

7.8 The Track Info pane appears on the right side of the GarageBand window.

You can click the Edit tab at the top of the Track Info pane to display the Edit tab (see figure 7.9), which lets you choose effects for the track.

The other GarageBand component that occupies the same part of the GarageBand window as the loop browser and the Track Info pane is the Media Browser. You use the Media Browser to add photos, audio clips, and movies to podcasts, so we'll leave this component till Chapter 11 (which covers creating podcasts).

Connecting Your Audio Instruments

You can make great music in GarageBand by using its audio loops, but to get the most out of GarageBand, you'll need to connect your own instruments.

Connecting a MIDI keyboard

The first essential is a MIDI keyboard. If you buy a MIDI keyboard that connects via USB (such as the M-Audio KeyStation models that

7.9 Display the Edit tab of the Track Info pane when you need to set effects manually.

the Apple Store sells), you connect the keyboard via a single USB cable and don't even need to use a power supply because the keyboard gets power from the USB cable. Other MIDI keyboards connect to a MIDI controller, which you then connect to your Mac via USB.

Genius

If possible, connect your MIDI keyboard directly to a USB port on your Mac rather than to a USB hub connected to your Mac.

When you connect a keyboard or other MIDI instrument, GarageBand lets you know instantly by displaying a dialog telling you that the number of MIDI inputs has changed and how many there now are. Figure 7.10 shows an example of this dialog.

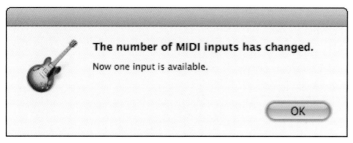

The number of MIDI inputs has changed.

Now one input is available.

OK

7.10 GarageBand tells you when the number of MIDI inputs changes — for example, when you connect a MIDI keyboard.

Connecting a microphone

To record live instruments such as drums, acoustic guitar, or vocals, you'll need to use one or more microphones. If your Mac has a built-in microphone, you can use that in a severe pinch, but for high-quality results you should use an external microphone that you can position exactly where you need it. hoose a microphone designed for recording music rather than a general-purpose microphone.

If you're using a single microphone, you can connect it directly to your Mac's audio input socket. To use two or more microphones, you'll need to use an audio interface, discussed next.

Connecting an audio interface

When you need to connect other instruments or audio equipment to your Mac so that you can direct their output into GarageBand as input, you need to use an *audio interface* — an electronic box that accepts the input from the instrument or audio kit, processes it as needed, and then passes it along to your Mac. You can get Mac-compatible audio interfaces that connect via either USB or FireWire; USB ones are usually easier.

Genius

When choosing an audio interface, figure out how many audio inputs you'll need, including high-impedance (for instruments) and lower-impedance (for lower-powered devices) inputs. Decide whether you need audio outputs (for example, for playback through an amplifier) as well as the USB output, and whether you need "phantom" power that will allow you to use a dynamic microphone.

For most audio interfaces, you need to install a driver so that Mac OS X can recognize the interface. After you install the driver, you typically manage the audio interface either through a custom panel in System Preferences or via a custom application provided by the interface's manufacturer. Figure 7.11 shows an example of a control panel in System Preferences.

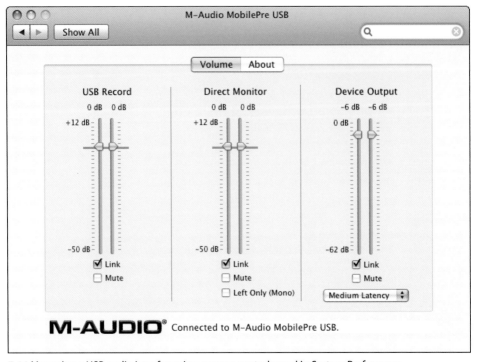

7.11 Managing a USB audio interface via a custom control panel in System Preferences

Setting Preferences to Suit the Way You Work

To enable yourself to work as fast and smoothly as possible in GarageBand, it's a good idea to spend a few minutes setting the application's preferences to suit the way you work. Even if you choose not to change the default settings at first, knowing which preferences you can change will be helpful when you find you do need to alter GarageBand's behavior.

Start by pressing ⌘+, (⌘ and the comma key) or choosing GarageBand ➪ Preferences to open the Preferences window.

Setting General preferences

If GarageBand doesn't displays the General preferences (see figure 7.12) at first, click the General button to display them.

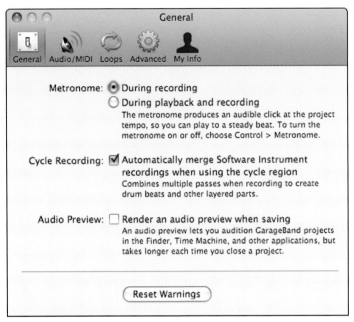

7.12 GarageBand's General preferences let you decide when to use the metronome, choose whether to use cycle recording, and create an audio preview of your projects.

- **Metronome.** Select the During recording option button if you want to hear the metronome's click only while you're recording. Select the During playback and recording option button if you want to hear the click during playback as well — useful when you're playing along with the song.

- **Cycle Recording.** Select the Automatically merge Software Instrument recordings when using the cycle region check box when you want to loop through a section of a Software Instrument track and add what you play to what's already there. This technique is useful for creating complex parts. For example, when recording a drum beat, you can play the bass drum on the first pass, add the snare drum on the second pass, add the hi-hat and cymbals on the third pass, and have all of them merged into a single track. The alternative is to have GarageBand record each pass through the region as a separate take; you can then select the take you want to keep.

● **Audio Preview.** Select the Render an audio preview when saving check box if you want GarageBand to create a preview that you can listen to from the other iLife applications or from the Finder. Creating this preview is usually a good idea, but it means that each time you close a project in GarageBand, saving the file takes a little longer because of creating the preview.

Note   If you don't select the Render an audio preview when saving check box in General preferences, GarageBand prompts you to decide whether to create a preview until you tell it to stop prompting you. So normally it's best to select the check box.

● **Reset Warnings.** You can click this button to reset GarageBand's warning messages to their default settings. Normally, you won't want to do this because it causes all the warning dialogs you've suppressed to start springing out of the woodwork again.

Setting Audio/MIDI preferences

Next, click the Audio/MIDI tab to display the Audio/MIDI preferences (see figure 7.13), and then choose settings:

● **Audio Output.** In this pop-up menu, choose where you want to direct GarageBand's output. Select System Setting to use the output selected on the Output tab in Mac OS X's Sound preferences in System Preferences. Select Built-In Audio or Built-In Output (depending on your Mac) to use your Mac's speakers or output jack. If you have connected an audio interface, you can select it from this pop-up menu to send the audio to the interface (and then to whichever amplifier or speakers you've connected to it).

● **Audio Input.** In this pop-up menu, choose which audio input GarageBand should use. Select System Setting to use the input selected on the Input tab in Mac OS X's Sound preferences in System Preferences. Select Built-In Microphone to use your Mac's built-in microphone, or Built-In Audio to use the input jack. If you have connected an audio interface, select it from this pop-up menu.

● **Optimize for.** Select the Maximum number of simultaneous tracks option button when you're working with a large number of tracks. Select the Minimum delay when playing instruments live option button when you're recording from a MIDI keyboard.

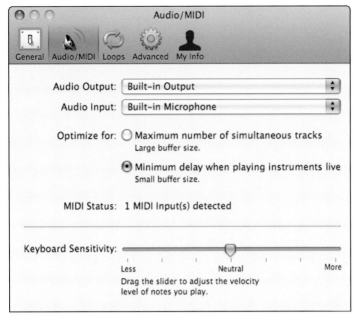

7.13 In Audio/MIDI preferences, choose your Mac's inputs and outputs, decide how to optimize GarageBand's playback, and set the keyboard sensitivity.

Caution If you select the Maximum number of simultaneous tracks option button in the Optimize for area in Audio/MIDI preferences, you may find there's a delay between your pressing a key on your MIDI keyboard and GarageBand playing it. If this problem, which is called *latency*, occurs, choose the Minimum delay when playing instruments live option button instead.

- **MIDI Status.** This readout shows how many MIDI devices GarageBand has detected. You can't change it directly, only by plugging in or unplugging MIDI devices. Use this readout to make sure GarageBand is aware of all the MIDI devices you're using.

- **Keyboard Sensitivity.** Drag the slider to choose how sensitive GarageBand should treat your keyboard as being. Finding the best setting for yourself depends on the keyboard and your playing style, so you'll probably need to experiment with this setting. Start with the slider at the Neutral position (in the middle), and then drag toward the Less end or the More end as needed.

Setting Loops preferences

Now click the Loops tab to display the Loops preferences (see figure 7.14), and then choose settings for working with loops:

- **Keyword Browsing.** Select the Filter for more relevant results check box if you want to return only search results that are within two semitones of the song key you're using. This setting is useful when you've installed many loops and need to whittle down your search results.

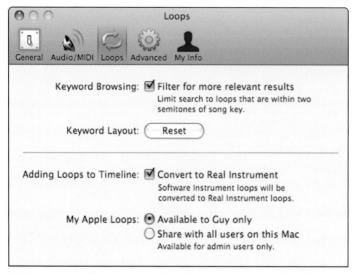

7.14 In Loops preferences, choose how to browse loops, whether to convert Software Instruments to Real Instruments when you add them to the timeline, and whether to share your loops.

- **Keyword Layout.** Click the Reset button to reset the keyword layout to its default after you've customized it.

- **Adding Loops to Timeline.** Select the Convert to Real Instrument check box if you want GarageBand to automatically convert Software Instrument loops to Real Instrument loops when you add them to the timeline. Real Instrument loops take less processor power to play than Software Instrument loops, so converting Software Instrument loops to Real Instrument loops can be a good move if your Mac is struggling to play a song. You can override this setting by Option-dragging a loop to the timeline.

- **My Apple Loops.** Select the Available to *Your Username* Only option button if you want to keep your selection of Apple loops to yourself. Select the Share with all users on this Mac option button if you want to share the loops with others. Two things to note here: First, this setting applies only to extra loops you add, not to GarageBand's main set of loops (which are available to all users of your Mac). Second, only administrator users can make this choice; standard users can't.

Setting Advanced preferences

Moving along, click the Advanced tab to display the Advanced preferences (see figure 7.15), and then choose settings that suit you:

- **Real Instrument Tracks.** In this pop-up menu, choose how many Real Instrument tracks to allow in a song: 8, 16, 32, 64, or 255. If your Mac is struggling to run GarageBand, try reducing the number as far as your songs permit.

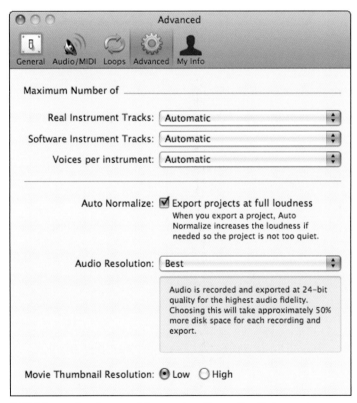

7.15 Advanced preferences let you reduce GarageBand's demands on your Mac, normalize projects automatically, and choose resolution for audio and for movie thumbnails.

If you leave any of the three "Maximum Number of" pop-up menus set to Automatic (the default), GarageBand assesses your Mac's performance and limits the number accordingly.

- **Software Instrument Tracks.** In this pop-up menu, choose how many Software Instrument tracks to allow in a song: 8, 16, 32, or 64. Software Instrument tracks are more demanding for your Mac than Real Instrument tracks, so keep the number low if your Mac is struggling.

- **Voices per instrument.** In this pop-up menu, choose whether to limit the number of voices (notes) each instrument can use. Your choices are 10 sampled, 5 other; 20 sampled, 10 other; 32 sampled, 16 other; or 64 sampled, max other (max being unlimited). Again, if your Mac is having trouble playing back your songs, reducing the number of voices may help. (The "other" voices are synthesized rather than sampled.)

- **Auto Normalize.** Select the Export projects at full loudness check box if you want GarageBand to automatically adjust the volume on projects you export. Unlike the normalization in iTunes that tends to wreck the dynamic range of songs, GarageBand's normalization is usually a good idea because it enables you to export songs at around a standard volume even if you've mixed them at a lower volume.

- **Audio Resolution.** In this pop-up menu, select Good, Better, or Best, as appropriate. Good resolution records and exports at standard CD audio quality (16-bit), which is enough for any projects you're planning to put on CD. Better resolution records at 24-bit quality and exports at 16-bit, allowing you to keep higher-quality versions in GarageBand than you're outputting. Best resolution both records and exports at 24-bit quality; use this for songs you'll distribute at higher quality than CDs.

The disadvantage to using Better or Best audio resolution is that your GarageBand files take up half as much space again because of being higher quality.

- **Movie Thumbnail Resolution.** For your podcast projects, select the Low option button or the High option button to control the resolution of the movie thumbnail image that GarageBand creates.

Setting My Info preferences

Lastly for the preferences, click the My Info tab (see figure 7.16) and set the information you want to use to tag your songs and podcasts in iTunes:

- **iTunes Playlist.** This setting tells iTunes which playlist to place your songs in. If the playlist doesn't exist yet, iTunes creates it when you export the first song from GarageBand.

- **Artist Name.** This setting tells iTunes which artist name to assign to the song.

- **Composer Name.** This setting tells iTunes what to write in the Composer tag.

- **Album Name.** This setting controls the album name that iTunes applies.

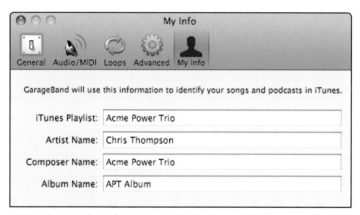

7.16 In the My Info preferences, provide the information for tagging your songs and podcasts in iTunes.

Kick-Starting a Song with Magic GarageBand

Have you ever needed to put together a backing track in a minute so that you can play along and develop an idea you've had on the guitar or piano?

If so, you can use Magic GarageBand to quickly create a custom backing track from generic ingredients. The "magic" part is that GarageBand automatically picks sequences of instrumental loops that work together, quickly creating a viable custom backing track for the combination of instruments and musical genres you choose.

Here's how to get started with Magic GarageBand:

1. **Press ⌘+N or choose File ➪ New to display the GarageBand opening screen.** If you've got a project open that contains unsaved changes, GarageBand prompts you to save them.

2. **Click the Magic GarageBand button in the left panel to display the Magic GarageBand music choices.**

3. **Click the icon for the music genre you want to create: Blues, Rock, Jazz, Country, Reggae, Funk, Latin, Roots Rock, or Slow Blues.** To preview the type of music, move the mouse pointer over an icon and click the Play icon on the Preview button that appears; click the Stop icon to stop the preview.

4. **Click the Create button.** GarageBand displays the Magic GarageBand and loads a standard set of instruments for the musical genre you chose. Figure 7.17 shows the selection you get for Rock.

7.17 Magic GarageBand loads a standard set of instruments for music of the genre you chose.

5. **Choose your instrument from the My Instrument pop-up menu on the left.** You can choose Keyboard, Guitar, or a microphone. From the same menu, you can turn the monitor on (so that you hear the instrument through GarageBand) or off (so that you hear the instrument only through your other audio equipment).

6. **Tune your instrument (or your voice).** Click the tuning-fork icon to the right of the My Instrument pop-up menu, and then use the controls that appear to make sure GarageBand agrees the note you're playing or singing is what you intend. Click the icon again when you've finished tuning.

7. **Click the icon for the subtype of instrument you're using.** For example, for Keyboard, choose Grand Piano, Electric Piano, or Arena Run. You can also click the Customize button to display further choices.

8. **Decide whether to create a snippet or an entire song by moving the switch on the bottom of the window frame to Snippet or Entire Song.** Entire Song usually gives better results, because you can hear more of the music. If you choose Snippet, click the section of the song in the gray bar: Intro, Verse 1, Chorus, Verse 2, or Ending.

From here, you pick a sound for each instrument you want to include, and knock out any instruments you don't need. Exactly how you proceed depends on the genre of music you're creating, your musical skills, and what kind of music you like. But here's an example of setting up a rock backing track to which you will add a lead guitar line.

Note You can simply start the music playing by clicking the Play button and work from there, but many people find it easier to start with a single instrument as described in this example.

1. **Silence all the instruments except the one you want to start with.** Click each instrument to display its name, click the disclosure triangle to the left of the name to display a set of controls, and then click the Mute button on the left (see figure 7.18).

Note Instead of silencing an instrument, you can get rid of it. Click the instrument, and then click the No Instrument button on the toolbar. The instrument disappears, leaving an empty spotlight on the boards as its placeholder.

2. **When you've silenced all the instruments except the one you want to start with, click the Play button, and then click the toolbar button for the style you want.** Drag the instrument's volume control if you need to increase or decrease the volume.

3. **Click the instrument you want to add next, turn off its muting, and then click the toolbar button for the style.**

7.18 It's usually easiest to start by silencing most of the instruments so that you can gradually build up the sound you want. You can play along on your instrument to help choose the right backing tracks.

Genius

You can change an instrument's style at any point by clicking the instrument, and then clicking the style you want.

4. **Repeat step 3 as needed to add each other instrument you want to the song and choose the style you'd like it to play.** To focus on one instrument, you can click its Solo button (the button that shows a pair of headphones).

Note

To switch to another genre, you can click the Change Genre button at any time.

5. **When you're satisfied with your choices, click the Open in GarageBand button to create the project.** Magic GarageBand pulls together the files, and then displays the song in the GarageBand window. Figure 7.19 shows an example.

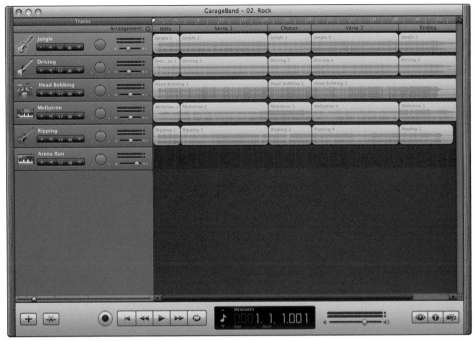

7.19 When your song appears in the main GarageBand window, you can customize it manually to get exactly the structure and sound you're looking for.

From here, you can adjust the song as needed. For example:

- **Rename it.** Magic GarageBand gives the song a generic name based on the genre. To rename it, choose File ➪ Save As.

- **Customize your instrument.** Double-click the track header for your instrument to open the Track Info pane, click the Edit tab, and then pick your preferred settings.

- **Change some of the loops.** If you find that a particular section doesn't fit the song you're trying to create, you can change it or simply delete it. See the next chapter for details.

- **Add other tracks as needed.** See the next chapter for details.

241

Using the Learn to Play Feature and the Lesson Store

One of GarageBand '09's most exciting features is Learn to Play, which gives you lessons in instruments such as piano and guitar right through GarageBand. GarageBand includes the first couple of basic lessons, and you can download further basic lessons for free from the Lesson Store. The Lesson Store also sells artist lessons, in which artists give you a walkthrough of how to play a particular song.

Genius

The Learn to Play feature needs a Mac with a dual-core or better Intel processor. If you're running iLife on a PowerPC Mac or a single-core Intel processor, you'll need to upgrade to use this feature.

To get started with Learn to Play, simply choose File ⇨ New (or press ⌘+N), and then click the Learn to Play button on the left of the opening GarageBand screen. Click the lesson you want, and then click Choose. GarageBand opens the lesson full screen (see figure 7.20) and starts teaching you.

7.20 GarageBand's Learn to Play feature helps you get up to speed on piano or guitar — and even teaches you how to play popular songs.

To get more lessons for Learn to Play, choose File ⇨ New (or press ⌘+N), and then click the Lesson Store button on the left of the opening GarageBand screen. Click the Basic Lessons tab to download free lessons, or the Artist Lessons tab (see figure 7.21) to buy lessons on individual songs.

7.21 The Lesson Store provides basic lessons for free, but you must pay to learn to play individual songs.

How Do I Record a Song in GarageBand?

With your music studio set up on your Mac as described in the previous chapter, you're ready to record an original song. If you want to begin by assembling tracks from loops, start at the beginning; if you want to start using the arrange track to structure your song, or if you're ready to record either Software Instrument or Real Instrument tracks, jump straight into the middle of the chapter. And if you've wondered how to create your own custom Software Instruments, go to the end of the chapter to find out.

Creating a New Track

If you've come straight from Chapter 7 and you already have GarageBand running with a music project open — either a new project from exploring GarageBand or a project you've kick-started using Magic GarageBand — you're ready to start. Otherwise, launch GarageBand from the Dock or from the Applications folder, click the New Project button on the opening screen and click Choose, and then use the New Project from Template dialog box to set up your new music project.

This chapter starts off with a new project that uses the default settings from the New Project from Template dialog box: 4 / 4 time signature at 120 beats per minute and the C major key.

When you start most new projects, GarageBand gives you a single track for the instrument you chose. For example, if you choose Piano in the New Project from Template dialog box, GarageBand gives you a Grand Piano track to start off with. For other projects, such as Keyboard Collection, GarageBand starts you off with multiple tracks.

To pick a different type of instrument, double-click the track header to open the Track Info pane with the Browse tab selected. You can then change the instrument to another Software Instrument as described later in this chapter.

Note

To get rid of a track, click its header and press ⌘+Delete or choose Track ⇨ Delete Track.

Beginning to add a track

Here's how to add a new track to your music project and choose the instrument for it:

1. **Click the New Track button in the lower left corner of the GarageBand window, or choose Track ⇨ New Track, or simply press ⌘+Option+N.** GarageBand displays a dialog prompting you to choose between a Software Instrument track, a Real Instrument track, or an Electric Guitar track.

2. **Select the option button for the track type you want to add:**

   ● **Software Instrument.** Select this option button if you want to add a track consisting either of Software Instrument loops or of a Software Instrument that you'll play using either one of GarageBand's on-screen keyboards (see the previous chapter for details) or an external musical keyboard you connect via USB.

● **Real Instrument.** Select this option button to add a track that you will use either to play Real Instrument loops or to record a real instrument such as an electric guitar or bass, vocal track, or any other track that uses an external microphone (for example, a piano, an acoustic guitar, or a woodwind instrument).

● **Electric Guitar.** Select this option button to add a track specifically for electric guitar. This option enables you to use GarageBand's built-in amplifiers and stompbox effects.

3. **Click Create.** GarageBand adds the track and displays the Track Info pane. You can now choose settings for the Software Instrument track (as discussed in the next section), the Real Instrument track (as discussed after that), or the Guitar Track (discussed even later).

Setting up a Software Instrument track

Use the Track Info pane (see figure 8.1) to set up a Software Instrument track like this:

1. **In the left column, click the instrument category you want — for example, Drum Kits.** The list of available instruments (or kits, for drums) appears in the right column.

8.1 Choose the instrument category and the specific instrument for a Software Instrument track on the Browse tab of the Track Info pane.

2. **In the right column, click the instrument you want — for example, Rock Kit.** GarageBand applies the instrument. If an instrument is grayed out, you may need to install extra GarageBand files from your iLife install DVD or from Software Update.

3. **Test the instrument's sound by playing your keyboard.** Use either the Onscreen Keyboard, the Musical Typing keyboard, or your external musical keyboard. If you don't like the sounds, you can either choose another instrument by repeating Steps 2 and 3, or change its sound as described later in this chapter.

4. **If you want to change the icon for the instrument, click the instrument icon near the bottom of the Track Info pane, and then choose an icon on the pop-up panel.**

5. **Click the Track Info button if you're ready to hide the Track Info pane again.** (If you have enough screen space, you can leave the Track Info pane open if you prefer.)

Setting up a Real Instrument track

Here's how to set up a Real Instrument track in the Track Info pane (shown in figure 8.2):

1. **If you will play an instrument through this track instead of playing loops, connect the instrument as described in the previous chapter.** If the instrument is already connected, you're set.

2. **In the left column, click the category of loop or instrument you will play through this track — for example, Bass.** The list of available effects appears in the right column.

3. **In the right column, click the effect you want to apply to the instrument — for example, Edgy Rock Bass for a bass.**

4. **For a musical instrument or microphone, open the Input Source pop-up menu and choose the source.** For example, choose the stereo input from your audio interface for a guitar track.

5. **For a musical instrument or microphone, choose whether to monitor the input in the Monitor pop-up menu.** Select Off, On, or On with Feedback Protection, as needed. If you're planning to use this Real Instrument track only for GarageBand's Real Instrument loops, make sure the Monitor pop-up menu is set to Off.

Turn GarageBand's monitor off if you put the musical instrument through an audio interface that lets you monitor it outside the Mac. For example, if your audio interface can drive an amplifier, you can monitor the instrument through the amplifier rather than through GarageBand.

8.2 On the Browse tab of the Track Info pane for a Real Instrument, choose the instrument type, the effect you want, and the input source and recording level if you're using an instrument rather than loops.

6. **For a musical instrument or microphone, drag the Recording Level slider to set the recording level.** Select the Automatic Level Control check box if you want GarageBand to set the level for you. If these settings aren't available, you'll need to control the input volume manually on your audio interface.

7. **Click the Track Info button if you're ready to hide the Track Info pane again.**

Genius Avoid using GarageBand's Automatic Level Control if possible. GarageBand doesn't know how loud you're going to play, so it will need to adjust the level as the input volume changes. You'll get much better results by setting the Recording Level control manually to a level that allows your loudest playing without distortion but that doesn't adjust automatically for quieter passages.

Setting up an Electric Guitar track

Here's how to set up an Electric Guitar track in the Guitar Track pane:

1. **If you haven't already connected the guitar, connect it as described in the previous chapter.**

2. **In the pop-up menu at the top of the pane, choose the sound on which you want to base this guitar track.** For example, choose Classic Crunch, Seventies Metal, or Woodstock Fuzz. GarageBand displays an amplifier with the effects pedals used for the sound. Figure 8.3 shows an example.

3. **To change one of the existing settings, click the effects pedal you want to change, and then use your mouse to change the knobs, switches, and other controls.**

4. **To change the pedals used for the sound, click the Edit button to the right of the pop-up menu that shows the sound's name.** The Guitar Track pane shows the selection of available pedals (see figure 8.4). Drag a pedal up to a space on the stage to add it, or drag a pedal down off the stage to remove it. Click the Done button when you've finished.

8.3 In the Guitar Track pane, choose the basic sound, and then customize it as needed while you play.

5. **If you've customized the sound, save the changes.** Click the Save Setting button, type a name for the new sound in the Save Instrument dialog box, and then click the Save button. You can then reapply your sound quickly by choosing it from the My Settings section at the bottom of the pop-up menu.

6. **Click the Track Info button if you're ready to hide the Track Info pane again.**

Browsing and Auditioning Loops

The quick way to build a track in GarageBand is by using its prerecorded loops of music. These loops, which are called Apple Loops, contain chunks of music that you can assemble into the order you want to create a track. GarageBand lets you change the tempo and pitch of loops, so you can make them sound substantially different to suit the needs of a song.

8.4 You can add or remove effects pedals to produce exactly the sound you want.

To work with loops, you use the loop browser, which lets you audition loops, add them to your song, and view their original tempo, key, and duration.

Start by opening the loop browser in one of these ways:

- Click the loop browser button.
- Press ⌘+L.
- Choose Control ⇨ Show loop browser.

251

Figure 8.5 shows the loop browser in its normal view with the Guitars button clicked. The icons that appear in green indicate Software Instrument loops and work only in Software Instrument tracks. The icons that appear in blue indicate Real Instrument loops and work only in Real Instrument tracks.

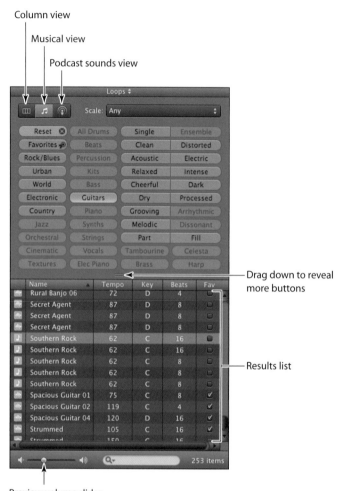

Column view

Musical view

Podcast sounds view

Drag down to reveal more buttons

Results list

Preview volume slider

8.5 The loop browser open in Musical Button view

Choosing a view and finding loops

You can find loops in three easy ways in the loop browser:

- **Musical Button view.** Click a button to display the list of loops tagged with that keyword — for example, Guitars. Click another button to narrow the selection farther.

Genius

You can swap the positions of any two buttons in Musical Button view by clicking a button, dragging it onto another button, and dropping it there. You can also change a button by Control-clicking or right-clicking it and choosing the item you want it to bear.

- **Column view.** Click the keyword type in the first column, click the category in the second column, and then click the keyword in the third column. The results then appear in the results list.

- **Searching and sorting.** To search, click in the Search box, type one or more keywords, and then press Return. To sort the loops you've found, click a column heading.

Note

The loop browser also has Podcast Sounds view, which shows only jingles, stingers, sound effects, and favorites. See Chapter 11 for coverage of Podcast Sounds view.

Auditioning a loop by itself

To audition a loop by itself, simply click it in the list in the loop browser. GarageBand starts playing the loop repeatedly until you stop it by clicking again, by clicking another loop to start that loop playing, or by dropping the loop on a track in the song (as discussed next).

Genius

When you audition a loop and find you like it, select its check box in the Fav (Favorites) column. You can then find it quickly by clicking the instrument type (for example, Bass) and then clicking the Fav column heading to bring your favorites to the top.

Adding a loop to your song

When you find a loop you want to use in your song, drag the loop from the Results List to the Track List:

- **To use an existing track, drop the loop on that track.** GarageBand displays a black vertical bar that shows the bar at which you place the loop's start (see figure 8.6). If you need to change the settings for the track, double-click its header and work in the Track Info pane, as described earlier in this chapter.

- **To create a new track, drop the loop below the last track you used in the Track List.** GarageBand automatically creates a new track of the right type (Software Instrument or Real Instrument) for the loop you dropped.

8.6 When you add a loop to an existing track, the black vertical bar shows where the loop's region will begin.

When you add a loop like this, GarageBand creates a *region* containing the loop. The region is a copy of the loop that you can adjust without changing the original version of the loop.

If the region ends up in the wrong track bar, click it and drag it to where you want it.

Playing back the song

When you've placed one or more loops in your song, listen to it so that you can judge how the loops work together.

1. **Move the Playhead to where you want to start playback.** For example, click the Go to Beginning button in the transport controls (see figure 8.7) to move the Playhead to the beginning of the song.

2. **Click the Play button to start playback.**

3. **Click the Play button again when you want to stop playback.**

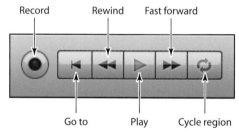

8.7 Use the transport controls to play back the song.

Repeating, shortening, and extending regions

Next, adjust the duration of the region as needed for your song:

⦿ **Repeat the region.** To make the region play back more than once, position the mouse pointer over the upper part of the region's right border so that the pointer changes to a curling arrow. Drag the border to the right as far as you want the region to repeat. GarageBand shows a notch at the end of each full repetition (see figure 8.8), so you can easily end the region right at the end of a repetition if you need to.

8.8 Drag the upper part of a region's right border to the right to repeat the region. The notches at the top and bottom indicate complete repetitions of the loop.

Note You can't shorten a region that you've repeated. Instead, reduce the length of the last repetition by dragging to the left with the curling arrow.

● **Shorten a region.** To play only part of the region, position the mouse pointer over the lower part of the region's right border so that the pointer changes to a bracket with two arrows. Drag to the left to shorten the region (see figure 8.9).

Joining two or more regions into a single region

After you adjust two or more regions so that they play just right in sequence, you can join them together so that you can repeat the sequence more easily in another part of the song.

8.9 Drag the lower part of a region's right border to the left to shorten the region.

Genius You can also *extend* a Software Instrument region by dragging the lower part of its right border to the right. Extending the region is different from looping it because you add empty air to the end of the region. This sounds pointless, but it lets you join two regions together, as described next. You can't extend a Real Instrument region.

Here's how to join adjacent regions together:

1. **Select the regions you want to join.**

2. **Choose Edit ⇨ Join.** GarageBand joins the regions together and gives the joined region the name that the first region had.

Splitting a region in two

Other times, you may need to split a region into two parts. Splitting is especially useful with regions you record and then find you want to use in separate parts, but you can also split GarageBand's prerecorded regions if you want.

1. **Position the Playhead where you want to split the region.**

2. **Click the region you want to split.**

3. **Choose Edit ⇨ Split or press ⌘+T.** GarageBand splits the region and gives each new region the same name.

4. **Rename the regions to indicate the change.** This step is optional, but if you don't rename the regions, it's easy to get confused by their having the same name but different contents.

Auditioning a loop with your song

Auditioning a loop by itself lets you focus on how it sounds, but often you'll be able to judge its suitability better by listening to how it sounds with the rest of your song so far. You can do this easily:

1. **Move the Playhead to just before the part of the song where you want to try out the loop.**

2. **Click the Play button to start playback.**

3. **When playback reaches the bar before where you want to hear the loop, click the loop in the results list.** GarageBand starts playing the loop when the new bar begins.

4. **Drag the Preview Volume slider as needed to change the loop's volume.** For example, you may need to increase its volume so that you can hear it more clearly over the other tracks.

Auditioning multiple loops with the cycle region

If you need to audition several loops, turn on the cycle region so that GarageBand repeatedly plays back the part of the song you want to hear. Follow these steps:

1. **Click the Cycle Region button (the button with two gray arrows at the right of the transport controls) to turn on the cycle region.** GarageBand changes the arrows to blue and displays a golden bar below the timeline indicating the extent of the cycle region.

2. **To change the region, position the mouse pointer over the start or finish, and then drag the region to where you want it (see figure 8.10).**

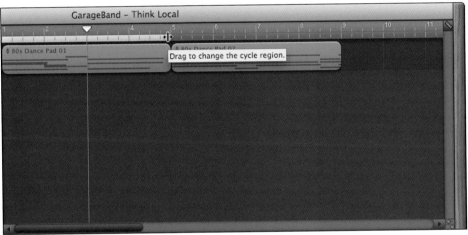

8.10 Drag either end of the yellow cycle region to tell GarageBand which part of the song to repeat.

3. **Move the Playhead to where you want to start play, and then click the Play button.** GarageBand starts playing the cycle region, and loops back to the start when it reaches the end.

Note When you turn on the cycle region, clicking the Go to Beginning button in the Transport Controls moves the Playhead to the beginning of the cycle region rather than the beginning of the song.

4. **Click the first loop you want to play.** When you're ready to start the next loop, click it. Click the Play button when you want to stop playback.

Switching to another loop in the same family

If two arrows appear in the upper left corner of the loop's region, that means the loop is part of a *family* of loops, a group of loops that are related to each other.

You can switch quickly to another loop in the same family by clicking the arrows and then choosing the loop from the pop-up menu (see figure 8.11).

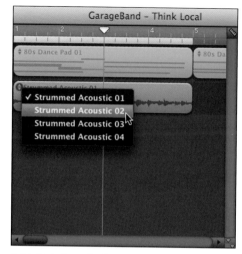

8.11 Click the pair of arrows in the upper left corner of a loop to switch quickly to a related loop.

Genius

Switching loops like this can give strange effects, but it's well worth a try, especially because you can switch back to the previous loop in moments.

Filtering loops

To cut down on the number of results in the results list, you can filter the results by scale type. To do so, open the Scale pop-up menu and choose Major, Minor, Good For Both, or Any. Filtering by scale is helpful with harmonic loops such as bass lines or melodies; don't use it for rhythmic loops such as drums, where it won't help.

To turn off filtering by scale type, choose None in the Scale pop-up menu.

Note

You can filter loops further by selecting the Filter for more relevant results check box in Loops preferences (choose GarageBand ⇨ Preferences, and then click Loops). This setting restricts the display to loops within two semitones of the song key and is useful when you have many loops in your GarageBand library.

Adding loops to your collection

GarageBand comes with plenty of loops to get you started, but if you get heavily into GarageBand, you'll want to add further loops. You can add other people's prerecorded loops as described here, or you can create your own custom loops, as described next.

You can add loops to GarageBand in three ways:

- **Run an installation routine.** If you buy one of the GarageBand Jam Packs from the Apple Store (http://store.apple.com), run the installation routine to install the loops.

- **Add individual loops or folders of loops to the loop browser.** Open a Finder window to the folder that contains the individual loops or the folders of loops. Select the loops or the folders you want to add, drag them to the loop browser, and drop them there. GarageBand displays the Importing Loops sheet while it imports the loops and categorizes them.

- **Add a loop to a song.** Instead of adding one or more loops to the loop browser, you can insert a single loop directly in a song. When you do this, the loop doesn't appear in the loop browser, so you can use it only in the song to which you added it. Chances are you won't want to do this often, but when you do, open a Finder window to the folder that contains the loop, drag the loop to the existing track in which you want to use it in the GarageBand window, and then drop it. To create a new track using the loop, drop the loop below the last track in the track list.

Creating your own loops

One of the best things about GarageBand is that you can create your own loops from either Real Instrument or Software Instrument recordings you make. We're getting a bit ahead of ourselves here because you probably haven't made any recordings yet, but when you have, come back to this section and try making a loop.

Follow these steps to create a loop:

1. **Record the loop and edit it as necessary to make a region the right length for the loop.**
   Use the editing techniques described in this chapter and the next chapter.

2. **Click the region in the Timeline to select it.**

3. **Choose Edit ⇨ Add To Loop Library to display the sheet shown in figure 8.12.**

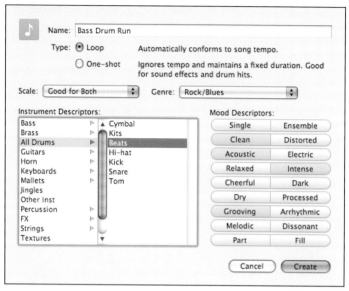

8.12 You can quickly create a loop from a Software Instrument region or a Real Instrument region.

4. **Type the name you want to give the loop in the Name box.** GarageBand suggests the instrument's name, but giving it a more descriptive name is better. Name your loops consistently (for example, Storming Electric Lead 1, Storming Electric Lead 2) to make them appear next to each other in the results list.

5. **In the Type area, choose whether to create a loop or a "one-shot" sound:**

   - **Loop.** This is what you'll normally create — a region that GarageBand automatically manipulates to make it match the song's tempo.

   - **One-shot.** This is a sound file that you want to always play back at the tempo at which you recorded it — for example, a cymbal smash, a guitar riff that you want to use only at a specific tempo, or a sound effect that always needs to play at the same speed.

6. **Open the Scale pop-up menu and choose which scales you want to use the loop or sound with: Any, Minor, Major, Neither, or Good For Both.** This setting controls when the loop shows up when you filter the loops by the Scale pop-up menu in the loop browser.

7. **Open the Genre pop-up menu and choose the genre: Rock/Blues, Electronic, Jazz, Urban, World, Cinematic, Orchestral, Country/Folk, Experimental, or Other Genre.** Specifying the genre lets you browse the loops by genre, which can save time.

8. **In the Instrument Descriptors box, click the instrument type on the left, and then click the specific instrument on the right.** For example, choose All Drums on the left and Kick on the right.

9. **In the Mood Descriptors area, click the button for each descriptor you want to apply to the loop.** When you click a button, it turns blue; click it again if you want to turn it off. The buttons are arranged in opposing pairs by row, so clicking one button in a pair turns off the other button if it's on. For example, Single and Ensemble are opposites, so you can select only one of them at once.

10. **Click Create to close the sheet and add the loop to GarageBand's library.**

Working with the Arrange Track

If your song follows a normal pattern, it will have several components that repeat one or more times, either identically or with variations. GarageBand lets you break your song up into different sections that you can copy and repeat as needed. For example, you can divide your song into an intro section, a verse section that repeats, a chorus section that repeats, a bridge between some of the repetitions, and an ending.

To define and manipulate the different sections of the song, you create what GarageBand calls *arrange regions* in the Arrange Track. An arrange region acts as a vertical section of the Timeline — you choose how many beats or bars it lasts — and gives you a way of grabbing all the loops you've positioned in that part of the Timeline. You can then move or copy all the contents of the arrange region at once.

Setting up arrange regions

First, set up arrange regions within the Arrange Track like this:

1. **Display the Arrange Track at the top of the Timeline by choosing Track ⇨ Show Arrange Track or pressing ⌘+Shift+A.** The Arrange Track appears as a gray bar below the beat ruler, with a single button — the New button — on it(see figure 8.13).

2. **Click the New button to create a new arrange region.** GarageBand adds an eight-bar region and names it *untitled*.

3. **If you need to change the start position of the arrange region, drag the bar so that its beginning is in the appropriate place.**

Arrange track   New

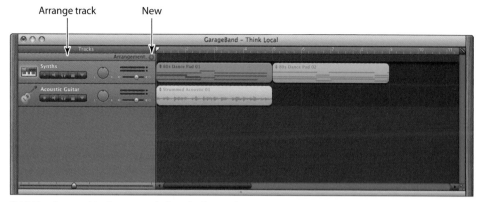

8.13 The Arrange Track appears below the beat ruler.

Note If you move the first arrange region from the beginning of the song, GarageBand automatically creates a new arrange region at the beginning of the song to occupy whatever space is available.

4. **To change the duration of the arrange region, drag its right border to where you want the region to end.**

5. **Rename the arrange region by double-clicking the "untitled" name, typing the new name, and then pressing Return.** Make sure the arrange region is selected before you double-click; if it's not, the double-click won't register correctly.

6. **To create a new arrange region, click the New button.** GarageBand adds the new arrange region after the one you just renamed. Adjust the new arrange region and rename it as before.

Moving and copying arrange regions

After you create arrange regions, you can quickly rearrange your song by dragging them in these ways:

- **Copy an arrange region.** Option-drag the arrange region to where you want the copy. GarageBand creates a copy and adds "copy" to the original name. Rename the copy with a more descriptive name.

- **Move an arrange region.** Drag the arrange region to where you want it. GarageBand moves the other arrange regions out of the way as you drag (see figure 8.14).

8.14 Drag an arrange region to move its section of your song to another position.

● **Swap the positions of two arrange regions.** Drag one of the arrange regions and drop it on the other arrange region. GarageBand swaps the two arrange regions over.

● **Overwrite an arrange region with another arrange region.** ⌘-drag the arrange region and drop it on the arrange region you want to overwrite.

Joining and splitting arrange regions

You can join two or more arrange regions together like this:

1. **If the arrange regions aren't adjacent, drag one or more of them so that they are.**

2. **Click the first arrange region, and then Shift-click each other arrange region to select all the ones you want to join.**

3. **Choose Edit ➪ Join or press ⌘+J to join the regions.** GarageBand gives the joined arrange region the name of the first arrange region. Rename it if necessary.

Similarly, you can split an arrange region into two arrange regions:

1. **Position the Playhead where you want to split the arrange region.**

2. **Choose Edit ➪ Split or press ⌘+T.** GarageBand splits the arrange region and gives each new arrange region the same name.

3. **Rename one or both of the arrange regions as needed.** Leaving both with the same name is a recipe for confusion.

Changing the Song's Tempo, Signature, and Key

When you first created the song project, you chose the tempo, the time signature, and the key for it. But often, as you assemble the song, you'll realize that you need to change one or more of these elements.

GarageBand makes it easy to change the tempo, the time signature, and the key. However, it's important that if you do need to make one of these changes, you do so before you record any Real Instrument tracks into your song. This is because GarageBand can't change the tempo, time signature, and key of audio you record in Real Instrument tracks.

To change the tempo, time signature, or key, choose Project in the LCD Mode pop-up menu at the left side of the display. You can then use the Key pop-up menu, the Tempo pop-up menu, or the Signature pop-up menu (see figure 8.15) to make the change.

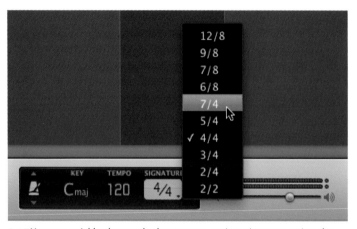

8.15 You can quickly change the key, tempo, or time signature using the Project LCD.

Recording Software Instruments and Real Instruments

GarageBand's wide selection of Software Instruments lets you play everything from grand piano to bass and drums using your musical keyboard, the Onscreen Keyboard, or the Musical Typing keyboard. This is great for composing music, but what's even better is adding a real musical instrument or a vocal part to your GarageBand song. This section shows you how to do both.

You can record either Software Instruments or Real Instruments in a single take or in multiple takes. With Software Instruments, you can also combine multiple passes through a cycle region into a single recording.

Preparing to record a Software Instrument

Start by getting your keyboard and the Software Instrument track ready like this:

1. **Get your keyboard ready.** Connect your musical keyboard via USB if it's not already connected. Or, if you're using the Onscreen Keyboard or the Musical Typing keyboard, display that keyboard.

2. **Add a Software Instrument track for the instrument you want to play, as described earlier in this chapter.** If your song already contains a Software Instrument track for the instrument, click that track's header to activate it.

3. **Make sure the dot on the Record button for the track is red to indicate that the track is set for recording.** If the dot is gray, click it to turn it red.

4. **Position the Playhead where you want to start playing.** For example, click the Go to Beginning button to move the Playhead to the beginning of the song.

Preparing to record a Real Instrument or Electric Guitar

Follow these steps to get a musical instrument ready for recording:

1. **Connect your instrument to your Mac as discussed in Chapter 7.** For example, plug your electric guitar into an audio interface connected via USB to your Mac, and check that the Audio Input pop-up menu in GarageBand's Audio/MIDI preferences is set to use that audio interface.

2. **Add a Real Instrument track of the appropriate type to the song, as discussed earlier in this chapter.** Choose the right input source in the Input Source pop-up menu in the Track Info pane, and choose whether to turn the monitor off, on, or on with feedback protection. For an electric guitar, add an Electric Guitar track.

3. **Play your instrument, and set the recording level.** Look at the level meter in the Mixer column for the track you're recording. You need to have the green LEDs and some of the orange LEDs lighting up while the input plays, but not have all the red on constantly, or you'll get distortion. To adjust the recording level, drag the Recording Level Slider in the Track Info pane for the track or change the volume on the instrument or the audio interface.

4. **If you want to change the track's name, double-click the default name in the track header, type the new name, and then press Return.**

5. **Make sure the dot on the Record button for the track is red to indicate that the track is set for recording.** If the dot is gray, click it to turn it red.

Genius

To give yourself a heads-up of when to start playing, turn on the count-in feature by choosing Control ⇨ Count In or pressing ⌘+Shift+U. GarageBand then gives you a one-bar count-in when you click the Record button. The count-in works only when the metronome is turned on (choose Control ⇨ Metronome or press ⌘+U).

Recording in a single take

The straightforward way of recording a track is by using a single take, either for part of the song or (if you prefer) for the whole song. Follow these steps:

1. **Click the Record button to start recording.** Alternatively, press R.

2. **Play your part on the keyboard (for a Software Instrument) or on the musical instrument (for a Real Instrument).**

3. **Click the Record button to stop recording, or click the Play button to stop both recording and playback.**

Recording multiple takes with cycle recording

If you prefer, you can record multiple takes for the same part of the song by turning on the cycle region. This works for both Software Instrument tracks and Real Instrument tracks.

Caution

Before recording multiple takes with Software Instruments, make sure that you have cleared the Automatically merge Software Instrument recordings when using the cycle region check box in the General preferences. If this check box is selected, you will create a single layer part instead (as discussed next). This setting doesn't apply to Real Instruments.

Here's how to record multiple takes:

1. **Click the cycle region button to turn on the cycle region.** Drag the ends of the cycle region so that it will repeat the part of the song you want to record.

2. **Click the Record button to start recording.**

3. **Play your part on the keyboard or musical instrument.** When the Playhead reaches the end of the cycle region, it loops back to the start of the region. GarageBand starts recording a new take, so you can just keep playing.

4. **Click the Record button to stop recording, or click the Play button to stop both recording and playback.** The yellow icon in the upper left corner of the recorded region shows how many takes you've recorded (see figure 8.16).

Now play back the song and decide which take you want to keep. You can switch from take to take by clicking the icon and choosing the take from the pop-up menu (see figure 8.17).

8.16 The yellow icon shows how many takes you've recorded for the region.

Creating a layered part with cycle recording

With Software Instruments, the alternative to recording multiple takes with cycle recording is to use multiple passes through the same region to build a layered part. Each time GarageBand loops through the cycle region, it merges the new notes you play with those you recorded on previous passes.

8.17 Use the pop-up menu to switch from one take to another and to delete the takes you don't want to keep.

This technique is especially useful for creating drum parts because it lets you record using several passes rather than a single pass. For example, you can record hi-hat and bass drum on the first pass, snare drum and ride cymbal on the second pass, tom-toms on the third pass, and extra cymbals and percussion on subsequent passes. You end up with a single region that contains all the drums instead of having a separate region for each pass.

Here's how to create a layered part:

1. **Choose GarageBand ➪ Preferences.** Select the Automatically merge Software Instrument recordings when using the cycle region check box in the General preferences, and then close the Preferences window.

2. **Click the Cycle Region to turn on the cycle region.** Drag the ends of the cycle region so that it repeats the part of the song you want to record.

3. **Click the Record button to start recording.**

4. **Play your first pass on the keyboard.** When the Playhead reaches the end of the cycle region, it loops back to the start of the region. Start your second pass, and repeat with as many passes as you need. As you play, GarageBand merges all the notes into the same region. Figure 8.18 shows this process on the Rock Kit track.

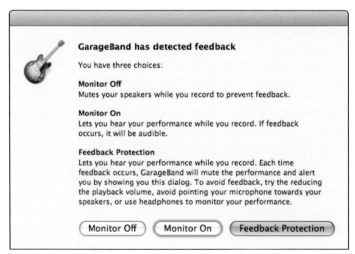

8.18 Creating a layered part by playing multiple passes through the same cycle region.

5. **Click the Record button to stop recording, or click the Play button to stop both record-ing and playback.**

After you finish recording, listen to the track. If you need to add further to it, you can do so by sim-ply starting recording again and playing the additions.

Dealing with feedback on Real Instruments

If you select the On setting or the On with Feedback Protection setting in the Monitor pop-up menu in the Track Info pane for a Real Instrument, you may get feedback during the recording. If GarageBand detects feedback, it displays the GarageBand has detected feedback dialog box (see figure 8.19) to warn you of the problem and let you decide what to do.

GarageBand has detected feedback

You have three choices:

Monitor Off
Mutes your speakers while you record to prevent feedback.

Monitor On
Lets you hear your performance while you record. If feedback occurs, it will be audible.

Feedback Protection
Lets you hear your performance while you record. Each time feedback occurs, GarageBand will mute the performance and alert you by showing you this dialog. To avoid feedback, try the reducing the playback volume, avoid pointing your microphone towards your speakers, or use headphones to monitor your performance.

(Monitor Off) (Monitor On) (**Feedback Protection**)

8.19 GarageBand helps you avoid ruining your recordings with feedback. If this dialog box keeps reappearing, click the Monitor Off button.

Normally, you'll want to click the Feedback Protection button, but if the dialog box reappears even after you do this, click Monitor Off instead. If you can quickly suppress the feedback manually (for example, by turning down the input volume on your audio interface), do so, and then click Monitor On.

Creating Custom Software Instruments

GarageBand comes with a great set of Software Instruments that you can use straight out of the box, but if you want to make your music sound special, you can build your own Software Instruments. The process is quick and easy, especially if you start from an existing Software Instrument, as this section shows you how to do.

Follow these steps to create a custom Software Instrument from an existing Software Instrument:

1. **Click the New button, or press ⌘+Option+N, to display the sheet for creating a new track.**

2. **Select the Software Instrument option button, and then click the Create button.** GarageBand creates a new Grand Piano track and displays the Track Info pane showing its settings.

3. **Switch to the instrument on which you want to base your new instrument.** In the left list box, select the category of instrument — for example, Guitars. In the right list box, select the instrument itself — for example, Big Electric Lead.

4. **Click the Edit tab to display the settings for the instrument you chose.** Figure 8.20 shows an example.

5. **Play the instrument using your musical keyboard (or one of GarageBand's keyboards) and see how it sounds.** Continue to play as you make changes so that you can judge their effects.

6. **If you want to make sweeping changes, change the sound generator used to create the sound.** In the Sound Generator area, choose the generator from the

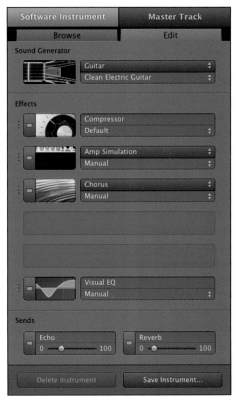

8.20 Use the controls on the Edit tab of the Track Info pane to create a new custom Software Instrument that sounds just the way you want it to.

upper pop-up menu and the sound from the lower pop-up menu. You can also click the picture under the Sound Generator text and use the dialog box that appears to customize the sound of the instrument. The dialog box contains different controls depending on the instrument; figure 8.21 shows an example of the Guitar dialog box. Click the close button (the red button) to close the dialog box when you finish.

7. **Adjust or remove the effects already applied to the instrument:**

   ● To adjust an effect, choose a different sound in the pop-up menu below its name.

   ● To edit the sound in the pop-up menu, click the picture button to its left, and then work in the dialog box that appears. Figure 8.22 shows the Amp Simulation dialog box for adjusting guitar sounds. Click the close button (the red button) to close the dialog box when you're done.

   ● To turn an effect off, click the green light on the left side of the picture button so that the light goes off.

8. **Add other effects as needed:**

   ● Click one of the unused buttons in the Effects area, and choose the effect from the pop-up menu that appears.

   ● Choose a sound or setting in the pop-up menu below the name of the effect you added.

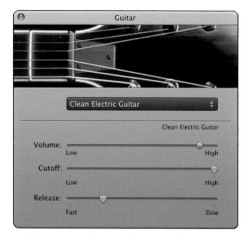

8.21 To change the overall sound of an instrument, open its dialog box and adjust the controls.

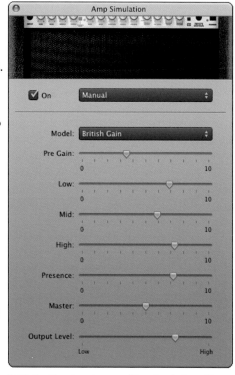

8.22 Configuring the amplifier simulation effect for a guitar.

- If necessary, edit the sound or setting by clicking the picture button and working in the resulting dialog box.

9. **To make your custom instrument easy to recognize in the track list, click the Browse tab, click the icon button at the bottom, and choose a distinctive icon from the panel.**

10. **Click Save Instrument at the bottom of the Details pane, type a descriptive name in the Save Instrument dialog box, and then click Save.**

If you switch to another instrument without saving the changes you made to the instrument you were working on, GarageBand displays a dialog box to let you decide whether to save changes. To save the changes, click Save As, type the instrument name in the Save Instrument dialog box, and then click Save. If you want to discard the changes, click Continue. You can then go on to work with a different instrument.

Normally, you'll want to keep the Software Instruments you create, but if you decide you no longer need one, you can delete it by clicking it in the Track Info window and then clicking Delete Instrument. GarageBand confirms the deletion; click Remove to get rid of the instrument.

How Can I Make My Song Sound Great and Then Share It?

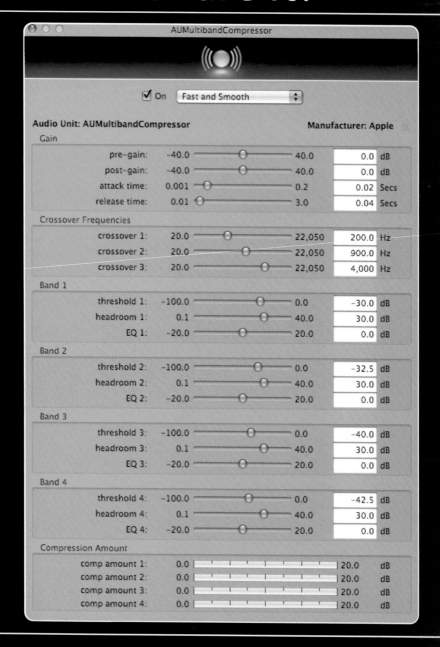

Recording a song is half the battle won, but if you want to grab your listeners by the ears and not let them go, you'll need to edit and mix the song as well. GarageBand provides powerful tools for editing both Software Instrument tracks and Real Instrument tracks to remove unwanted parts and change the pitch. You can then mix the song by changing the volume, panning, and effects of both individual tracks and the master track that controls the song's overall sound. When the song is finished, you can use it in the other iLife applications directly from GarageBand; but what you'll probably want to do is export the song to iTunes, give it a full set of tags, add lyrics and artwork, and then share the song with friends or the world via the Internet.

Editing a Song

To edit a song, you'll need to pick out the tracks you want to work on, either individually or together. You can then open a track in the Track Editor and edit it. You can change Software Instrument tracks extensively, even changing the pitch and velocity of individual notes; for Real Instrument tracks, including Electric Guitar tracks, your options are more limited, but you can move sections of audio, delete them, and change the track's tuning or timing.

Muting and soloing tracks

When you edit a song, you'll often need to focus on a single track or just a handful of tracks. You can do this by using GarageBand's Mute and Solo controls, which appear in the track header (see figure 9.1).

To mute a track so that you hear the other tracks without it, click the track's Mute button once to turn on muting. Click a second time to turn muting off again.

To solo a track so that you hear that track without the others, click the Solo button. Click the Solo button a second time to turn soloing off.

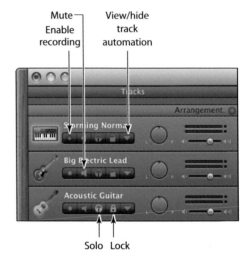

9.1 Use the buttons in the track header to mute and solo tracks so that you can hear exactly what you need to.

Genius

If you need to listen to several tracks but not all of them, you can either solo each of those tracks or mute all the other tracks.

Editing Software Instrument tracks

Recording Software Instrument instruments is pretty wonderful because you can either record multiple takes (and choose the best) or record a single take using multiple passes. But what's even better is that you can edit a region you've recorded, adjust the notes it contains, and even change their length and velocity.

Opening a region for editing in the Track Editor

To open a region for editing, double-click the region in the timeline. Figure 9.2 shows a Software Instrument region open for editing in Piano Roll view, the view in which Garage Band first opens the region. The other view is Score view, and you'll meet it shortly.

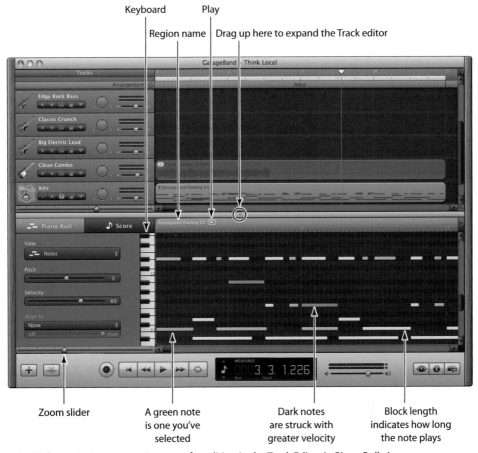

Keyboard   Play

Region name | Drag up here to expand the Track editor

| Zoom slider | A green note is one you've selected | Dark notes are struck with greater velocity | Block length indicates how long the note plays |

9.2 A Software Instrument region open for editing in the Track Editor in Piano Roll view.

Editing individual notes in Piano Roll view

Here's how to edit individual notes in Piano Roll view:

- **Select multiple notes.** Either drag a selection box around the notes (see figure 9.3), or click the first note, and then Shift+click each of the other notes.

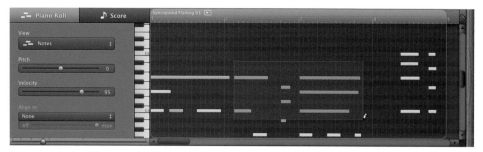

9.3 Selecting multiple notes in Piano Roll view in the Track Editor.

- **Copy a note.** Option+click the note and drag it to where you want the copy.

- **Change the pitch.** Select the note, and then drag it up or down. As you drag, GarageBand plays the note you've reached.

- **Change the velocity.** Select the note, and then either drag the Velocity slider or type a new value in the Velocity box.

- **Change the length.** Select the note, and then drag the right end of its length bar to the right or to the left.

- **Add a note.** ⌘+click where you want to place the note. Drag the right edge of the note to change the length as needed, and change the velocity by dragging the Velocity slider or typing in the Velocity box.

Editing individual notes in Score view

Score view shows notes as they appear on sheet music, with musical note symbols placed on staves to indicate their timing and pitch. Here's how to edit individual notes in Score view:

- **Select multiple notes.** Either drag a selection box around the notes (see figure 9.4), or click the first note, and then Shift+click each of the other notes.

9.4 When you select multiple notes in Score view, GarageBand displays the length of each note as a box attached to its note character.

- **Copy a note.** Option+click the note head and drag it to where you want the copy.

- **Change the pitch.** Select the note, and then press Up Arrow or Down Arrow. Alternatively, drag the note head up or down. As you move the note, GarageBand plays the note you've reached.

- **Change the velocity.** Select the note, and then either drag the Velocity slider or type a new value in the Velocity box.

- **Change the length.** Select the note, and then drag the right end of its length bar to the right or to the left.

- **Add a note.** Open the Insert pop-up menu and choose the note length you want, then ⌘+click where you want to place the note.

- **Change the note value.** Ctrl+click or right-click the existing note you want to change, and then choose the note value from the menu that appears (see figure 9.5).

9.5 Changing the length of an existing note in the region.

Changing the timing for a track

If you've recorded a Software Instrument track that's not perfectly in time, you may be able to fix it by using the Enhance Timing feature. Follow these steps:

1. **Set the song playing so that you can judge the effect the timing change produces.**

2. **Open the track in the Track Editor by double-clicking one of the track's regions in the timeline.**

3. **Open the Enhance Timing pop-up menu at the bottom of the pane and choose the note value you want to use.** For Software Instrument tracks, this menu offers a wide range of choices, from 1/1 Note through 1/64 Note, from 1/4 Triplet through 1/16 Triplet, and from 1/8 Swing Light through 1/16 Swing Heavy.

4. **Drag the Enhance Timing slider to adjust the timing.** Listen to the effect the change produces, and adjust it if necessary.

Changing the modulation, pitchbend, sustain, expression, or foot control

To make your tracks sound more lively, you can change the modulation, pitchbend, sustain, expression, or foot control for a region. If you recorded this controller information by using the controls on your keyboard, you can edit the existing movements of the controls. If not (for example, because your keyboard doesn't have a foot control), you can add controller information manually using your mouse.

To change the controller information, follow these steps:

1. **Set the song playing so that you can judge the effect of the changes you make.**
2. **Open the track in the Track Editor by double-clicking one of the track's regions in the timeline.**
3. **In the View pop-up menu, choose the controller you want to work with.** The controller information appears in the Track Editor. Figure 9.6 shows an example of changing the pitchbend on a track.
4. **Adjust the curve as needed:**

   - Remove unneeded control points, the points at which the curve changes. Click a control point and press Delete to delete it.
   - Change the value of a control point. Drag the control point up or down.
   - Alter when a change occurs. Drag a control point to the left or right.
   - Draw a new line. ⌘+click an empty area in the control track. You can then drag the control points for the line.

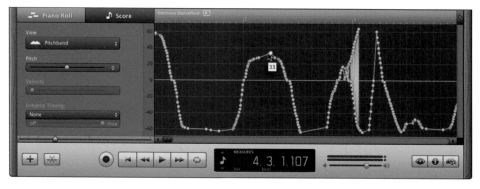

9.6 You can change the pitchbend of a track by choosing Pitchbend in the View pop-up menu and moving the control points.

Editing Real Instrument tracks

What's even neater than editing the notes in a Software Instrument track is being able to edit the regions in a Real Instrument track — either a region you create from a loop or one you record using a musical instrument. You can edit out mistakes (or mis-takes) and sew together your best performances to produce a seamless track.

Selecting the audio you want to edit

Here's how to select the audio you want to edit in a Real Instrument track:

1. **Double-click the region you want to edit to open it for editing in the Track Editor.**
   Figure 9.7 shows the Track Editor with a Real Instrument region ready for editing.

2. **Drag the Zoom slider in the Track Editor to zoom in or out so that you can see as much of the region as you need to.**

Playhead

Zoom slider

9.7 The Track Editor with a Real Instrument region ready for editing.

3. **Move the mouse pointer into the region in the Track Editor so that it appears as a cross.** As long as the pointer isn't right at the top of the track or right at the start or finish, it'll appear as a cross-hair — so anywhere in the middle is fine.

4. **Drag left or right to select the section you want.** Figure 9.8 shows an example.

Changing the tuning for a track

If you record a Real Instrument track that's in time but not fully in tune, try using the Enhance Tuning feature to fix the tuning like this:

1. **Set the song playing so that you can judge the effect that the tuning change produces.**

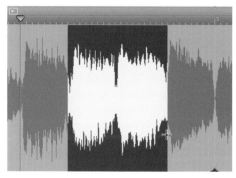

9.8 Drag with the cross-hair pointer to select a section of a Real Instrument region in the Track Editor.

Caution

Changing the tuning can save a track, but you need to understand the limitations. First, tuning works accurately only on regions that contain single notes rather than chords. Second, changing the tuning affects all the regions in the track, not just a single region.

2. **Open the track in the Track Editor by double-clicking one of the track's regions in the timeline.**

3. **Drag the Enhance Tuning slider to the right from the leftmost position (in which it is off).** Listen to the effect the change produces, and adjust it if necessary.

4. **If you want to restrict the tuning to the project's key instead of using the 12-note chromatic scale, select the Limit to Key check box.** Again, listen to the effect of the change and decide whether you want to keep it.

Changing the timing for a track

If you recorded a Real Instrument track that's not perfectly in time, you may be able to fix it by using the Enhance Timing feature. Follow these steps:

1. **Set the song playing so that you can judge the effect that the timing change produces.**

2. **Open the track in the Track Editor by double-clicking one of the track's regions in the timeline.**

3. **Drag the Enhance Timing slider to the right from the Off position.** Listen to the effect the change produces, and adjust it if necessary.

4. **If necessary, open the Enhance Timing pop-up menu at the bottom of the pane and choose a different note value from it.** For example, choose 1/8 Triplet or 1/8 Note rather than 1/16 Note.

Editing an audio file outside GarageBand

When GarageBand's editing capabilities aren't enough to fix a problem with a Real Instrument region you've recorded, you can use an external audio editor to fix the problem instead.

GarageBand saves your recorded Real Instrument regions within a package file, so you need to use the Finder to open the package and locate the region file like this:

1. **Close the project file in GarageBand.**

2. **Open a Finder window to the folder that contains the song.** For example, open a window to the ~/Music/GarageBand folder.

3. **Ctrl+click or right-click the song and choose Show Package Contents.** Mac OS X opens a new Finder window showing the files contained in the song's package.

4. **Open the Media folder to locate the audio file containing the region.**

5. **Ctrl+click or right-click the audio file, highlight Open With, and then choose the audio editor.**

6. **When you have finished editing the audio, save the file:**

   - If you save the file under the same name, GarageBand simply loads the new version of the file when you open the project.

   - If you save the file under a different name, you must replace the version that's in the timeline with the new version. This extra step is often a good idea in case editing the file doesn't produce exactly the result you want; if this happens, you can return to the original file (or try editing it again).

Locking a track

When you finish setting up a track, you can lock it to prevent yourself from changing it inadvertently. To lock the track, click the Lock button in the track header so that the button glows green. Click the Lock button again to remove the locking.

Mixing a Song

To mix the tracks of your song into the arrangement you want, you use GarageBand's mixer controls (see figure 9.9). These allow you to adjust the volume and control the left-right panning of each track automatically as the track plays. You can also add other automation curves to a track to control other effects, such as echo, reverberation, or the intensity and speed of a tremolo effect.

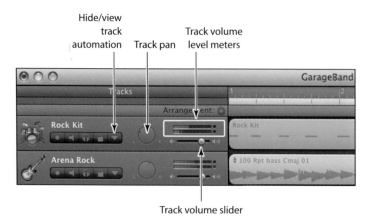

9.9 The mixer's deceptively simple controls can make all the difference to the sound of a track.

Adjusting the volume of individual tracks

GarageBand lets you adjust the volume either for the whole of a track or for parts of it. By using both techniques, you can set the track's volume exactly the way you need it.

Start by using the Track Volume slider to set the relative volume of the track. When you add the track, GarageBand sets the slider to 0 decibels (dB), which means the track's loudness is not increasing or decreasing.

To reduce the track's volume, drag the slider to the left; to increase the volume, drag it to the right. GarageBand displays a tooltip showing the decibel measurement you're setting (as shown in figure 9.10), but normally you'll do better to rely on your ears to judge whether the track is as loud as you want it.

9.10 Changing a track's volume using the Track Volume slider.

That sets the track to play at the same level. Often, you'll want finer control than this. For example, you may want to fade into the song rather than start with a bang, fade out to a whimper, or play parts of the track at a lower volume so that other tracks can come to the fore.

To make different parts of a track play at different volumes, use the track's volume curve like this:

1. **If the Automation track isn't displayed, click the View/Hide Track Automation button on the track header to display it.** Figure 9.11 shows the Automation track with the Track Volume automation curve displayed and turned on.

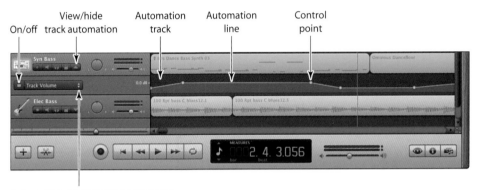

9.11 The Automation track displays a single automation effect at a time — Track Volume, Track Pan, or another automation effect you add.

2. **In the Automation Parameters pop-up menu, choose Track Volume if it's not already selected.** The line along the Automation track shows the volume level. Unless you've set a volume curve already, this line will be horizontal, maintaining a steady volume. You can increase the volume by dragging the first control point up or decrease it by dragging down. This first control point controls the overall volume of the track until you create a volume curve, so dragging it has the same effect as moving the Track Volume slider for the track.

3. **To create a volume curve, place control points on the volume line like this:**

   - Set the song to cycle through the section you're working with so that you can hear the effects of the changes you make. Start playback.

Note

When you create an automation curve for a track, GarageBand automatically turns on that automation parameter and displays the green On light (for a Software Instrument track) or blue On light (for a Real Instrument track) when that parameter is selected in the Automation Parameters pop-up menu. You can turn the automation parameter off by clicking the On light so that it goes off.

● Click where you want to place a control point. Each control point appears as a blue dot for a Real Instrument track or a green dot for a Software Instrument track (see figure 9.12).

9.12 Dragging a control point to create a volume curve on an Automation track.

● Drag a control point up to increase the volume at that point, or drag it down to decrease the volume.

● To change when a control point alters the volume, drag the control point to the left or right along the volume curve.

● To get rid of a control point, drag it along to the next control point, which swallows it like Pac-Man.

4. **When you finish setting the volume curve, click the View/Hide Track Automation button to hide the Automation track again.** If you're going to change panning (discussed next) or automation (discussed later in this chapter), you may want to leave the Automation track displayed.

Controlling panning

To control the left-right placement of the sound on tracks, use the panning controls. These let you position different tracks where you want them around the panorama of the song, so that the tracks sound as though they're coming from different directions. For example, you may choose to place your drum track, lead instrument, and vocals centrally and pan the backing tracks to the left and right.

You can set a track panning position for the track as a whole, or you can create a custom panning curve that moves the track to different pan positions at different points in the timeline as needed.

Genius

Go easy on the panning — you seldom need to pan a track all the way to the left or the right. Doing so can make the song sound stretched and odd.

For example, you can make your edgy guitar line move from one side of the mix to the other — and then back again.

To set a track panning position for the track as a whole, click the Track Pan knob and drag downward to pan to the left or upward to pan to the right.

To create a custom panning curve for the track, follow these steps:

1. **If the Automation track isn't displayed, click the View/Hide Track Automation button on the track header to display it.**

2. **In the Automation Parameters pop-up menu, choose Track Pan.**

   - The line along the Automation track shows the panning for the track, with panning to the left appearing above the 0 mark (with positive values) and panning to the right appearing below the 0 mark (with negative values).

   - Until you set a custom pan curve for the track, the panning line is horizontal, maintaining a steady position that you set by dragging the Track Pan knob.

   - You can adjust the panning for the whole track by dragging the first control point up (to pan to the left) or down (to pan to the right). This first control point controls the overall panning of the track until you create a custom panning curve, so dragging the control point has the same effect as dragging the Track Pan knob.

3. **To create a panning curve, place control points on the track like this:**

   - Set the song to cycle through the section you're working with so that you can hear the effects of the changes you make. Start playback.

   - Click where you want to place a control point. Each control point appears as a blue dot for a Real Instrument track or a green dot for a Software Instrument track.

   - Drag a control point up to pan to the left at that point, or drag it down to pan to the right.

   - To change when a control point alters the panning, drag the control point to the left or right along the panning curve.

   - To get rid of a control point, drag it along to the next control point.

4. **When you finish setting the panning curve, click the View/Hide Track Automation button to hide the Automation track again.** If you're going to change automation (discussed next), you may want to leave the Automation track displayed.

Adding automation parameters to a track

A volume curve and custom panning curve can make a big difference to a track's sound, especially when you set them for most or all of the tracks in the song. But GarageBand also lets you add other automation curves to each track as needed. You can add an automation curve for visual equalization (to control, say, bass frequency or treble gain), echo, reverberation, or any of the other effects you apply to the track.

Adding an automation parameter

Here's how to add an automation parameter to a track:

1. **If the Automation track isn't displayed, click the View/Hide Track Automation button on the track header to display it.**

2. **In the Automation Parameters pop-up menu, choose Add Automation to open the Add Automation dialog box.** Figure 9.13 shows the Add Automation dialog box for a guitar track with several effects.

3. **If the category for the automation parameter is collapsed, click the disclosure triangle to expand it.** For example, click the sideways triangle next to Echo & Reverb to display the Echo and Reverb automation controls.

4. **Select the check box for each automation parameter you want to give a custom curve.**

5. **Click OK to close the Add Automation dialog box.** If you selected a single automation parameter, GarageBand displays the Automation track for it. If you selected more than one, Garage Band displays the Automation track for the first parameter. To choose a different parameter, open the Automation Parameters pop-up menu and choose the automation parameter you want to change first (see figure 9.14).

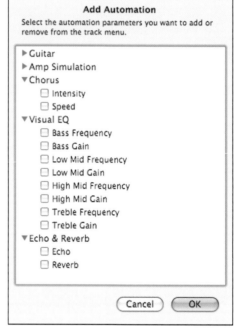

9.13 Choose the automation parameter in the Add Automation dialog box.

6. **Add control points and position them as described earlier in this chapter.**

7. **Work with other automation parameters as needed, or click the View/Hide Track Automation button on the track header to hide the Automation track again.**

Removing an automation parameter

If you need to remove an automation parameter from a track, open the Add Automation dialog box, expand the category if necessary, and clear the check box for the automation parameter. GarageBand prompts you to confirm the decision. Click the Continue button in the You are about to remove automation dialog box, and then click OK to close the Add Automation dialog box.

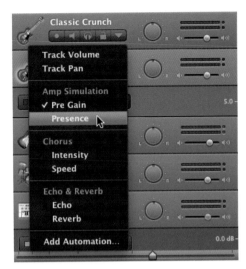

9.14 Choose the automation parameter for which you want to create an automation curve.

Setting up the master track

When you've arranged the volume and panning for the individual tracks within the song and applied such effects as are needed, you're ready to do the same for the master track. This is the track that controls the volume, panning, automation, and effects for the song as a whole.

Deciding how to arrange the master track

Given that the master track controls the overall sound of the song, you normally need to treat it differently than the individual tracks.

1. **Choose track info settings for the master track.** GarageBand comes with a stack of preset settings for different types of track, and you can customize them as needed.

2. **Set a volume curve for the master track to control the overall volume of the song and to implement any fade in, fade out, or volume changes that apply song-wide.**

3. **You may need to create a master pitch curve for the song (varying the pitch as the song plays) or a master tempo curve (so that some parts of the song play faster than others).**

4. **You may need to apply automation parameters to control the effects used for the track.** For example, you may need to change the amount or *color* (feeling) of echo in different parts of the track.

By contrast, you seldom need to set a panning curve for the master track. If you already panned the individual instruments to where they belong in the mix, you won't need to pan the whole track unless you're trying to disorient the listener.

Similarly, you will normally do best to go easy on the effects you apply to the master track, because these effects build on the effects you already applied to the individual tracks.

Displaying the master track

The master track is normally hidden until you display it by choosing Track ⇨ Show Master Track or pressing ⌘+B. The master track appears at the bottom of the Track List, separated from the other tracks by open space (see figure 9.15).

9.15 The master track appears at the bottom of the track list and has no Mixer controls.

Setting track info for the master track

What you normally need to do first is set track info for the master track. The track info lets you quickly switch the overall feel of your song, so it's great for creating different edits of the song.

To set the track info for the master track, follow these steps:

1. **Double-click the track header for the master track to display the Track Info pane with the Master Track button selected (see figure 9.16).**

2. **In the left list box, click the sound category you want — for example, Pop or Stadium Rock.** The list of available sounds appears in the right box.

3. **In the right list box, click the sound you want.** For example, if you choose Stadium Rock, you have choices such as Stadium Rock Basic, Large Arena, and Stadium Empty.

4. **Play the song and make sure the effect is what you want.** If not, choose another sound and test it.

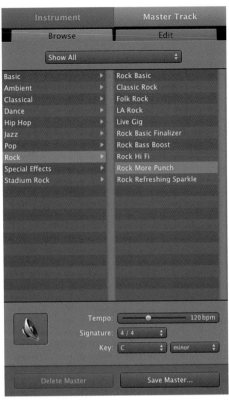

9.16 The master track lets you quickly change the overall feel of the song.

Note

From the Master Track info pane, you can also adjust the song's tempo, time signature, or key. Usually, you'll want to fix these elements earlier in the process of creating your song because changing them now can wreck the whole song. But sometimes you'll need to tweak a setting to make the song sound the way you want it to.

5. **If you want to fine-tune the sound, click the Edit tab to display the effects used (see figure 9.17).**

6. **Change or remove any of the effects applied to the master track using the techniques explained earlier in this chapter.** For example, choose a different preset for the Echo effect, or click the picture to the left of the Reverb effect and use the resulting Reverb window to set the reverb time, color, and volume you want.

7. **If necessary, add another effect in an empty row in the Master Effects list.** For example, you may want to apply the AUMultibandCompressor effect. This offers preset compressions such as Fast and Smooth, Sub Control, and Gentle, or you can click the Edit button and use the AUMultibandCompressor dialog box (shown on the opening page of this chapter) to create custom multiband compression.

9.17 Use the Edit tab in the Master Track info pane to fine-tune the effects for your song.

8. **If you customized the sound in a way you want to be able to use again for other songs, save the master track settings as a preset.** Click Save Master, type a descriptive name in the Save Master dialog box, and then click Save.

Creating a volume curve for the master track

After choosing the effects for your master track, create a volume curve for it like this:

1. **Open the Automation Parameters pop-up menu and choose Master Volume to display the volume curve (unless it's displayed already).**

2. **Set control points as described earlier in this chapter to create the volume curve you want.** For example, create a swift fade in at the beginning of the track and a gradual fade out at the end.

Genius   GarageBand can create a fade out for you automatically. Just click the track and then choose Track ➪ Fade Out. But because GarageBand doesn't know your music, you should always listen to the effect and customize it as necessary.

Changing the tempo during the song

Many songs work well at a standard tempo, but for others, you can add variation and aural excitement by changing the tempo during the song. For example, you may want to speed up the tempo during the climax of a song or wind it down toward the end.

To change the tempo during the song, create a custom Master Tempo curve like this:

1. **Open the Automation Parameters pop-up menu and choose Master Tempo from it.** GarageBand displays the Master Tempo track.

2. **Set control points as usual to create the tempo curve you need.** Drag a control point upward to increase the tempo or downward to decrease it; GarageBand displays the bpm value as you drag. Figure 9.18 shows an example of a tempo curve that makes a section of a song faster before gradually returning to the previous tempo. The change appears minor in the timeline, but the listener hears a dramatic difference.

9.18 Creating a custom Master Tempo curve to add variation to a song.

Changing the master pitch of the song

Besides letting you change the pitch of a region or track, GarageBand also lets you change the master pitch of the song. This basically means grabbing all the regions that it makes sense to shift and moving them up or down the musical scale. GarageBand doesn't change drum tracks or Real Instrument regions you've recorded.

As with the other Automation tracks, you can either change the pitch for the whole song or create an automation curve that changes the pitch for only the parts of the song that you specify. Here's what to do:

1. **Open the Automation Parameters pop-up menu and choose Master Pitch from it.** GarageBand displays the Master Pitch track.

2. **If you want to change the pitch of the entire song, drag the first control point (which GarageBand creates automatically) up or down.** When you drag the first control point, the automation curve remains straight, so the pitch changes evenly throughout the whole song.

3. **If you want to change the pitch of parts of the song, set control points as for any other automation curve.** Drag a control point upward to increase the pitch or downward to decrease it. GarageBand displays a tooltip showing the number of musical half-steps by which you're moving the control point (for example, +1 or -2).

Adding automation to the master track

You can add automation to the master track by using the same techniques as for the other tracks:

1. **Open the Automation Parameters pop-up menu and choose Add Automation to display the Add Automation dialog box.**

2. **Select the check box for each automation parameter you want to add, and then click OK.**

3. **Open the Automation Parameters pop-up menu and choose the parameter you want to work with.**

4. **Add control points and create an automation curve for the parameter.**

For the master track, GarageBand offers four echo automation parameters rather than the one echo automation parameter that's available for other tracks:

- **Echo Time.** This parameter controls how long each echo lasts (whether it is faster or slower).

- **Echo Repeat.** This parameter controls how many times the echoes repeat.

- **Repeat Color.** This parameter controls whether the echoes are *dark*, with each repetition sounding duller than the previous one, or *bright*, with each repetition sounding thinner than the previous one.

- **Echo Volume.** This parameter controls how loud the echoes are.

By working with the different echo parameters, you can produce a wide variation of echo effects that enhance the song.

Sharing a Song

When you finish a song, you'll probably want the world to know about it. GarageBand makes it easy to export a song to iTunes, share it with other people on the Internet, or put it to use in a slideshow, a movie, or a DVD.

Note

If you create an iPhone ringtone with GarageBand, you can export it to iTunes in moments. Just open the ringtone project and choose Share⇨Send Ringtone to iTunes. Next time you connect your iPhone, click its entry in iTunes' Source list, then click the Ringtones tab. Your new ringtone appears there, and you can sync it like any other ringtone.

Exporting a song to iTunes

If you want to listen to your song using iTunes, put it on your iPod or iPhone, or burn it to CD, export the song to iTunes like this:

1. **Choose Share ⇨ Send Song to iTunes to open the Send your song to your iTunes library sheet shown in figure 9.19.**

2. **Change the text in the iTunes Playlist, Artist Name, Composer Name, and Album Name boxes as needed.** Garage Band pulls this info from the My Info preferences, but you'll often want to give songs different artist and composer credits or put them in different albums.

9.19 Exporting a song to iunes. The Compress Using pop-up menu and Audio Settings pop-up menu appear only when you select the Compress check box.

3. **If you want to compress the song to reduce the file size, select the Compress check box and choose the compression method:**

  - Select AAC Encoder or MP3 Encoder in the Compress Using pop-up menu. AAC gives marginally higher quality than MP3 and is great for iPods, iPhones, and iTunes, but MP3 files are playable in more hardware and software players than AAC files, so it's a trade-off.

Note

If you clear the Compress check box in the Send your song to your iTunes library sheet, GarageBand exports the song as an AIFF file.

  - Choose the quality from the Audio Settings pop-up menu. Good Quality (64 Kbps) is suitable for voice recordings (such as podcasts) but not for music. High Quality (128 Kbps) gives good results for songs, but Higher Quality (192 Kbps) is usually the best choice.

Genius

If you want to compress your song at the highest possible quality, export it from GarageBand without compression, and then compress it using Apple Lossless Encoding in iTunes. In GarageBand, clear the Compress check box on the Send your song to your iTunes library sheet and click Share. In iTunes, open the General preferences and click Import Settings. Choose Apple Lossless Encoder in the Import Using pop-up menu, and then click OK to close each dialog box. Ctrl+click or right-click the file you imported and choose Create Apple Lossless Encoding Version.

4. **Click Share.** GarageBand mixes down the song and adds it to your iTunes library. iTunes starts playing the new song automatically, no matter if you were listening to something else at the time.

Tagging a song

When you send a song to your iTunes library, GarageBand fills in the Name, Artist, Composer, Album, BPM, and Year tags.

This is a good start, but it's only a start. Before distributing a song, Ctrl+click or right-click it in iTunes, choose Get Info, and then use the tabs of the Item Info dialog box (shown in Chapter 1) to edit these tags (if needed) and to add further tags and information to the song. Consider adding the following:

- **Genre.** It's vital to set the genre so that people find the song when they browse by genre.

- **Track Number.** Fill this in so that the listener can sort your songs in the order you intended.

- **Artwork.** Drag one or more pictures to the box on the Artwork tab of the Item Info dialog box, or click the Add button and use the Open dialog box to pick the pictures. If you add multiple pictures, drag them into the order in which you want the audience to see them.

- **Album Artist.** Set this tag if the album artist is different from the artist.

- **Sorting tags.** If you want your song to be sorted by a different name, artist name, album artist, album, or composer, enter the appropriate tags on the Sorting tab.

- **Lyrics.** If your song has words, add them on the Lyrics tab. Not only do most people like to know a song's lyrics, but you'll avoid the heartache of seeing your lyrics mangled by well-intentioned listeners on the Web's lyrics sites.

Using a song in other iLife applications

Even without exporting a song from GarageBand, you can use it in your projects in the other iLife applications as long as you saved an iLife preview of the song (as GarageBand prompts you to do when you close a project).

To use the song, simply open the Media Browser in the application, and select the song in the GarageBand category.

If you haven't saved an iLife preview for the song, you won't be able to preview it in the Media Browser. Instead, when you select the song in the Media Browser, the application you use prompts you to open the song in GarageBand so that you can create a preview (see figure 9.20). Click Yes if you want to use the song.

9.20 The iLife application (here, iPhoto) prompts you to open GarageBand and save an iLife preview for a song project that lacks one.

295

How Do I Build a Web Site with iWeb?

Have you ever wanted to create your own Web site easily, without having to learn the HTML markup language? Apple's iWeb application lets you put together a sleek, well-designed Web site in minutes, publish it to the Web, and quickly update it with new information whenever you need to. Whether you just want to display your own photos and writings or you want to include advanced features like online maps, videos from YouTube, and revenue-generating advertisements, this chapter shows you what you need to know.

Getting Started with the iWeb Interface

To get started with iWeb, launch the application by clicking the iWeb icon on the Dock (if there is one) or by opening the Applications folder and double-clicking the iWeb icon.

Launching iWeb and choosing a template

iWeb expects you to start creating a Web site automatically if you don't already have one, so it displays the sheet shown in figure 10.1. This is called the Template Chooser, and it lets you choose the theme and template for each Web page.

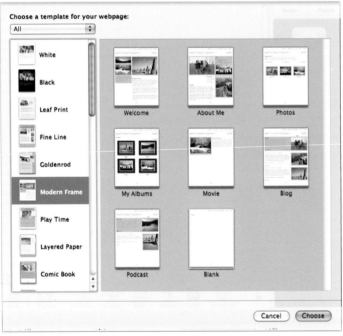

10.1 iWeb displays the Template Chooser the first time you launch the application so that you can create your first Web page immediately.

The *theme* is the overall design of the Web page. For example, the White theme has a white background, the Black theme has a black background, and the Goldenrod theme features golden tones. Each theme contains several different templates, each of which holds the layout for a particular type of page: the Welcome page, the About Me page, the Photos page, and so on.

If you click the Cancel button in the Template Chooser when your site doesn't contain a page, iWeb simply closes, so go ahead and start creating a page:

1. **Make sure All is selected in the pop-up list at the top of the Template Chooser.**

Genius

The pop-up menu above the left list box lets you choose among showing all iWeb themes, the themes in iWeb 3.0, those in iWeb 2.0, those in iWeb 1.1, and those in iWeb 1.0. Choose All in the pop-up menu to give yourself the widest choice of templates. Choose one of the other selections if you want to see only the themes from an earlier version of iWeb.

2. **In the list box on the left, click the theme you want to use for your Web site.** Each theme contains the same set of templates, so you can switch easily from one theme to another.

3. **In the box on the right, click the Welcome page.** This is usually the best starting point for a Web site.

4. **Click Choose.** iWeb closes the template chooser and starts a Web page using the template you chose.

Meeting the iWeb interface

Now that you've got iWeb open, let's look at the user interface. Figure 10.2 shows the main areas of the iWeb window and the items you'll see at first.

- **Sidebar.** This area contains your Web sites, blogs, and Web pages. You can expand or collapse any item that has a gray disclosure triangle next to it. You can display any page on the Web page canvas by clicking it in the Sidebar.

- **Web page canvas.** This the area on which you create the Web page.

- **Navigation area.** This area contains links to the different pages in your Web site, plus the text indicating the current page. Whichever page you're currently viewing doesn't have a link because you're already on it and don't need to navigate to it.

- **Toolbar.** This bar contains tools for quickly giving the most widely used commands in iWeb.

- **New button.** Opens the Template Chooser so that you can create a new Web page.

- **Text placeholders.** These predefined areas contain sample text that you replace with your custom text.

- **Picture placeholders.** These predefined areas contain sample pictures that you replace with your own pictures.

Sidebar   Navigation area   Web page canvas   Picture placeholders

Text placeholders   Toolbar

10.2 The main components of the iWeb user interface

Understanding the four regions of the Web page canvas

In iWeb, each Web page is divided up into four regions:

- **Header.** This area appears at the top of the page and contains the title of the page.

- **Navigation area.** This area appears near the top of the page — exactly where depends on the template used for the Web page — and contains links to the other main pages in the Web site.

- **Body.** This is the main part of the page. The body usually contains multiple placeholders for text and images.

- **Footer.** This area appears at the bottom of the page. Its contents depend on the Web page's template.

To see the divisions between the different areas of a page, choose View ⇨ Show Layout or press ⌘+Shift+L. iWeb displays narrow lines marking out the different areas (see figure 10.3). Press ⌘+Shift+L again or choose View ⇨ Hide Layout when you want to hide the lines again.

10.3 Displaying the layout lines with the View ➪ Show Layout command lets you see the divisions between the header, footer, body, and navigation area.

Setting Preferences to Suit the Way You Work

Compared to most other applications, iWeb has refreshingly few preferences, so you can set them in moments. The preferences make a big difference to the way iWeb behaves, so it's worth taking those moments.

Press ⌘+, (⌘ and the comma key) or choose iWeb ➪ Preferences to pop open the Preferences window (see figure 10.4).

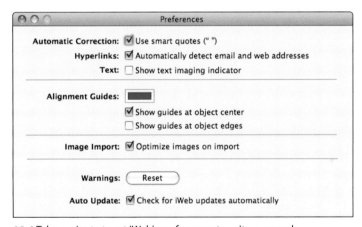

10.4 Take a minute to set iWeb's preferences to suit your needs.

Here's what the iWeb preferences do, with suggestions of how you'll probably want to set them:

- **Use smart quotes (" ").** Select this check box to make iWeb automatically turn straight quote marks into "smart" quotes that curl the right way, just like in Pages or Microsoft Word.

- **Automatically detect email and Web addresses.** Select this check box to have iWeb automatically create a link when you type an e-mail address or a Web URL. You can adjust the link afterward if you need to.

● **Show text imaging indicator.** This check box's name seems puzzling, but it's easy enough. When you use custom fonts in your Web pages rather than special fonts, Web browsers on computers that don't have the fonts won't be able to display the text. To avoid this problem, iWeb converts text in custom fonts to images, which any Web browser can download. When you select this check box, iWeb displays a yellow picture icon on any text box that it will convert to an image. This gives you a heads-up and lets you change the font if you want to keep the text as text.

Genius

iWeb's trick of converting text in custom fonts to images makes sure anybody can see that text. But be aware that search engines normally don't read text in images. So if you want to make sure your Web site can be read by search engines, avoid using custom fonts for important text.

● **Alignment Guides.** Choose the color you want to use for alignment guides. You may need to change to a color that stands out against the template you're using.

● **Show guides at object center.** Select this check box to make iWeb show guidelines at the center of objects (see figure 10.5). Whether you want the guides at the object center, edges, or both depends on which you find easiest.

10.5 Guides at the object center (as shown here) or object edges help you align objects quickly.

● **Show guides at object edges.** Select this check box to make iWeb show guidelines at the edges of objects.

● **Optimize images on import.** Select this check box if you want iWeb to alter images you include so that they're suitable for Web use. This feature is helpful because it helps you avoid lumbering your Web site with huge image files that will take ages to download to a viewer's computer.

● **Reset.** Click this button to reset iWeb's various warnings to their default settings.

● **Check for iWeb updates immediately.** Select this check box if you want iWeb to automatically alert you to updates.

Planning Your Web Site

iWeb's flexibility and ease of use enable you to plunge straight into creating a Web site and feel your way along, but you'll probably make better progress if you take a minute to plan the pages you will create and the material you will use on them.

iWeb offers eight different kinds of pages (see Table 10.1) for your Web sites. That may not seem like many, but they cover the full range of content you're most likely to use — and you can customize the pages if you need to create different looks.

Table 10.1 iWeb's Eight Kinds of Web Pages

Template name	Explanation
Welcome	The Web page on which the user arrives if he or she simply types the address of your site rather than the address of a specific Web page on it. Other applications call this the *index page*.
About Me	A page for describing yourself, showing a few pictures, and providing links to some of your favorite items (for example, songs or Web sites).
Photos	A page for showing a selection of your photos.
My Albums	A page that contains a summary of your photo pages and links to them.
Movie	A page on which you can present a video or movie.
Blog	A page for creating entries in your blog, your online journal. We'll look at how to create blog entries in the next chapter.
Podcast	A page for creating audio or video podcasts. We'll look at how to create podcasts in the next chapter.
Blank	A blank (or mostly blank, depending on the theme) page on which you can place whichever elements you need.

Choosing where to host your Web site

iWeb is built to make the most of MobileMe, so if you have a MobileMe account, this will normally be your first choice for hosting your Web site. You can sign up for a 60-day trial of a MobileMe account by choosing Apple menu ➪ System Preferences and clicking the MobileMe icon.

If you don't have a MobileMe account, you can use iWeb with other Web hosts easily enough, as you'll see later in this chapter.

Creating Web Pages

After setting preferences, get right down to work and create your first few Web pages. iWeb makes the process as easy as possible, but this section gives you a few pointers.

Choosing a template

If you want to go ahead and create your first page using the Web page template you chose after you opened iWeb, stick with that. Otherwise, click it in the Sidebar and press Delete to delete it. That leaves you with no Web pages in your site, so iWeb opens the Template Chooser automatically to get you started creating a new page.

Choose a theme that suits the character you're planning for your Web site, choose the template for the page, and then click Choose. For example, if your Web site's focus is showcasing your talents in the hope of landing you a job, choose a theme such as Elegant or Formal. For something more free-wheeling, try a theme such as Road Trip. Or for an events site, try Main Event.

Choose the template for the page, and then click Choose. iWeb creates the site and adds the page to it.

Genius Don't worry too much about choosing the right template. You can change templates for a page at any time by clicking the Theme button on the toolbar and choosing another template from the panel that appears. You may have to rearrange your content to suit the new template, but usually that doesn't take long.

Adding text

Next, add text to the Web page. Simply click to select a text placeholder, click again to select the text in it, and then start typing your own text over the custom text.

If the text you type is too long for a placeholder, you have a couple choices:

- Resize the placeholder to make it big enough for the text. To resize, click and drag one of the sizing handles on the corners or on the sides of the placeholder. To reposition, simply click and drag the placeholder wherever you want it to be.

- Select the text and make it smaller. Triple-click the placeholder to select the text. Press ⌘+– (⌘ and hyphen) to reduce the text to the next available size, or click the Fonts button on the toolbar to open the Fonts window, and then choose a different size.

Resizing and repositioning placeholders

You can resize and reposition any of the placeholders in the template you're using.

To resize a placeholder, click it, and then drag one of the sizing handles that appears. Drag a corner handle to resize the placeholder both horizontally and vertically at once, or drag a side handle to resize it only horizontally or only vertically.

To reposition a placeholder, click it and drag it to where you want it to appear. To help you position the placeholder accurately, iWeb displays alignment guides at the center of the placeholder, at the edges, or both, depending on the Alignment Guides choices you made in iWeb's Preferences.

Replacing the placeholder images

Your next move is to replace the placeholder images on the Web page with images of your own. To do so, follow these steps:

1. **Click the Show Media button on the toolbar to open the Media Browser.**

2. **Click the Photos button at the top if it's not already selected (see figure 10.6).**

3. **Navigate to the iPhoto album or other item that contains the photo you want.**

4. **Drag a photo from the Media Browser to the placeholder in which you want to display it.**

10.6 The Media Browser opens at a small size, but you can drag the shaded handle in the lower right corner to expand it and improve your view.

Note If you prefer, you can drag a photo from iPhoto and drop it on a placeholder in iWeb. This move is handy when you've already got iPhoto open and showing a photo you want to use — you don't need to open the Media Browser and navigate to the photo again.

5. **If necessary, resize the placeholder to accommodate the image better.** Click the place-holder, and then drag one of its sizing handles.

6. **Zoom in on the image if necessary.** Drag the Zoom slider on the black pop-up window to zoom in or zoom back out.

7. **Change the part of the image displayed if necessary.** If the image is a different shape than the placeholder, part of it will be masked, so that it lies behind other elements on the Web page and isn't visible. If you zoom in on the image, much of it may be masked. To change the part of the image displayed:

   • Click the Edit Mask button on the black pop-up window to reveal the whole image behind other objects.

   • Click within the image placeholder.

   • Drag the image until the part of it you want appears in the placeholder. Figure 10.7 illus-trates dragging an image within a placeholder.

   • Click the Edit Mask button again to restore the mask.

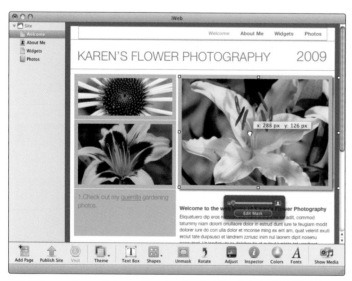

10.7 When an image is larger than its placeholder, click the Edit Mask button and drag the image to display a different part of it.

Placing Images in Text Boxes

iWeb doesn't limit you to placing images in image placeholders. You can place an image in a text box if you like. When you do this, iWeb treats the image as a floating object, which means it's not fixed in place and gets moved along as you edit the text.

Here's how to place an image in a text box:

1. Click the text box to select it.
2. Click to place the insertion point between the characters where you want the image to appear.
3. Choose Insert ⇨ Choose to open a sheet for choosing the image.
4. Select the image. For example, scroll down in the Sidebar, click the Photos item to display the contents of your iPhoto library, and then click the photo.
5. Click Insert to insert the image. You can then click the image within the text box and resize it as needed to suit the text box.

Adding your own text boxes and images

After replacing the placeholder text and images with your own content, you may need to add more text boxes and images to provide further content.

To add a text box:

1. **Make sure the insertion point isn't positioned in another text box (unless you want to place the new text box within that text box).**
2. **Click the Text Box button on the toolbar.** iWeb adds a new text box.
3. **Drag the new text box to where you want it to appear, and then resize it by dragging its corner handles or side handles.**
4. **Type the text you want in the text box.**

Genius

You can easily create a new text box or image by Option-dragging an existing one (to make a copy) and then changing its contents.

To add a new image, drag it from the Media Browser or from a folder and drop it where you want it to appear. You can then resize the image and adjust its mask as described earlier in this chapter.

Making text look the way you want

When you add text to a text box, iWeb automatically gives the text the formatting applied to the text box. If you want to change formatting or layout, you can do so easily by using the Text Inspector. Follow these steps:

1. **Select the text you want to affect.** To affect all the text in a text box, click the text box. To affect just some text within a text box, click the text box, and then drag to select the text.

2. **To change the font, click the Fonts button on the toolbar, and then work in the Fonts window (see figure 10.8).**

   - **Font.** Choose a font collection in the Collections box (or simply choose All Fonts), then choose the font family in the Family box. In the Typeface box, choose the typeface — for example, Regular, Italic, Bold, or Bold Italic. Then choose the Size in the Size list, or drag the Size slider beside the Size list.

   - **Underline and Strikethrough.** Use the Text Underline pop-up menu and the Text Strikethrough menu if you need to apply these effects.

   - **Text Color and Document Color.** Click the appropriate button to open the Colors window, pick the color, and then click the close button (the red button) to return to the Fonts window.

   - **Text Shadow.** Click the Text Shadow button to toggle text shadow on. You can then use the Shadow Opacity slider, Shadow Blur slider, Shadow Offset slider, and Shadow Angle knob to adjust the shadow.

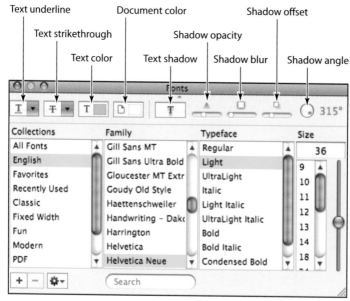

10.8 The Fonts window includes controls for applying and adjusting text shadows.

3. **To change alignment, spacing, wrapping, or bullets and numbering, click the Inspector button to display the Inspector window.** The Inspector window provides eight different Inspectors for different aspects of your Web site, including the pages, text, photos, and links. Figure 10.9 shows the button bar at the top of the Inspector window, which you use to choose the Inspector you need.

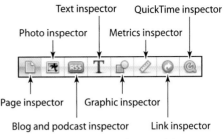

10.9 Use the button bar at the top of the Inspector window to select the Inspector you need. The title bar shows the current Inspector.

4. **Click the Text Inspector button to display the Text Inspector.**

5. **To change alignment and spacing, you use the Text tab of the Text Inspector (see figure 10.10).** Click the Text button if it's not already selected.

   - **Alignment.** Choose the horizontal alignment — Align Left, Center, Align Right, or Justify — and the vertical alignment (Align Top, Align Middle, or Align Bottom).

   - **Color.** Click the button to display the Colors window, then choose the color and close the window. If you've already set the color using the Fonts window, you won't need to set it again.

   - **Background Fill.** Select the Background Fill check box, then use the color button to choose the color. Again, if you've already set the background color using the Fonts window, you won't need to do this.

   - **Spacing.** Drag the Character slider, Line slider, Before Paragraph slider, After Paragraph slider, and Insert Margin slider to set the spacing you want. Alternatively, use the spin boxes and the Line Spacing pop-up menu. The Inset Margin measurement is the distance between the edge of the text box and the beginning of the text.

10.10 The Text tab of the Text Inspector lets you change color, alignment, spacing, and margins.

6. **If you've added an image or shape to a text box, click the Wrap button and set wrapping on the Wrap tab.** Select the Object causes wrap check box, click the alignment button, and then use the Extra Space box to change the amount of space if necessary.

7. **If you want to add bullets or number-ing, click the List button, and use the controls on the List tab.** The controls that appear depend on which type of list you choose. Figure 10.11 shows the List tab for creating numbered lists.

8. **When you've finished formatting the text, close the Inspector window by clicking its close button (the red but-ton) or by clicking the Inspector but-ton on the toolbar in the main iWeb window.**

Adding shapes to your Web pages

To give a page visual interest, you can add a shape to it. iWeb provides 15 assorted shapes that range from a plain line and arrows to squares, circles, speech bubbles, stars, and pentagons.

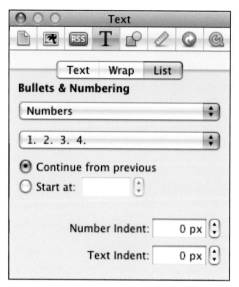

10.11 You can choose from various formats for numbered lists.

To add a shape, click the Shapes button on the toolbar, and then choose the shape you want from the pop-up panel. iWeb plunks the shape down in the middle of the page, leaving you to resize it and reposition it as needed.

You can add text to a shape by double-clicking the shape and then typing the text. If there's too much text to fit in the shape, iWeb displays a boxed plus (+) sign at the bottom of the shape. You can then either resize the shape to accommodate the text or reduce the text size to make it fit in the shape.

Adding hyperlinks to your Web pages

To enable visitors to navigate from one Web page to another. iWeb automatically creates a hyper-link in the navigation area for each main Web page you add to the site. iWeb doesn't create a navi-gation-area hyperlink in the navigation area to lower-level Web pages. For example, when you add a My Albums Web page, iWeb creates a hyperlink to that Web page, but not to the Web pages for the individual albums.

Adding hyperlinks manually from text or images

You can also add hyperlinks manually, either to your own Web site or to other sites. Here's what to do:

1. **Click the object (for example, an image) or select the text from which you want to create the hyperlink.**

2. **Click the Inspector button on the toolbar to open the Inspector window.**

3. **Click the Link Inspector button to display the Link Inspector.** Click the Hyperlink tab (see figure 10.12) if it's not displayed at first.

4. **Select the Enable as a hyperlink check box to turn the object or text into a hyperlink.**

5. **In the Link To pop-up menu, choose the type of link you want to create.** The pop-up menu below the Link To pop-up menu changes its name depending on the choice you make:

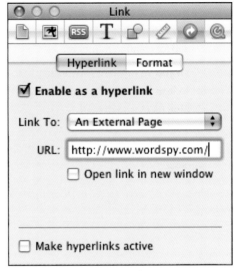

10.12 Use the Hyperlink tab of the Link Inspector to turn an object into a hyperlink.

- **One of My Pages.** A page on your iWeb site. Choose the page by name from the Page pop-up menu.

- **An External Page.** Any Web page outside your Web site. Type the URL in the URL box.

- **A File.** In the Open dialog box that iWeb displays, click the file, and then click the Open button. iWeb enters the filename in the Name box.

- **An Email Message.** Type the e-mail address in the To box, and then type the default subject in the Subject box. (The visitor can change both the address and the subject if he or she wants.)

Formatting your hyperlinks

If you want to control the way a hyperlink appears on a Web page, follow these steps:

1. **Select the hyperlink you want to format.**

2. **Click the Inspector button on the toolbar to open the Inspector window.**

3. **Click the Link Inspector button to display the Link Inspector.** Click the Format tab to display its contents (see figure 10.13).

4. **For each hyperlink state, choose the color you want to use, and decide whether to underline the hyperlink:**

   - **Normal.** This is the color in which hyperlinks the visitor hasn't yet hovered the mouse over or clicked appear.

   - **Rollover.** This is the color a hyperlink turns when the visitor moves the mouse pointer over it.

   - **Visited.** This is the color a hyperlink turns after the visitor has clicked it.

   - **Disabled.** This is the color in which an unavailable hyperlink appears.

5. **If you want to use these same colors for other links you create on this Web page, click the Use for New Links on Page button.**

6. **Close the Inspector window.**

Making an image's colors match your Web page

To make an image fit in better with a Web page, you have two choices:

- **Adjust the image's colors to suit the Web page.** Click the image, click the Adjust button on the toolbar, and then use the controls in the Adjust Image window (see figure 10.14) to change the image's colors. These controls work in

10.13 You can customize the colors iWeb uses for hyperlinks.

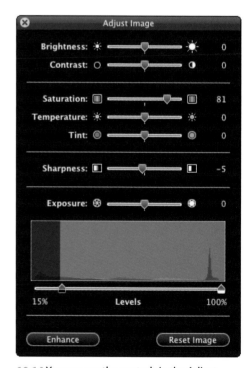

10.14 You can use the controls in the Adjust Image window to make an image fit its background better.

the same way as those described in Chapter 3. For example, the Enhance button attempts to improve the color balance and lighting automatically.

● **Adjust the Web page's colors to suit the image.** Click the Inspector button on the toolbar to open the Inspector window, click the Page Inspector button to display the Page Inspector, and then click the Layout button to display the Layout tab (see figure 10.15). Use the Page Background controls to change the color of the page's background.

Creating an Email Me button on a Web page

One thing you'll want on many Web sites is a button that enables the visitor to start an e-mail to you. You can do this in moments by choosing Insert ➪ Button ➪ Email Me.

iWeb inserts the Email Me button in the footer (see figure 10.16), where some visitors may miss it. You can drag it to a different area of the Web page if you want.

To tell iWeb which e-mail address to use for your Web site, click Site (or whatever name you've given to your Web site, as described a bit later) at the top of the iWeb Sidebar to display the Site Publisher Settings, and then type the e-mail address in the Contact email box.

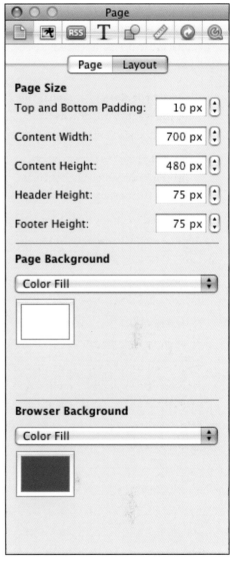

10.15 Alternatively, use the Page Background controls to change the page's background color to suit an image.

Adding a hit counter to a Web page

iWeb also makes it easy to add a hit counter to a Web page, allowing visitors to see how many visits that page has received. Simply choose Insert ⇨ Button ⇨ Hit Counter.

iWeb inserts the hit counter in the footer, but you can drag it to a different area of the Web page.

10.16 Add an Email Me button if you want to give visitors an easy way to contact you.

Genius Having a very low score on a hit counter can make your Web site look unloved. You can increase the score of a hit counter by refreshing the display of the Web page in your Web browser. For example, in Safari, press ⌘+R to refresh the display.

Renaming your Web site and Web pages

iWeb names your first Web site simply Site (and subsequent sites, if you create them, Site 2, Site 3, and so on). To give your site a snappier name, double-click the name in the Sidebar, type the new name in the edit box that appears, and then press Return.

Each Web page you add to the Web site receives its template name — for example, Welcome or About Me. You can rename a Web page by double-clicking its name in the Sidebar, typing the new name, and then pressing Return.

Rearranging your Web pages

As you create new Web pages to your Web site, iWeb adds them to the list in the Sidebar in the order you create them.

If you want to rearrange the Web pages in a site, drag them up and down in the Sidebar. When you rearrange the Web pages, iWeb automatically changes the order of the links in the Navigation area to reflect the new order.

Creating a New Web Site

iWeb is happy to let you create two or more Web sites if you want. To create a new site, either choose File ➪ New Site or Ctrl+click (or right-click) in the Sidebar and choose New Site from the menu that appears.

Each Web site appears as a separate collapsible tree in the Sidebar. You can move a Web page, or even a folder full of Web pages, from one site to another by dragging the page or folder from one site's entry in the Sidebar to the other site's entry.

Adding Photos and Albums from iPhoto

Since they consist of your own content and are (usually) personal, photos and albums from iPhoto make great content for your Web site. iWeb makes it simple to create Web pages that contain your photos or your albums.

Working with photo pages

You can create a Web page containing individual photos in a few moments:

1. **Click the Add Page button to open the Template Chooser.**

2. **Click the theme you want, click the Photos template, and then click Choose.** iWeb adds a My Photos Web page to the Web site.

3. **Click the Media button to open the Media Browser, and then click Photos to display your photos.**

4. **Drag a photo or an album over the placeholder (see figure 10.17).** iWeb replaces all three sample photos with what you dragged and displays the Photo Grid dialog box (see figure 10.18).

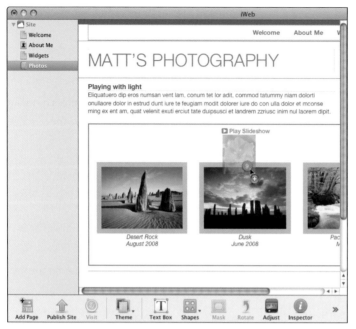

5. Choose settings in the Photo Grid dialog box:

● **Album Style.** Click the pop-up button and select the style you want — for example, with drop shadows or with rounded corners on the photos.

● **Columns.** In this box, set the number of columns of photos to have on the page.

● **Spacing.** Drag this slider to increase or decrease the distance between photos.

● **Photos per page.** Choose how many photos to display on each page. The default setting is 99, but having more pages with fewer photos on each is usually easier to browse. If you add more photos to the page than the number set here, iWeb automatically creates multiple linked pages.

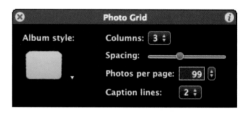

10.18 From the Photo Grid dialog box, you can quickly change how the photos are displayed and how many lines of text they include.

● **Caption lines.** Choose how many lines of text to display below each photo. (Choose 0 if you want no captions.)

316

6. **Drag the photos into the order you want, and edit the captions as needed.**

7. **Edit the text of the Web page as usual.**

Creating an overview page of your photos

If you create several photo pages, you can create a single overview page to let visitors navigate among them easily. iWeb calls this page the My Albums page, but you can change the name in seconds.

Here's how to create an overview page:

1. **Click the Add Page button to open the Template Chooser.**

2. **Click the theme you want, click the My Albums template, and then click Choose.** iWeb adds a My Albums Web page to the Web site.

3. **Drag each of your photos pages from the Sidebar to the Album placeholder on the My Albums page.** iWeb creates an album for each page you drag.

4. **To rearrange your overview page, click an album on it, and then choose settings in the Media Index dialog box (see figure 10.19):**

   - **Index style.** Click the pop-up button and select the design or colored background you want to use for the album pictures.

10.19 Use the controls in the Media Index dialog box to change how your overview page looks.

   - **Columns.** In this box, set the number of columns of album photos to display on the page.

   - **Spacing.** Drag this slider to increase or decrease the space between album photos.

   - **Album animation.** In this pop-up menu, choose the animation to use for the album: None, Dissolve, Random, Reveal, Push, Fade Through Black, or Skim.

   - **Show title.** Select this check box to display each album's title on the overview page.

   - **Show number.** Select this check box to display the number of photos each album contains.

   - **Allow subscribe.** Select this check box to include a Subscribe link that visitors can click to subscribe to your albums (so that they receive updates when you post new photos).

5. **To change the order in which the albums appear, drag the albums to where you want them.**

6. **If you want to rename the overview page, double-click its name in the Sidebar, type the new name, and then press Return.**

Putting Web Widgets on Your Web Pages

Text, photos, and photo albums can make a great-looking Web site — but what if you want to take your Web site to the next level with active content? iWeb lets you easily add YouTube videos, Google Maps, AdSense ads, RSS feeds, and other items to your Web site.

Genius

You can find other Web widgets at sites such as Widgetbox (www.widgetbox.com) and SpringWidgets (www.springwidgets.com/widgets/).

Adding a YouTube video to a Web page

Adding a video from YouTube to a Web page is a great way of illustrating a point or bringing a topic to life. Here's how to add a video:

1. **Steer your Web browser (for example, Safari) to YouTube and locate the video you want to add to your page.**

2. **Copy the address of the YouTube page.**

3. **In iWeb, choose Insert ➪ Widget ➪ YouTube.** You can also click Widgets in the Media Browser and then double-click the YouTube widget. The YouTube window appears.

4. **Paste the embed code into the YouTube URL text box (see figure 10.20), and then click Apply.**

5. **Click the X button to close the HTML Snippet dialog box.**

Now you can test the YouTube clip by clicking the Play button in its lower right corner.

10.20 It takes only moments to add a YouTube video to a Web page in iWeb.

Inserting a Google Map into a Web page

If you want to show someone where to find a particular place — your home, say, or the beach on which you're meeting for a party — you can add a map from Google Maps to a Web page. To do so, follow these steps:

1. **Create a new Web page if necessary, or make space on an existing page.**

2. **Choose Insert ➭ Widget ➭ Google Maps to open the Google Maps dialog box.** You can also click Widgets in the Media Browser, and then double-click the Google Maps widget.

3. **Type the address (see figure 10.21) and choose options:**

   - **Zoom controls.** Select this check box to display controls for zooming in and out on the map. These are usually helpful.

   - **Search bar.** Select this check box to include a Google search bar in the bottom left corner of the map.

   - **Address bubble.** Select this check box to display a pop-up balloon showing the address. This too is usually helpful — and visitors can close it if it's in the way.

10.21 Adding a Google Map to a Web page is as simple as filling out the address.

4. **Click Apply to insert the map, and click the X button to close the Google Map dialog box.**

5. **Resize the map as needed by dragging a sizing handle, or simply test the map to make sure it's working.**

Inserting AdSense ads

If you need your Web site to pay its way, you can include AdSense ads on it. AdSense ads are relevant to a page's content (sometimes more relevant in theory than in practice) and earn you money from Google when visitors click them.

1. **Choose Insert ➭ Widget ➭ Google AdSense.** You can also click Widgets in the Media Browser, and then double-click the Google AdSense widget. iWeb adds a Google AdSense placeholder and opens the Google AdSense Ad dialog box (see figure 10.22).

319

2. **In the Select ad format pop-up menu, choose the type, size, and shape of the ad:**

   • **Type.** You can choose among text ads, text and image ads, and text links.

   • **Size and shape.** The ads come in various sizes and shapes, from the 125-x-125-pixel button to banner ads (wider than they're tall) and skyscraper ads (taller than they are wide).

10.22 Choosing the size and color scheme for a Google AdSense ad.

Note

To use AdSense ads, you need to have an AdSense account. If you don't have one already, iWeb displays the Set up a Google AdSense account dialog box when you give the Google AdSense Ad command. Make sure the Email box shows the e-mail address you want to use, and then click Submit. You'll then receive an e-mail message that tells you how to complete the sign-up process. After you finish jumping through the hoops, it takes a couple of days for Google to finish setting up your account and start serving money-making ads. In the meantime, Google displays public-service ads in the placeholders.

3. **In the Select ad color pop-up menu, choose the ad color.** You may want the ad to match your Web page's background — or to stand out against it.

4. **Drag the ad placeholder to where you want it to appear on the Web page, then click the X button to close the Google AdSense Ad dialog box.**

In iWeb, you see only the AdSense placeholders, not the ads themselves. When you publish your Web site to MobileMe, the ads themselves appear. The ads then change periodically without you needing to do anything.

Genius

iWeb lets you use only a single Google AdSense account at a time. To change the account you're using, choose File ➪ Set Up Google AdSense to open the Google AdSense dialog box. Click the Change Account button, and follow through the procedure for either specifying a different existing account or setting up a new account.

Inserting an iSight photo

If your Mac has an iSight camera attached, you can use it to capture a photo of yourself (for your About Me page, for example), or whatever you feel like sticking in front of the camera. Here's how it's done:

1. **Choose Insert ⇨ Widget ⇨ iSight Photo.** You can also click Widgets in the Media Browser, and then double-click the iSight Photo widget.. iWeb adds an iSight Photo placeholder and opens the iSight Photo dialog box (see figure 10.23).

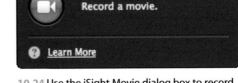

2. **Position yourself (or whatever) in the line of the iSight camera.**

10.23 Use the iSight Photo dialog box to take a photo to insert into your Web page.

3. **Click the Capture a photo button.** iWeb counts down from 3, snaps the photo, and inserts the shot into the iSight Photo placeholder.

4. **Drag the placeholder to where you want it to appear on the Web page, then click the X button to close the iSight Photo dialog box.**

Inserting an iSight movie

Your Mac's iSight camera isn't just good for photos: you can use it to capture short movies, as well. If you want to add such a movie to your Web site, you can use iMovie '09's new iSight Movie widget to do it. Here's what you do:

1. **Choose Insert ⇨ Widget ⇨ iSight Movie.** You can also click Widgets in the Media Browser, and then double-click the iSight Movie widget. iWeb adds an iSight Movie placeholder and opens the iSight Movie dialog box (see figure 10.24).

2. **Position yourself (or whatever) in the line of the iSight camera.**

10.24 Use the iSight Movie dialog box to record a movie to insert into your Web page.

3. **Click the Record a movie a photo button.** iWeb counts down from 3 and then starts recording.

4. **Do your thing in front of the camera, and then click the Stop button.** iWeb and inserts the video into the iSight Movie placeholder.

5. **Drag the placeholder to where you want it to appear on the Web page, then click the X button to close the iSight Movie dialog box.**

Inserting a Countdown widget

Have you got an upcoming event that you're discussing or promoting on your Web site? If so, then you might want to embellish your site with a reverse timer that counts down the number of days, hours, minutes, and seconds until the event happens. This is all made very easy by iMovie '09's new Countdown widget, which you insert by following these steps:

1. **Choose Insert ➪ Widget ➪ Countdown.** You can also click Widgets in the Media Browser, and then double-click the Countdown widget. iWeb adds a Countdown placeholder and opens the Countdown dialog box (see figure 10.25).

2. **Click Style and then click the style of timer you prefer.**

3. **Click and drag the ends of the Display control to specify the components you want to include in the timer: Years, Days, Hours, Mins, and Secs.**

4. **If you want the timer to include labels for each component (a good idea), leave the Labels check box selected.**

10.25 Use the Countdown dialog box to set up a countdown timer on your Web page.

5. **Use the controls in the Countdown To section to specify the date and time to countdown to.**

6. **Drag the placeholder to where you want it to appear on the Web page, then click the X button to close the Countdown dialog box.**

Inserting an RSS feed

A great way to add content to your site is to display posts from an RSS feed supplied by a blogger, news media organization, or other Web site that posts regular content. iMovie '09 lets you insert an RSS feed in seconds thanks to its new RSS Feed widget. Here's how to use it:

1. **Steer your Web browser (for example, Safari) to the page that contains the site's RSS feed.**

2. **Copy the address of the RSS feed page.**

3. **In iWeb, choose Insert ⇨ Widget ⇨ RSS Feed.** You can also click Widgets in the Media Browser, and then double-click the RSS Feed widget. iWeb adds an RSS Feed placeholder and opens the RSS Feed dialog box (see figure 10.26).

4. **Use the Subscription URL text box to paste the feed address.**

5. **Use the Number of Entries spin box to set the number of posts you want to display.**

6. **Leave the Show Date check box selected if you want to display the post date at the top of each entry.**

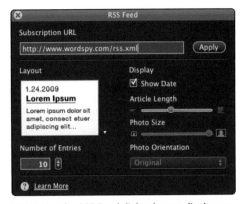

10.26 Use the RSS Feed dialog box to display an RSS feed on your Web page.

7. **Click and drag the Article Length slider to set how much of each post you want to display.**

8. **If the feed includes photos, click and drag the Photo Size slider to set the display size, and use the Photo Orientation pop-up menu to select how you want the photos to appear.**

9. **Drag the placeholder to where you want it to appear on the Web page, then click the X button to close the RSS Feed dialog box.**

Inserting an HTML snippet

The iWeb page-creation tools are certainly advanced, but there are still lots of page goodies that iWeb can't do. For example, it doesn't let you create a table, set up a form, define an image map, and so on.

Fortunately, you can still add any of these features yourself if you're conversant with HTML, which is the set of codes that defines most of what you see on the Web. iWeb lets you insert anywhere on a page a snippet of HTML that you write yourself. Here's how:

1. **Choose Insert ⇨ Widget ⇨ HTML Snippet.** You can also click Widgets in the Media Browser and then double-click HTML Snippet. The HTML Snippet window appears.

2. **Use the large text box to enter your HTML code.**

3. **Click Apply.** iWeb renders the HTML code, as shown in figure 10.27.

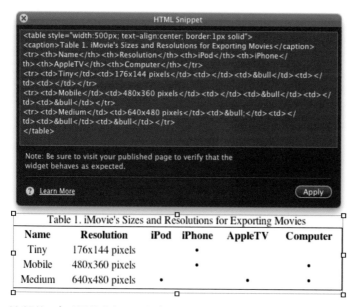

10.27 Use the HTML Snippet window to enter the HTML code that you want to add to your page.

4. **Drag the placeholder to where you want it to appear on the Web page, then click the X button to close the HTML Snippet dialog box.**

Previewing Your Web Site

iWeb lets you see roughly how your Web site appears, but you'll probably want to preview your Web site before you publish it. You can do this in two ways: by making hyperlinks active in iWeb, so that the links actually work, and by publishing the Web site to a folder.

Making your Web site's hyperlinks active

To make the hyperlinks in your Web site active, follow these steps:

1. **Click the Inspector button on the toolbar to open the Inspector window.**

2. **Click the Link Inspector button to display the Link Inspector.** Click the Hyperlink tab if it's not selected automatically.

3. **Select the Make hyperlinks active check box.** You can now position the mouse pointer over a hyperlink and click to jump to the linked page.

When you've finished testing the hyperlinks, clear the Make hyperlinks active check box again, and then close the Link Inspector window.

Publishing your Web site to a folder

If you want to test your Web site in a browser, publish it to a folder on your Mac like this:

1. **Click Site (or the name of your Web site) at the top of the Sidebar.**
2. **Click the Publish to pop-up menu and then click Local Folder.**
3. **Choose the folder in which to store the site — for example, in the Sites folder within your Home folder.** You can create a new folder by clicking the New Folder button, typing the name in the New Folder dialog box, and clicking Create.
4. **If you haven't yet provided a snappy name for your site, type the name in the Site text box.**
5. **Leave the Enter the URL for your site box blank.**
6. **Click the Publish Site button in the toolbar.** iWeb displays a notice asking you to confirm that you have permission to publish your Web content.
7. **Click Continue.** iWeb publishes the site to the folder and then displays the dialog box shown in figure 10.28.

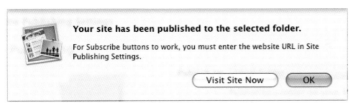

10.28 You can preview your Web site in a browser by publishing it to a folder and then clicking the Visit Site Now button.

8. **Click Visit Site Now.** iWeb opens your default browser (for example, Safari) and displays the site. You can then see exactly how it looks and test the hyperlinks.

Publishing Your Web Site to the Web

When you've finished creating your Web site to your satisfaction, you can publish it quickly, either to your account on Apple's MobileMe service (formerly .Mac) or on a different online service.

Note

If you use MobileMe, your Web site appears at http://Web.me.com/*YourMobile MeName*/Site.

Publishing your Web site to MobileMe

Here's how to publish your Web site to MobileMe:

1. **Click Site (or the name of your Web site) at the top of the Sidebar.** iWeb displays the Site Publishing Settings page.

2. **Click the Publish to pop-up menu and then click MobileMe.**

3. **If you haven't yet provided a name for your site, type the name in the Site text box.**

4. **Click the Publish Site button in the toolbar.** iWeb displays a notice asking you to confirm that you have permission to publish your Web content.

5. **Click Continue.** iWeb then displays the Publishing will now continue in the background dialog box (see figure 10.29) to warn you that publishing may take a few minutes, during which time you can't quit iWeb.

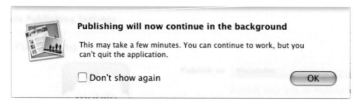

Publishing will now continue in the background

This may take a few minutes. You can continue to work, but you can't quit the application.

☐ Don't show again

OK

10.29 iWeb warns you that you can't quit while publishing is in progress.

6. **Click OK.**

Genius

If you look at the File menu, you'll see there's a Publish Entire Site command as well as the Publish Site Changes command. You use the Publish Entire Site command if your Web site has become corrupted and you need to publish all the pages again. Normally, you use the Publish Site Changes command to publish only the pages that have changed since the last time you published.

Viewing your Web site

After uploading the files for your site, iWeb displays the Your site has been published dialog box (see figure 10.30). Click the Visit Site Now button to open the Web site in your default Web browser (for example, Safari) so that you can make sure it looks the way you want it to.

Your site has been published.

Your site is located at:

http://web.me.com/guy_hd/Site

You can announce your website with an email message containing your website address, or view the website in your browser.

(Announce)   (Visit Site Now)   (OK)

10.30 After publishing your site, you'll probably want to visit and check it out before announcing it to the world.

Note After you've published your site, you can view it at any time by clicking the Visit button in the toolbar or by choosing File ⇨ Visit Published Site.

Announcing your Web site or your new pages

Alternatively, click the Announce button to start a canned e-mail message using your default e-mail application (for example, Mail or Entourage). The message says that you've just updated your Web site, invites the recipients to check it out, and includes the URL for your site and URLs for new Web pages you've added.

Customize the message as needed, put your own address in the To box, add the recipients to the Bcc box (so each recipient sees only his or her own address), and then send it.

Publish on MobileMe with Your Own Domain Name

If you have your own domain name with another domain registrar, you can use it for your Web site on MobileMe. To make this work, you tell your domain registrar to redirect Web browser requests for your domain name to MobileMe.

That sounds awkward, but Apple has made the process as easy as possible. Here's what to do:

1. **In iWeb, choose File ⇨ Set Up Personal Domain on MobileMe.** iWeb launches your default Web browser, which connects to the MobileMe Web site.

2. **Log in with your MobileMe username and password (unless you've configured Mac OS X to log you in automatically).** Your Web browser displays your MobileMe account page.

continued

327

continued

3. **Click Personal Domain.** Your browser displays the Personal Domain page in Account Settings.

4. **Click the Add Domain button to display the Add Personal Domain page.**

5. **Type your domain name in the Domain Name box, confirm it in the Confirm Domain box, and then click Continue.** Your browser displays an information page with instructions.

6. **Open a browser tab or window manually and go to your domain registrar's Web site.** Log on to your account, and then set Web .me.com to be the CNAME for your domain name. A CNAME (short for Canonical Name) is a sort of alias that you use to tell Web servers where to look for a Web site.

7. **When your domain registrar has updated your domain with the CNAME change, return to your MobileMe account, and click the Done button on the Add Personal Domain page.**

Deleting a Web page from iWeb and from MobileMe

When you want to delete a Web page from your Web site, you first need to delete it from your site in iWeb, and then publish the changes.

To delete the page, Ctrl+click or right-click it in the Sidebar, and then click Delete Page. Alternatively, click the page in the Sidebar, and then press Delete. iWeb deletes the page and removes all links to it from other pages.

Note If you delete a page in error, choose Edit ⇨ Undo Delete Page before you do anything else in iWeb.

After deleting the page in iWeb, publish the changes to MobileMe as described earlier in this chapter.

Protecting your site with a password

Most Web sites are wide open to the entire wired world, but if you want, you can protect your iWeb site with a password. Anyone who wants to view your Web site must enter the password first. This feature works only on MobileMe, not on other Web hosts.

Here's how to protect your site with a password:

1. **Click your site in the Sidebar.** iWeb displays the Site Publishing Settings page, shown in figure 10.31.

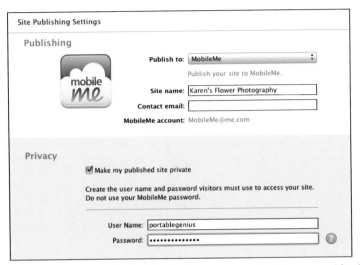

10.31 Use the Password tab of the Site Inspector to set up the password for the site.

2. **Select the Make my published site private check box.**

3. **Type the username and password that visitors will use.**

Note

When you create a password, the site uses the same password for all visitors. You can't create a site that uses different usernames and passwords.

Publishing your Web site to a different online service

If you prefer to publish your Web site on a different online service than MobileMe, here's what to do:

1. **Click Site (or the name of your Web site) at the top of the Sidebar.** iWeb displays the Site Publishing Settings page.

2. **Click the Publish to pop-up menu and then click FTP Server.** iWeb reconfigures the Site Publishing Settings page as shown in figure 10.32.

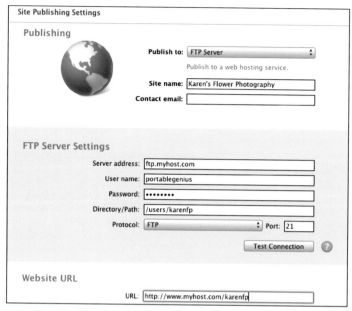

10.32 Choose FTP Server in the Publish to menu and then fill in your FTP settings.

3. **Use the Server address text box to type the address of your Web host's FTP server.**

4. **Use the User name and Password text boxes to type your FTP login credentials.**

5. **Use the Directory/Path text box to type the path to the server directory that you want to use to store your Web site files.**

Caution

The path you type in the Directory/Path text box must point to an existing directory.

6. **Use the Protocol pop-up menu and Port text box to specify your FTP connection settings.**

Note

At this point, it's a good idea to click the Test Connection button to make sure your FTP settings are configured properly. iWeb logs in to your FTP server and attempts to upload a file. If all goes well, click OK and continue publishing. Otherwise, double-check your settings and try again.

7. **In the Web site URL section, use the URL text box to type the main (root) URL of your site.** iWeb uses this URL to set up your links correctly.

8. **Click the Publish Site button in the toolbar.** iWeb displays a notice asking you to confirm that you have permission to publish your Web content.

9. **Click Continue.** iWeb then displays the Publishing will now continue in the background dialog box to warn you that publishing may take a few minutes, during which time you can't quit iWeb.

10. **Click OK.** iWeb uploads your pages and then displays the Your site has been published dialog box.

11. **Click Visit Site Now to load your site into your default Web browser.** Alternatively, click OK to return to iWeb.

Updating your Facebook profile each time you publish your Web site

If you have a Facebook account, iWeb '09 lets you send an update to your friends whenever you publish your Web site. Here's how to set this up:

1. **Click Site (or the name of your Web site) at the top of the Sidebar.** iWeb displays the Site Publishing Settings page.

2. **Select the Update my Facebook profile when I publish this site check box.** iWeb prompts you to log in to your Facebook account.

3. **Type your Facebook e-mail address and password, and then click Login.** Facebook asks whether you want to allow iWeb access to your profile.

4. **Click Allow**.

5. **Click Finish.**

How Do I Publish Blogs and Podcasts with iWeb?

Do you have information to share with people frequently? If so, you can go beyond the limits of standard Web pages by publishing your own blog or podcasts on your Web site. A blog is a great way of distributing text-based information quickly, but you can also include photos, audio, or movies as needed. A podcast lets you quickly distribute either audio-based content or video-based content to listeners or viewers worldwide. Visitors can either browse or subscribe to your blog entries and podcasts on your Web site so that they automatically receive news of new entries and podcasts.

Publishing a Blog

A *blog* (short for *Web log*) is a journal that you keep on a Web site. A blog is a great way to communicate with your family and friends — or, in a business setting, with your colleagues and customers.

iWeb makes it easy to set up a blog, make it look good, and keep it updated with attractive content. When you add a new entry to a blog, it automatically appears at the top of the blog, so that visitors see it first. Below it appear other recent entries, and older blog posts appear on archive pages.

Adding a blog to your iWeb site

Here's how to add a blog to your iWeb site:

1. **Click the Add Page button in the iWeb toolbar (or choose File ⇨ New Page) to open the Template Chooser.**

2. **In the list box on the left, choose the theme you're using for your Web site.**

3. **In the larger box, click the Blog item, and then click Choose.** iWeb closes the Template Chooser, adds a Blog item (containing an Entries item and an Archive item) to the Sidebar, and starts creating your first entry (see the chapter-opening illustration).

4. **Double-click the title placeholder to select it, and then type the name you want to give your blog.**

Understanding the Blog, Entries, and Archive items

When you start creating a blog, iWeb adds three items to the Sidebar:

- **Blog.** This is a collapsible item that contains the Entries item and Archive item (discussed next). Click this item to view the main page that visitors will see when they access your blog. This page contains the latest entries you've created.

- **Entries.** This is the page you use in iWeb to create new blog entries and manage older ones. This page appears only in iWeb, not on your Web site.

- **Archive.** This page contains all the entries in your blog — both those on your Blog page and older entries that don't appear there.

Creating a blog entry

You can now create a blog entry as follows:

1. **Click Entries.** If you're working with the initial entry created by iWeb, skip steps 1 and 2.

2. **Click Add Entry.** iWeb creates a new blog entry and adds some default content.

3. **Double-click the default title in the entry to display an edit box.** (If the title's already selected and displaying an edit box, you're all set.) Type the title you want, and then press Return to apply it. iWeb automatically applies the change to the entry's title in the Title box at the top of the window.

4. **If you want to change the date from today's date, double-click the date to display a date picker (see figure 11.1).** Choose the date you want the blog entry to show.

5. **Double-click the placeholder text for the entry, and then type your entry.**

January 2009

S	M	T	W	T	F	S
				1	2	3
4	5	6	7	8	9	10
11	12	13	14	15	16	17
18	19	20	21	22	23	24
25	26	27	28	29	30	31

1/ 8/2009   4:17 PM

Choose a date format:

Thursday, January 8, 2009

11.1 Use the date picker to change the blog entry's date if necessary or to choose a different date format.

Genius

In the date picker, you can also change the date format the blog uses if you want to.

6. **Replace the placeholder image with a photo of your own.** Click the Media button to open the Media Browser, display the Photos tab, and then drag the photo across. If necessary, zoom, re-center, or otherwise adjust the image as you learned in Chapter 10.

If you need to delete a blog entry, click it in the list of blog entries, and then click the Delete Entry button. iWeb doesn't confirm the deletion, but if you delete the wrong entry, you can undo the deletion by choosing Edit ⇨ Undo Delete Blog Entry immediately.

Setting up the main page for the blog

Next, set up the main page of the blog — the page that visitors will see when they first go to your blog. Follow these steps:

1. **Click the Blog item in the Sidebar to display the main page.** Figure 11.2 shows an example using the Modern Frame theme. Some of the blog themes are much busier and have many more elements that you can customize.

Caution
Beware choosing a busy theme for your blog. While being able to add more photos and other elements is fun, they may distract readers from the text.

11.2 The entry or entries you just created appear on your blog's main page, but you need to customize all the other elements.

2. **Change the title, main picture, description, and other elements on the main page.** As usual, double-click a text placeholder to select its contents, and then type the text you want. Replace the placeholder images by dragging photos from the Photos tab of the Media Browser.

3. **Click the Inspector button to open the Inspector window.** Click the Blog & Podcast Inspector button on the toolbar, and then click the Blog tab to display its contents (see figure 11.3).

4. **In the Blog Main Page area, set the Number of excerpts to show value and drag the Excerpt Length slider to choose how much of each entry to show.** You'll see the changes in the entry or entries you've created so far.

11.3 Use the Blog tab of the Blog & Podcast Inspector to choose whether to allow comments and attachments on your blog.

5. **In the Comments area, choose whether to allow comments and attachments:**

   - Select the Allow comments check box if you want to allow visitors to leave comments. iWeb displays the Allow Comments sheet to make sure you know how to manage comments. Click OK.

   - If you selected the Allow comments check box, you can select the Allow attachments check box if you want visitors to be able to leave attachments as well. iWeb pops up the Allow Attachments warning sheet to make sure you're aware that you might get objectionable attachments or ones for which you don't have distribution rights.

6. **Select the Display search field check box if you want to allow visitors to search through your blog.** Usually, searching is helpful.

Caution

Each attachment can be up to 5MB in size. That's enough for a high-resolution photo or a four-minute song at reasonable quality (for example, 128 Kbps in AAC or MP3 format), but if your site gets a lot of 5MB attachments, it can chew through your MobileMe storage allowance and transfer allowance quickly.

Changing the layout of your blog template

From the main page of your blog, you can also change the layout of the entry pages. Here's how to do this:

1. **Click anywhere in the blog entries area on the main page to open the Blog Summary dialog box (see figure 11.4).**

2. **Clear the Show Photos check box if you want to hide the photo from the blog entry.** You can then skip the rest of this list because clearing this check box disables the other controls.

3. **To change the placement of a photo, open the Placement pop-up menu and click the placement you want to apply.**

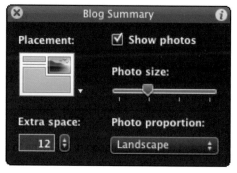

11.4 Use the Blog Summary dialog box to rearrange the photos in your blog.

4. **To make the photo bigger or smaller, drag the Photo size slider.**

5. **To increase or decrease the amount of space around a photo, adjust the number in the Extra space box.** (This measurement is in pixels.)

6. **To change the shape of the photo box, open the Photo proportion pop-up menu and choose Original, Square, Landscape, or Portrait.**

7. **Click the X button in the upper left corner to close the Blog Summary dialog box.**

Adding multimedia to a blog entry

Blog entries are often text-only or text and pictures, but iWeb lets you easily add audio or video to your blog entries if you want.

To add an audio file, follow these steps:

1. **Click Entries and then click the blog entry to which you want to add the audio file.**

2. **Click the Show Media button to open the Media Browser, and then click the Audio tab.**

3. **Drag the audio file to the blog entry and drop it there.** iWeb displays a Drag image here placeholder.

4. **If you want to add a photo to provide visual interest while the audio plays, click the Photos tab in the Media Browser, and then drag a photo to the placeholder.** Resize the photo as needed. Figure 11.5 shows an example of a photo with the audio controls under it.

Unexpected Snowfall

Thursday, November 20, 2008

11.5 When you include an audio file in a blog entry, you can add a picture to give visitors something to look at.

To add a video file from your Mac to a blog entry, follow these steps:

1. **Open the blog entry to which you want to add the audio file.**

2. **Click the Show Media button to open the Media Browser, and then click the Movies tab.**

3. **Drag the movie file to the blog entry and drop it there.** Resize the movie as needed.

Publishing your blog

When you've created your blog entries, click the Publish Site button to publish your blog together with all the other changes you've made to your Web site. When iWeb tells you it has finished publishing the Web site, click the Announce button and send an e-mail to encourage friends and family to read your blog. If your blog is gripping, your visitors will subscribe for updates, so you may not need to send announcements via e-mail after your first few entries.

Managing visitor comments

One of the most compelling features of blogs is that visitors can contribute to them by adding comments. If you want, you can also let visitors attach files to their comments so that other people can download the files.

Visitor comments can greatly add to the appeal of your blog. But if you allow comments, you will need to review them frequently and delete any unsuitable comments.

Similarly, if you allow attachments, you must check the files frequently to make sure that none contain offensive material or copyrighted material that is being distributed without adequate permission. You will also need to make sure that attachments don't take your MobileMe account over its monthly storage limit or data-transfer limit.

Note   iWeb helps to protect you against "comment spam" by making anyone who tries to submit a comment type a displayed sequence of characters first. This "captcha," or Completely Automated Public Turing Test to Tell Computers and Humans Apart, aims to prevent automated programs from posting spam comments to your site. Some programs have been written that break captchas by deciphering and typing the word automatically, but these are not widespread at this writing.

Reviewing and removing comments and attachments

If you do permit comments (and maybe attachments) on your blog, you should review them regularly to make sure there's nothing you need to remove.

When visitors add comments to your blog, the Archive displays a telltale red icon showing the number of comments, just like Mail does for unread e-mail messages. You can force iWeb to check for comments by choosing File ⇨ Check for New Comments.

Figure 11.6 shows an example of comments in iWeb. One comment includes an attachment; the other does not.

To delete a comment, click the Delete button (the round button with an X on it). As long as your Mac is connected to the Internet, iWeb deletes the comment from the published version of your blog immediately as well as from the iWeb version. You don't need to publish your blog again to get rid of the comment from the published version.

Deleting comments from your blog using a browser

Because the live version of your blog (on the Web) isn't kept strictly in sync with the version in iWeb, you can get into the situation where your blog has comments but you can't read them in iWeb because you've deleted the entries.

11.6 Viewing the comments and attachments that visitors have left.

When this happens, you can use Safari or another Web browser to read the comments — and to delete them if necessary. Follow these steps:

1. **In iWeb, click the Visit button or choose File ⇨ Visit Published Site to open your blog in your default Web browser.**

2. **Click the Blog link, and then go to the blog entry that contains the comments.**

3. **Click the lock icon next to the number of comments.** The browser displays the Site Owner Login screen.

Understanding Your Blog's RSS Feed

RSS (short for Really Simple Syndication) is the group of standards used for blog subscriptions. By subscribing to your blog's RSS feed, a visitor can automatically receive news of your latest posts.

iWeb automatically provides an RSS link on your blog's main page and on the archive page, and most Web browsers display an RSS icon in the address box when you open one of these pages in them.

4. **Type your MobileMe ID and password, and then click the Login button.** The browser displays the Manage Comments page (see figure 11.7).

5. **Select the check box for the comment (or comment and attachment) you want to delete, or select the Select All check box, and then click Delete.** Click OK in the confirmation dialog box that the browser displays.

6. **Click the Return to Entry link if you want to return to the blog entry.**

11.7 You can also manage comments and attachments from Safari or another Web browser.

Creating Podcasts

Podcasts give you a way of broadcasting your own audio or video content easily on the Internet. You create a podcast episode and post it to your Web site, where anyone worldwide can download it. And if that person enjoys the podcast, he or she can subscribe and receive automatic notification of future episodes when you post them.

Putting a podcast up on the Web is a four-stage process:

1. **Add a podcast to iWeb.** Start by creating your Podcast item in iWeb.

2. **Create the podcast.** To create a podcast, you use an audio or video application such as GarageBand.

3. **Create a Web page for the podcast.** In iWeb, you create a Web page using one of the Podcast templates. You then place the podcast episode on the page, together with any explanatory text it needs.

4. **Publish the podcast to the Web.** You publish the podcast from iWeb in exactly the same way as you publish other Web pages.

Genius

If you want, you can also submit your podcasts to the iTunes Store. This can be a great way of putting your material in front of a larger audience than you can reach via your own Web site.

Add a podcast to iWeb

To add a podcast to your Web site in iWeb, follow these steps:

1. **Click the Add Page button in the iWeb toolbar (or choose File ⇨ New Page) to open the Template Chooser.**

2. **In the list box on the left, choose the theme you're using for your Web site.**

3. **Click the Podcast item, and then click Choose.** iWeb adds three items to the Sidebar:

   - **Podcast.** This is a collapsible item that contains the Entries item and Archive item (discussed next). Click this item to view the main page that visitors will see when they access your podcasts. This page contains an overview of your last few podcasts.

   - **Entries.** This is the page you use in iWeb to create new podcasts and manage older ones (for example, deleting them). This page appears only in iWeb, not on your Web site. iWeb creates a new entry for you by default.

   - **Archive.** This page contains all your podcasts — both those on your Podcast page and older podcasts that no longer appear on that page.

4. **Click the Podcast page, and then customize the text and image placeholders using the techniques you've learned in this chapter and the previous chapter.** This is the first page that visitors see when they click the Podcast link in your Web site.

5. **To change the layout of the podcast entry pages, click one of the entries, and then use the Blog Summary dialog box as discussed earlier in this chapter.**

6. **When you finish customizing the Podcast page, click the Entries page in the Sidebar, and then delete the entry that iWeb created for you.** You'll create a real podcast entry from GarageBand next.

Creating a podcast from GarageBand

GarageBand lets you create both audio podcasts and video podcasts. You can create a simple podcast that contains only audio or only video and audio, but GarageBand makes it easy to create enhanced podcasts that include artwork (in audio podcasts), navigation markers, and URLs the viewer can visit. This section shows you how to create enhanced podcasts.

Start creating a podcast

Here's how to start creating a podcast:

1. **Launch GarageBand from the Dock icon or the Applications folder.** If GarageBand is already open, choose File ➪ Close to close the open project.

2. **On the GarageBand opening screen, click New Project, click Podcast, and then click Choose.** GarageBand displays the New Project from Template dialog box (see figure 11.8).

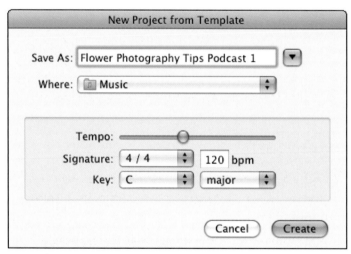

11.8 In the New Project from Template dialog box, name your podcast episode and pick the folder in which to store it.

3. **Type the name for the podcast episode in the Save As box, and pick the folder in the Where pop-up menu.**

4. **Click Create.** GarageBand creates the blank podcast project and displays it (see figure 11.9).

Zoom slider   Mixer   Playhead

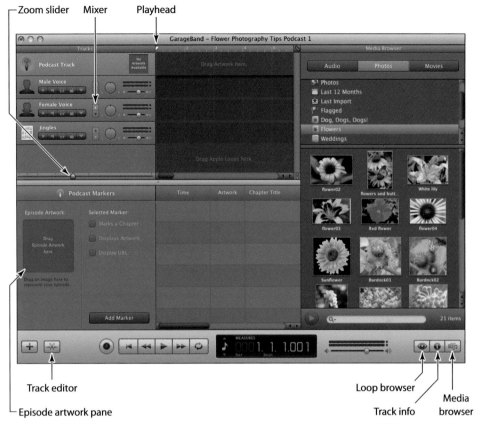

Track editor

Episode artwork pane

Loop browser

Media browser

Track info

11.9 A blank podcast project includes a Podcast Track, a Male Voice track, a Female Voice track, and a Jingles track.

Here are the details of what you see in the figure:

- **Podcast Track.** This is the track that contains the audio for the podcast. If you want to create a video podcast instead, you replace the Podcast Track with a Movie Track. A podcast can have only one of these at a time.

- **Male Voice track.** This is a Real Instrument track with settings optimized for making a male voice clearly audible in the podcast.

- **Female Voice track.** This is a Real Instrument track with settings optimized for making a female voice clearly audible in the podcast.

- **Jingles.** This track is for adding jingles, sound effects, and other short audio items to the podcast.

345

- **Podcast pane.** This pane contains the opening artwork for the podcast episode.

- **Markers pane.** This pane lets you create and work with markers in the podcast.

- **Media Browser.** As normal in the iLife applications, this browser lets you add audio, photos, and movies to your podcast.

- **Mixer.** As usual in GarageBand, the mixer controls let you adjust the volume, balance, and panning of different tracks in your podcast.

Adding audio to the podcast

You can add audio to the podcast either by recording narration or by adding musical tracks or loops.

Here's how to record narration:

1. **Double-click the Male Voice track header or the Female Voice track header (depending on the voice that will narrate) to display the Track Info pane (see figure 11.10).**

2. **In the Input source pop-up menu, choose the microphone you will use — for example, your Mac's built-in microphone, recording in stereo.**

3. **If you want to hear what you're recording, choose On with Feedback Protection in the Monitor pop-up menu.** (You can also choose the On setting, but you may get feedback.)

4. **Drag the Playhead to the time at which you want to start the recording.** If you'll add introductory music or jingles, leave enough space at the start.

5. **Click the Record button to start recording, and then start your narration.** Click the Play button when you've finished recording.

11.10 To record narration, choose the input source in the Track Info pane.

To add an audio file to the podcast, display the Media Browser, click the Audio tab, and then drag the file across to the podcast. GarageBand creates a new track for it, which you can adjust as discussed in Chapter 8.

Similarly, you can add Software Instrument or Real Instrument tracks to the podcast. Just click the Loop Browser button to display the Loop Browser, select the loop, and drag it to the podcast.

Replacing the Podcast Track with a Movie Track

If you want to create a video podcast, you replace the Podcast Track with a Movie Track. To do so, choose Track ⇨ Show Movie Track, and then click the Replace button in the dialog box (see figure 11.11) that GarageBand displays.

A project can contain either a podcast track or a movie track. Do you want to replace the podcast track with a movie track?

If you replace the podcast track, all existing markers and artwork will be lost. This cannot be undone.

Cancel   Replace

11.11 To create a video podcast, you replace the Podcast Track with the Movie Track.

GarageBand displays the Movie Track at the top of the track list. You can then drag a movie from the Movies tab in the Media Browser and drop it on the Movie Track. GarageBand adds the movie to the Movie Track and adds a Real Instrument track named Movie Sound containing the audio from the movie. You can edit this track just like any Real Instrument track — you can even mute it if you want to suppress it altogether and accompany the movie with narration or other audio content instead.

Adding episode artwork

Each podcast can have one piece of *episode artwork* — the image that represents the episode and that appears on the podcast's Web page in iWeb and your Web site.

To add the episode artwork, follow these steps:

1. **If the Track Editor isn't already displayed, click the Track Editor button to display it.** If you don't see the Podcast Markers pane, click the Podcast Track.

2. **If the Media Browser isn't already displayed, click the Media Browser button to display it.** Click the Photos tab to display its contents.

3. **Find the photo you want, and then drag it to the Episode Artwork pane in the lower left corner of the GarageBand window.**

4. **If you need to edit the photo, double-click it in the Episode Artwork area to open the Artwork Editor window (see figure 11.12).** Drag the slider to resize the photo, and then drag the photo so that the border frames the part you want to display. Click Set when you've finished.

11.12 Use the Artwork Editor window to resize a photo and to select the part you want to display.

Adding markers to a podcast episode

If you're creating an enhanced podcast episode, you can add markers to it. The markers break up the podcast track into marker regions that show you how long each section lasts. You can move marker regions or resize them using the same techniques you use for audio clips.

Here's the easiest way to add a marker:

1. **Position the Playhead where you want the marker region to start.** Either drag the Playhead or play through the podcast to reach the right point, and then stop playback.

2. **Click the Add Marker button or choose Edit ⇨ Add Marker (or simply press P).** GarageBand adds a marker to the Track Editor (see figure 11.13).

3. **Add artwork for the marker by dragging it from the Photos tab of the Media Browser to the marker's placeholder in the Artwork column in the editing area.** If you need to edit the photo, double-click it in the Artwork column to open it in the Artwork Editor, and then resize it and select the part you want as described earlier in this chapter.

11.13 Markers make your podcast episode easier to navigate and let you add URLs the viewer can reach.

Genius

You can also create a new region and add artwork to it by dragging a photo from the Photos tab of the Media Browser to the appropriate point on the Podcast Track.

4. **Click in the marker's row in the Chapter Title column in the editing area, type the title, and then press Return to apply it.**

Genius

Adding a chapter title to a marker is optional, but it enables someone playing back the podcast in iTunes, iDVD, or QuickTime to move quickly from one marker to another.

5. **If you want to add a URL to the marker, click in the URL Title column in the marker's row, and then type the text you want to display for the URL.** Then click in the URL column and type the URL itself. The URL title can be the same as the URL itself if you want, but often it's helpful to display a URL title that's shorter than the URL, more descriptive, or both.

Adding sounds or jingles

To help you jazz up your podcasts, GarageBand also provides jingles, sound effects, and *stingers* (attention-grabbing sounds). Here's how to add these sounds to a podcast episode:

1. **If the loop browser isn't open, click the loop browser button.**

2. **Click the Podcast Sounds View button.** GarageBand displays the sounds in Podcast Sounds View (see figure 11.14).

3. **Navigate to the sound you want.** For example, click Sound Effects in the Loops column, click the category in the second column, and then click the sound. Or type a search term in the Search box and press Return to find sounds that match that term.

4. **Drag the sound to the Jingles track, and position its beginning at the time you want it to start.**

Ducking backing tracks to keep narration audible

If your podcast episode includes audio tracks as well as one or more narration tracks, you can *duck* the audio tracks to make sure that the narration is always audible. To do this, you tell GarageBand which tracks are lead tracks and which tracks are backing tracks. When playing or mixing your podcast episode, GarageBand ducks (lowers) the backing tracks when any of the lead tracks has a sound. You can adjust the amount of ducking to get the effect you need.

11.14 The loop browser's Podcast Sounds View lets you quickly browse through the jingles, stingers, and sound effects.

Here's how to duck the backing tracks:

1. **If GarageBand isn't displaying the ducking controls (see figure 11.15), choose Control ⇨ Ducking to display them.**

2. **To make a track a lead track, click the upper arrow button so that it turns yellow.** If the button is already yellow, the track is already a lead track.

3. **To make a track a backing track, click the lower arrow button so that it turns blue.** If the button is already blue, the track is already a backing track.

Play the episode back and see whether the ducking is how you want it to be. If not, adjust the ducking like this:

1. **Click the Track Info button to open the Track Info pane.**

2. **Click the Master Track tab.**

3. **Click the Edit tab.**

4. **In the Ducker pop-up menu, choose the preset you want — for example, Fast - Maximum Music Reduction:**

   - **Speed.** There are three speeds: Fast, Slow, and Slowest. These control how fast the ducking happens.

   - **Degree of reduction.** There are three degrees of reduction: Maximum Music Reduction, Moderate Music Reduction, and Slight Music Reduction.

5. **If none of the Ducker presets suits you, create your own setting like this:**

   - **Choose Manual in the Ducker pop-up menu.**

   - **Click the Edit button to the right of the Ducker pop-up menu to display the Ducker dialog box (see figure 11.16).**

Ducking controls

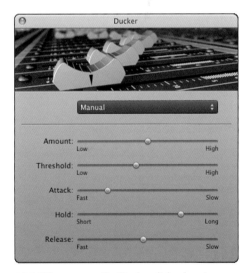

11.15 In the ducking controls, the yellow arrow pointing up indicates a lead track, and the blue arrow pointing down indicates a backing track.

11.16 You can use the Ducker dialog box to create custom ducking for your podcast episode.

351

● **Drag the sliders to set the amount of ducking you need, and then click the Close button (the red button in the upper left corner of the Ducker window).**

In the Ducker window, the Threshold slider controls the threshold level at which GarageBand starts to apply the ducking. The Attack slider controls the speed at which the ducking takes effect, and the Release slider the speed at which the duck-ing ceases. The Hold slider controls how long the ducking remains on.

Adding episode information to the podcast episode

After creating the content for your podcast episode, add the episode information like this:

1. **Double-click the Podcast Track to open the Episode Info pane (see fig-ure 11.17).**

2. **Type the title and adjust the artist and composer information as needed.**

3. **If you want to apply a parental advi-sory to the episode, open the Parental Advisory pop-up menu and choose Clean or Explicit, as appropriate.** If you don't want to apply a parental advisory, choose None.

4. **Click in the Description box and type a description of the episode's contents.**

11.17 Use the Episode Info pane to set the title, artist, and composer information, apply a parental advisory if needed, and add a description.

When you've finished creating your podcast episode, save it by pressing ⌘+S as usual.

Sending the podcast to iWeb

When you've completed the podcast, send it to iWeb like this:

1. **Choose Share ⇨ Send Podcast to iWeb.** GarageBand displays the Send your podcast to iWeb sheet (see figure 11.18).

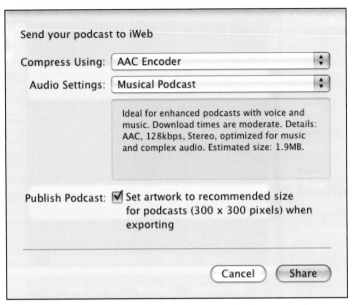

Send your podcast to iWeb

Compress Using: | AAC Encoder |

Audio Settings: | Musical Podcast |

Ideal for enhanced podcasts with voice and music. Download times are moderate. Details: AAC, 128kbps, Stereo, optimized for music and complex audio. Estimated size: 1.9MB.

Publish Podcast: ☑ Set artwork to recommended size for podcasts (300 x 300 pixels) when exporting

Cancel   Share

11.18 Before you can add your podcast to your Web site, you need to export it using this sheet.

2. **In the Compress Using pop-up menu, choose AAC Encoder if you want to use AAC format, or MP3 Encoder if you want to use MP3 format.** AAC gives marginally better quality, but MP3 is usually a better choice because many more players can play MP3 than AAC.

3. **In the Audio Settings pop-up menu, choose the quality:**

 - **Mono Podcast.** Uses the 32 Kbps bitrate and mono (one channel) rather than stereo. The files download quickly and help conserve Internet bandwidth, but the audio results are disappointing — as if you were podcasting on AM radio.

 - **Spoken Podcast.** Uses the 64 Kbps bitrate and stereo. This sounds fine for voice, but music and other complex audio suffers.

 - **Musical Podcast.** Uses the 128 Kbps bitrate and stereo. Music sounds fine to anyone except audiophiles.

 - **Higher Quality.** Uses the 192 Kbps bitrate and stereo. Music sounds great to most people, but the file sizes are that much larger.

● **Custom.** Opens the AAC Encoder dialog box or MP3 Encoder dialog box (depending on the encoder you chose in the Compress Using pop-up menu) so that you can choose exactly the settings you want. Figure 11.19 shows the MP3 Encoder dialog box. Click OK when you've made your choices.

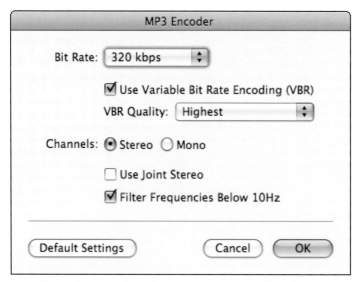

MP3 Encoder

Bit Rate: 320 kbps

☑ Use Variable Bit Rate Encoding (VBR)
VBR Quality: Highest

Channels: ⦿ Stereo ○ Mono

☐ Use Joint Stereo
☑ Filter Frequencies Below 10Hz

Default Settings   Cancel   OK

11.19 Use the MP3 Encoder dialog box or AAC Encoder dialog box when you need to create super-high-quality podcasts.

Genius

The normal reason for using custom audio settings is to crank the quality as high as possible. In the AAC Encoder dialog box or MP3 Encoder dialog box, choose a high bitrate — up to 320 Kbps if you can afford large file sizes. Turn on Variable Bit Rate Encoding when you need to squeeze the highest quality into your files. Choose the Stereo option button unless you need mono. For MP3, turn *off* joint stereo for bitrates over 160 Kbps — this is a space-saving measure that reduces audio quality.

4. **If you're using the AAC Encoder, select the Set artwork to recommended size for pod-casts when exporting check box if you want GarageBand to resize the art automati-cally.** This is usually a good idea. This setting doesn't apply to MP3 podcasts.

5. **Click Share.** GarageBand exports the podcast and passes it to iWeb, which prompts you to decide which blog you want to send it to.

6. **Choose the blog or podcast, and then click OK.** iWeb adds the podcast to the Entries list for the blog or podcast.

Publishing the podcast from iWeb

After you add the podcast episode to iWeb from GarageBand, you need to finalize its Web page, set series and episode information, and then publish it to your Web site.

Finalizing the podcast's Web page

When GarageBand creates an entry in iWeb's Podcast category for the podcast episode, it copies across the title and artist information you supplied. Often, you'll need to edit this information to make the entry's Web page look compelling. For example, you may want to improve the description, give the podcast a snappier title, or change the date.

Setting series and episode information

Next, set the series and episode information for the podcast like this:

1. **Click the Inspector button on the tool-bar to display the Inspector window.**

2. **Click the Blog & Podcast Inspector button to display the Blog & Podcast Inspector.** Click the Podcast tab to display it (see figure 11.20).

3. **Choose serieswide options in the Podcast Series area:**

   - **Series Artist.** Type the name you want to use for the artist for the podcast series. (This may be different from the artist for individual episodes.)

   - **Contact Email.** Type the address you want to use for the podcast series.

   - **Parental Advisory.** Choose Clean or Explicit if you want to apply a parental advisory to the series. Choose None if you don't.

11.20 Enter the series and episode information for your podcast on the Podcast tab in the Blog & Podcast Inspector.

- **Allow Podcast in iTunes Store.** Select this check box if you want the podcast series to appear in the iTunes Store for free download. This is a great way of getting distribution for your podcast.

4. **Choose options for this episode only in the Podcast Episode area:**

- **Episode Artist.** Type a different artist's name here if necessary.

- **Parental Advisory.** Choose Clean or Explicit if you want to apply a parental advisory to this podcast episode. (This rating can be different from that which you applied to the podcast series.) Choose None if you don't.

- **Allow Podcast in iTunes Store.** Select this check box if you want the podcast episode to appear in the iTunes Store for free download.

5. **Click the Close button (the red button in the upper left corner) to close the Inspector.**

Publishing the podcast

Your podcast is now ready for publishing. To publish it, click the Publish button in the lower left corner of the iWeb window.

How Do I Design, Build, and Burn DVDs in iDVD?

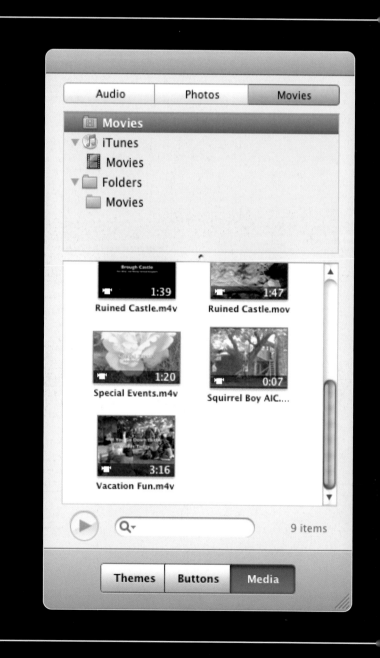

DVD lets you create professional-looking DVDs from your movies, photos, and compositions, complete with customized menu screens including pictures, video, and audio. You can either take full control of the process of creating the DVD, or use the Magic iDVD feature to jump-start the process for you and then finish it yourself. You can even use the OneStep DVD feature to burn a DVD directly from your DV camcorder without your intervention. The first essential is to understand the process of creating a DVD in iDVD. Let's look at that quickly, and then get to work.

Understanding the Process of Creating a DVD

Before we get into creating a DVD, let's go quickly through the steps you need to take. Even if you've worked with earlier versions of iLife, it's important to have the process straight because it changed considerably in iDVD '08 (but remains essentially the same in iDVD '09).

1. **Get your content ready in the other iLife applications:**

   - **Movies.** Create movies in iMovie and export them directly to iDVD or to the Media Browser. If you have movies already prepared in other folders, you can use them directly from there.

   - **Photos.** If you want to create slideshows in iDVD, prepare the photos in iPhoto. For example, put your edited photos in a photo album so that you can grab them all at once.

   - **Music.** Compose songs in GarageBand and save previews of them in the Media Browser so that iDVD can access them. You can also export the finished songs to iTunes and use them from there. And you can use any song or playlist from your iTunes library — so you may want to assemble a suitable playlist for a DVD.

2. **Start creating a DVD project in iDVD.** You can create either a regular DVD project, which gives you total control right from the word go, or use the Magic iDVD feature to jump-start creating the DVD. If you use Magic iDVD, you avoid Step 3 altogether, and Magic iDVD takes care of Step 4 for you.

Note The majority of this chapter shows you how to create a DVD manually. If you want to use the Magic iDVD feature to start your DVD project quickly, see the end of the chapter.

3. **Add content to the DVD.** At this point, you add your movies, photos, and music to the DVD. You may need to add chapter markers to a movie or create a scene selection menu for a movie; this involves a bit of work outside iDVD.

4. **Customize the menu screen for the DVD.** The menu screen is the background on which the various buttons for controlling the DVD appear. You can add movies and slideshows to the menu screen to give it more impact.

5. **Check the DVD's status and inspect the items it contains.**

6. **When the DVD project is ready, burn it to DVD.**

After skimming over the previous six steps, you may have already taken care of Step 1, preparing the contents. (If not, go and do so.) The following sections take you through the remaining five steps in turn.

Starting a DVD Project

Now that you understand the process of creating a DVD, it's time to launch iDVD and start a project.

Launch iDVD by either of these ways:

- Click the iDVD icon in the Dock.

- Click the desktop, choose Go ⇨ Applications, and then double-click the iDVD icon.

The first time you launch it, iDVD displays the iDVD '08 opening screen shown in figure 12.1.

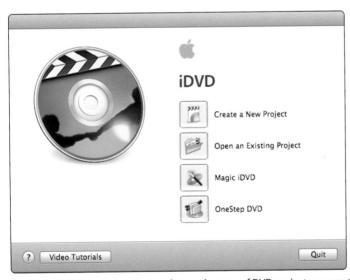

12.1 On the iDVD opening screen, choose the type of DVD project you want to create.

Note Once you've created a DVD project (or several), each time you launch iDVD, it opens the last project you were working with. If you close that project (by choosing File ⇨ Close Window), iDVD displays the iDVD '09 opening screen again.

Choosing which kind of DVD to create

Before you can get started with iDVD, you need to pick a task from the iDVD '09 opening screen. This screen lets you create three different kinds of DVD projects or open an existing project:

- **Create a New Project.** Click this button to start a new DVD that you create manually, as described in the bulk of this chapter. This is what you'll probably want to do most of the time.

- **Open an Existing Project.** Once you've started a DVD projects or two, you can click this button to open one of them to work on it further.

- **Magic iDVD.** Click this button to create a DVD the quick and easy way. Like the Magic GarageBand feature in GarageBand for starting custom songs in a snap, Magic iDVD lets you create a customized DVD with minimal effort, while providing you with control over the DVD's contents, menus, and appearance.

- **OneStep DVD.** Click this button to grab movie content from the tape on your DV camcorder and drop it directly onto a DVD. When you do, you don't get to use iMovie to edit the movie content and pretty it up, so OneStep DVD is best for content that's either final (for example, a movie project someone has exported to the DV camcorder) or that you're simply not planning to edit. You'll find details of OneStep DVD later in this chapter.

Creating a new project

Here's how to create a new project:

1. **Click the Create a New Project button from the iDVD '08 opening screen.** iMovie displays the Create Project dialog box (see figure 12.2).

2. **Type the name for the project in the Save As box in place of iDVD's suggestion (*My Great DVD*).**

Genius If you already have a DVD project open in iDVD, you can display the iDVD '09 opening screen by closing the open project. Alternatively, choose File ⇨ New to display the Create Project dialog box.

3. **In the Where pop-up menu, choose the folder in which to save the DVD project.** iDVD suggests the Documents folder, but it's better to use a different folder so that your Documents folder doesn't get cluttered. If necessary, expand the Create Project dialog box so that you can see the Sidebar and create a new folder.

Caution   Make sure the drive has plenty of free space for creating the DVD. You need 8 to 10 GB for burning a full single-layer disc and 15 to 20GB for burning a full double-layer disc.

12.2 Start by naming your DVD project, choosing its aspect ratio, and deciding where to save it.

4. **In the Aspect Ratio area, select the Standard option button if you're creating a DVD for standard-format screens.** Select the Widescreen option button if your audience will use wide screens.

5. **Click Create.** iDVD creates the project and displays it in the main iDVD window.

Setting preferences to meet your needs

Now that you have iDVD open, you can set preferences to tell iDVD how you want to work and how to encode your video. Choose iDVD ➪ Preferences to open the iDVD preferences window, and then click the General button on the toolbar if it's not already selected.

Setting General preferences

The General preferences (see figure 12.3) contain the following settings:

● **Show drop zone labels.** Select this check box to have iDVD label the areas on the menu screens where you can drop background music, photos, or movies. These labels are usually helpful.

● **Show Apple logo watermark.** Select this check box if you want to make an Apple logo appear as a watermark on the menu backgrounds of your DVD.

● **Fade volume out at end of menu loop.** Select this check box if you want iDVD to gradually fade out the volume at the end of each loop.

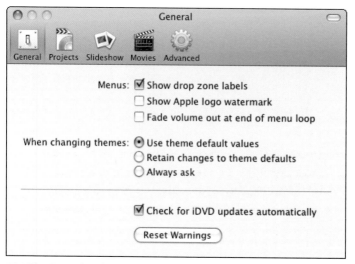

12.3 The General preferences include settings for fading out audio on menu loops and choosing how to handle theme changes.

● **When changing themes options.** Tell iDVD what to do about changes you've made to a theme when you switch a DVD project from one theme to another. Select the Use theme default values option button if you want to use the values in the new theme. Select the Retain changes to theme defaults option button if you want to keep your changes. Select the Always ask option button if you want iDVD to prompt you to decide at the time.

● **Check for iDVD updates automatically.** Select this check box if you want iDVD to automatically look for its own updates. Clear the check box if you prefer to check manually by choosing iDVD ➪ Check for Updates or by using Software Update.

● **Reset Warnings.** You can turn off many of iDVD's warnings by selecting a Don't ask me again check box in them. Click this button if you need to reset all iDVD's warnings.

Setting Projects preferences

The Projects preferences (see figure 12.4) let you choose the following settings:

- **Video Mode.** NTSC is the format generally used in North America, whereas Europe is PAL territory. The two formats use different numbers of frames per second of video and different numbers of horizontal lines, so a DVD in one format won't play properly on a TV that uses the other format.

Genius

The High Quality and Professional Quality settings in the Encoding pop-up menu in the Projects preferences give visibly better results than the Best Performance setting. The disadvantage is that, because neither of them starts encoding until you start burning the DVD project, the burning process takes that much longer. Professional Quality takes about twice as long as High Quality to encode the video, so plan ahead if you intend to use it.

- **Encoding.** This is a vital setting. Choose Best Performance if you want iDVD to encode movies for DVD as you work so that they're ready to burn when you finish the project. Choose High Quality to encode at higher quality when you start to burn your project. Choose Professional Quality to encode at the highest quality available, again when you start to burn your project.

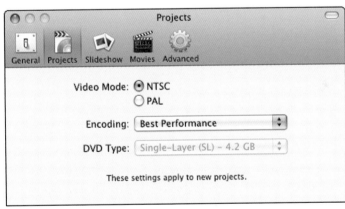

12.4 Choose the video mode and encoding type in the Projects preferences.

- **DVD Type.** Choose whether to create Single-Layer or Dual-Layer discs. If your Mac's SuperDrive can burn only Single-Layer discs, this pop-up menu is unavailable.

Setting Slideshow preferences

The Slideshow preferences (see figure 12.5) let you choose the following settings:

● **Always add original photos to DVD-ROM contents.** Select this check box if you want to include original, full-size photos on the DVD as well as the smaller versions used for the slideshows. This setting is helpful if you distribute the photos.

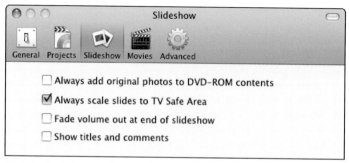

12.5 The Slideshow preferences let you add original photos to the DVD, stay in the TV Safe Area, fade the volume out, and include titles and comments.

● **Always scale slides to TV Safe Area.** The TV Safe Area is that part of a widescreen project that will appear on a standard-format TV screen (whose aspect ratio is 4:3 rather than 16:9). Select this check box if you want to make sure the full photo always appears on the TV screen. This is a good idea unless you're certain the DVD will be viewed only on widescreen monitors.

● **Fade volume out at end of slideshow.** Select this check box if you want iDVD to fade the volume out at the end of a slideshow. This effect can be useful with music, but you won't usually want to use it with voiceovers.

● **Show titles and comments.** Select this check box if you want to include the titles and comments with the photos. Having the titles and comments can be useful when you make DVDs for yourself, but you'll probably want to omit them when you make DVDs for other people.

Setting Movies preferences

The Movies preferences (see figure 12.6) let you choose the following settings:

● **When importing movies.** Select the Create chapter submenus option button if you want iDVD to automatically create a submenu screen to let the viewer access the chapters (the scenes) in the movie.

● **Look for my movies in these folders.** If you want iDVD to look for movies in other folders than your ~/Movies folder, your iTunes Movies, and the Media Browser, add the folders to this list.

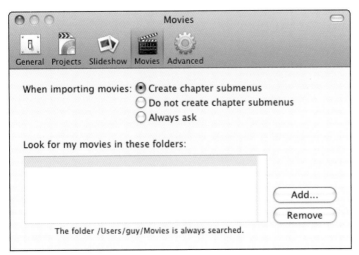

12.6 In the Movies preferences, choose whether to create chapter submenus. You can also add folders iDVD should scan automatically for movies.

Setting Advanced preferences

The Advanced preferences (see figure 12.7) let you choose the following settings:

● **Look for my themes in these folders.** iDVD automatically searches your Mac's /Library/Application Support/iDVD/Themes folder for themes. If you have themes in another folder, add that folder by clicking the Add button.

● **OneStep DVD capture folder.** The readout shows the folder iDVD is using to store the data it captures from your camcorder for creating OneStep DVDs. If you're running out of space on your Mac's hard drive, you may need to switch to a folder on an external drive. Click the Change button, select the folder in the Open dialog box, and then click the Open button.

● **Preferred DVD Burning Speed.** In this pop-up menu, choose the DVD burning speed you want to use. Usually, it's best to choose Maximum Possible and let iDVD handle the speed. But if you find that full-speed burning produces DVDs containing errors, choose a lower speed here.

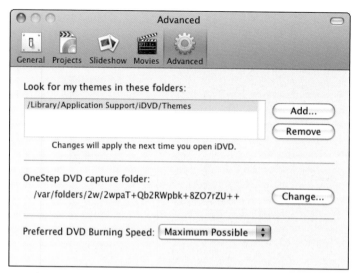

12.7 The Advanced preferences let you add themes, change your OneStep DVD capture folder, and set your preferred DVD burning speed.

Closing the Preferences window automatically saves your new preferences settings.

Genius

If you changed any of the Projects preferences, you have a chicken-and-egg situation here: The new settings you chose apply only to new projects you create from now on, not to the new project you just created in order to be able to set the preferences. To implement the changes, close your project (choose File ⇨ Close Window) and create a new one.

Navigating the iDVD interface

Now that you've got a project open in iDVD, it's time to get to grips with the application's interface. Figure 12.8 shows the main iDVD window.

Genius

If you find you've chosen Standard format for your DVD project instead of Widescreen, or vice versa, you can change by choosing Project ⇨ Switch to Widescreen or Project ⇨ Switch to Standard. You can also flip between the formats by pressing ⌘+Option+A.

Themes pop-up menu

Add

Inspector window

Map

Motion

Drop Zone

Volume slider

Preview

Burn

Themes pane

12.8 The main iDVD window.

Applying a theme

A *theme* is a complete set of formatting for the DVD, including the layouts, background, fonts, and background music.

Here's how to apply a theme:

1. **In the Themes pop-up menu at the top of the Themes pane, choose the category of themes you want to see:**

   - **All.** All the themes you've installed.

   - **7.0 Themes.** Themes from iDVD '08 and '09.

   - **6.0 Themes.** Themes from iDVD '06.

   - **5.0 Themes.** Themes from iLife '05.

   - **Old Themes.** Themes from earlier versions of iLife.

   - **Favorites.** Themes you've marked as your favorites.

Note   If you find iDVD's themes don't meet your needs, you can buy other themes online. (To find sites that sell themes, put the search term **iDVD themes** into your favorite search engine.). Usually, the easiest place to install them is in your Mac's /Library/Application Support/iDVD/Themes/ folder because iDVD then automatically adds them to the Themes pop-up menu.

2. **To see the other screens a theme includes, click the disclosure triangle next to it.**

3. **Click the theme you want.** iDVD applies the theme to the project. If the theme doesn't appear in the main iDVD window, try running Software Update from the Apple menu.

If you're creating a standard-format project and choose a widescreen-format theme, iDVD displays the Change Project Aspect Ratio dialog box (see figure 12.9) asking if you want to change aspect ratio and giving you three choices:

- **Keep.** Click this button to maintain the aspect ratio. This is usually the best choice because changing the aspect ratio gives the DVD the wrong aspect ratio for your movie.

- **Change.** Click this button to change the project to the theme's aspect ratio.

- **Cancel.** Click this button to cancel applying the theme. You can then pick another theme that uses the right aspect ratio.

Change Project Aspect Ratio
This is a standard project, but the theme you chose is designed for widescreen video. You can keep your project as standard (4:3), or change your project to widescreen video (16:9).

☐ Do not ask me again.

(Cancel)   (Keep)   (Change)

12.9 You may need to decide whether to change the project's aspect ratio to match the ratio of the theme you applied.

Note   As with most applications, you should save the changes you made to a DVD project when you're satisfied with them. Press ⌘+S or choose File ⇨ Save to save the changes.

Adding Content to the DVD Project

Now it's time to add the content to your DVD project. You'll probably want to add one or movies to the DVD project, but you can also create a powerful DVD by using slideshows either with movies or instead of them.

Adding a movie

To add a movie to your DVD, follow these steps:

1. **Click the Media button in the lower right corner of the iDVD window to display the Media pane.**

2. **Click the Movies button at the top of the Media pane to display the Movies tab (shown on the opening page of this chapter).**

3. **In the box at the top of the Movies tab, choose the source of the movies:**

   - **iMovie.** These are the movies you've added to the Media Browser from iMovie.

   - **Movies.** These are the movies stored in your Movies folder.

   - **iPhoto.** These are movies you've imported to iPhoto from your digital camera.

   - **iTunes.** These are movies you've exported to iTunes from iMovie or otherwise added to iTunes. Click the disclosure triangle to display the Movies category within iTunes.

   - **Folders.** These are movies in the folders you've told iDVD to search for movies. You can add other folders as described in the nearby sidebar.

4. **Click the thumbnail for the movie you want to add, and then drag it to the menu in the main part of the iDVD window.** You can drop it anywhere that the mouse pointer includes a green circle containing a + sign. iDVD adds a menu button with the movie's name on it. (You can change the name later.)

Caution

Make sure you don't drop the movie in one of the drop zones — if you do, iDVD makes it part of the menu screen rather than a separate movie.

5. **iDVD creates a button bearing the movie's name on the menu background.**

6. **If you want to change the button's text, click the button once, and then click it again to display the text-editing controls (see figure 12.10).** Edit the text as needed, choose the font, style, and size, and then click elsewhere to apply the changes.

12.10 You can easily change the text or formatting of a menu button.

Genius

If you find working on the main DVD screen confusing, try using the DVD map instead, as discussed later in this chapter. This shows you a layout of the DVD's contents that is much less graphical and (for many people) much easier to interpret.

Adding chapter markers to a movie

To break a movie up into scenes among which the viewer can easily navigate on a DVD, you add chapter markers to the movie. Unfortunately, iDVD's feature for adding chapter markers is severely limited: It lets you place chapter markers only at regular intervals — for example, every three minutes. This is better than nothing, but unless you've shot and edited your movie with unnatural precision, the chapter markers won't coincide with the beginning of scenes.

Here's how to add chapter markers in iDVD:

1. **Choose Advanced ⇨ Create Chapter Markers for Movie.** iDVD displays the dialog box shown in figure 12.11.

2. **Set the number of minutes in the Create marker every box**.

3. **Click OK.** iDVD adds the markers to the movie.

Adding Other Folders to the Movies Tab

If you keep your movies in various folders, you may want to make them appear on the Movies tab in the Media pane. You can add the folders like this:

1. Choose iDVD ⇨ Preferences to open the Preferences window.

2. Click the Movies button in the toolbar to display the Movies preferences.

3. Click the Add button to display the Open dialog box.

4. Select the folder that contains the movies, and then click Open. iDVD adds the folder to the Look for my Movies in these folders box.

5. Add further folders as needed, and then click the close button (the red button) to close the Preferences window.

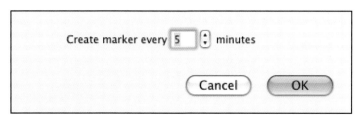

12.11 iDVD lets you add chapter markers to a movie, but they can only be at regular intervals.

These chapter markers give viewers a rudimentary way of navigating quickly through the movie on your DVD. But if you want to create a proper scene-selection menu tied to chapter markers that appear where you want them to, you need to do a bit more work, as described next.

Creating a scene selection menu

Here's the workaround for creating a scene selection menu tied to chapter markers that you position yourself instead of having iDVD position automatically. It takes more effort, but the results make it worthwhile.

Before you start this procedure, open iDVD preferences (choose iDVD ⇨ Preferences), click the Movies button, and make sure you've selected the Create chapter submenus option button in the When importing movies area of Movies preferences. This setting causes iDVD to create the scene selection menu when you import a movie that contains chapter markers.

Follow these steps:

1. **In iMovie, export the movie to the Media Browser.** You may have done this already.

2. **Launch GarageBand.** If GarageBand opens your last project, choose File ➭ Close to close it so that the GarageBand opening screen appears.

3. **Click New Project, click Podcast, and then click Choose.** GarageBand displays the New Project from Template dialog box.

4. **Type the name for the project and choose the folder in which to save it.** The best place to save the project is in your ~/Movies folder because then iDVD shows it automatically in the Movies pane.

5. **Click the Create button.** GarageBand creates the project.

6. **If the Media Browser isn't already displayed, click the Media Browser button (the button at the right end of the toolbar) to open it.**

7. **Click the Movies button at the top of the Media Browser.**

8. **Click the movie and drag it to the Podcast track at the top of the project.** GarageBand displays the dialog box shown in figure 12.12, asking if you want to replace the podcast track with a movie track.

A project can contain either a podcast track or a movie track. Do you want to replace the podcast track with a movie track?

If you replace the podcast track, all existing markers and artwork will be lost. This cannot be undone.

Cancel   Replace

12.12 Click the Replace button in this dialog box to turn your podcast project into a movie project.

9. **Click the Replace button.** GarageBand adds the movie to the project and creates thumbnails to represent it.

10. **Choose Edit ⇨ Add Marker (or press P) to display the chapter-editing pane (see figure 12.13).** GarageBand automatically adds a marker for the beginning of the movie. If you want to keep it, click in the Chapter Title box and type the name to give it. If you don't want the marker, click it, and then press Delete.

12.13 Creating chapter markers for a movie in GarageBand.

11. **Play the movie (click the Play button or press Spacebar) or drag the Playhead to where you want to create the next marker.** Drag the Zoom slider to zoom in on the thumbnails if you need to get a better view.

12. **Click the Add Marker button in the Markers pane to add a marker.** Click in the Chapter Title box and type the name for the marker.

13. **Continue until you've added all the markers you want.**

14. **Choose File ⇨ Save to save the project.**

15. **Choose Share ⇨ Send Project to iDVD to export the movie to iDVD.**

iDVD then opens, and you can add the movie to your project either by using the Media Browser (if you saved the movie in a folder that iDVD is monitoring) or by dragging it from a Finder window. iDVD automatically creates a scene selection menu, which you can customize as needed.

Adding a slideshow

Here's how to add a slideshow to your DVD project:

1. **Make sure you're on the main menu for your DVD project.**

2. **In the lower left corner of the iDVD window, click the Add button, and then choose Add Slideshow.** iDVD adds a button named My Slideshow to the menu.

3. **With the My Slideshow button still selected, click the button to select the text, and then type the name you want to give the slideshow.** You can also change the font, style, and size if you want. Click outside the button when you finish.

4. **Double-click the slideshow button.** iDVD opens the slideshow editor and selects the Photos tab in the Media pane.

5. **In the Photos pane, select the category or album that contains the photos you want.** For example, select the Flagged category if you want to use photos you flagged.

6. **Click and drag one or more photos — or an album — to the slideshow editor to add them to the slideshow (see figure 12.14).** To select multiple photos at once, click the first, and then ⌘+click each of the others.

    ● **If you add a photo you don't want, click it and press Delete to delete it.**

    ● **To view more photos at once, click the Grid View button in the upper right corner of the slideshow editor.**

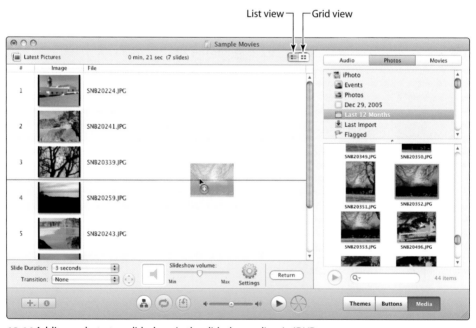

12.14 Adding a photo to a slideshow in the slideshow editor in iDVD.

7. **When you've added all the photos you want, click and drag them into the order you want.** You can play back your slideshow at any point by clicking the Play button. Click the Stop button to exit the preview window and return to the slideshow editor.

8. **If you want to add a song as the soundtrack for the slideshow, click the Audio tab at the top of the Media pane.** Locate the song in either GarageBand or your iTunes library, click it, and then drag it to the slideshow. Drop it anywhere, and iDVD applies it to the whole slideshow.

9. **Set the duration for each slide in the Slide Duration pop-up menu.** iDVD applies this duration to each slide; you can't set different numbers of seconds for different slides.

Genius

If you added a song in Step 8, iDVD automatically sets the Slide Duration pop-up menu to Fit to Audio. This setting automatically divides the length of the song equally among the slides. You can choose another setting if you want to end the slideshow earlier or make it carry on for longer.

10. **In the Transition pop-up menu, choose the transition to use for the slides, or choose None if you want no transition effect.** If the direction button to the right of the Transition pop-up menu is available, select the direction in which you want the transition to move — for example, a Push transition from the top or bottom.

11. **Set the volume for the slideshow by dragging the Slideshow Volume slider.**

12. **To choose other settings for the slideshow, click the Settings button, select the appropriate check boxes in the setting sheet (see figure 12.15), and then click OK:**

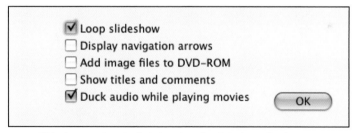

12.15 Slideshow options include looping the slideshow, displaying navigation arrows, and including titles and comments.

- **Loop slideshow.** Select this check box to make the slideshow repeat itself until the viewer stops it.

- **Display navigation arrows.** Select this check box to display forward and back arrow buttons on the slides.

- **Add image files to DVD-ROM.** Select this check box if you want to include original, full-size photos on the DVD as well as the smaller versions used for the slideshows.

- **Show titles and comments.** Select this check box if you want to include the titles and comments with the photos. This can be useful for your personal DVDs — for example, if you're reviewing the photos to pick the best.

- **Duck audio while playing movies.** Select this check box if you want iDVD to lower (*duck*) the volume on the slideshow when the viewer is playing a movie. This is almost always a good idea.

13. **When you finish setting up your slideshow, click the Return button to go back to the main menu screen.**

Customizing the Menu Screen for the DVD

Your next move is to customize the menu screen for the DVD by adding photos, slideshows, or movies to it. To add these items, you use the *drop zones*, the marked areas on the menu screen.

Finding out how many drop zones a menu screen has

iDVD's various themes have different numbers of drop zones in their menu screens, but all menu screens have at least one drop zone, and many have several. What's tricky is that in some menu screens, drop zones appear all at the same time, but in other screens, they play in sequence, so you see only one at a time.

To find out how many drop zones are in the menu screen you're using, click the Drop Zone button on the toolbar at the bottom of the iDVD window. iDVD displays the drop zone editor (see figure 12.16).

Adding a movie to a drop zone

A great way to add life to a menu screen is to place a movie in one of the drop zones. The movie then plays when the viewer opens the menu screen.

Genius

Use short movies for your drop zones because most viewers won't want to linger on the menu screens. You can also make iDVD play only part of the movie in the drop zone, as you'll see in a moment.

Drop zones for menu screen   Drop zone button

12.16 Use the drop zone editor to check how many drop zones a menu screen contains.

Here's how to add a movie to a drop zone and choose which part to play:

1. **If the drop zone editor isn't open, open it as explained in the previous section.**

2. **Click the Media button to display the Media pane, and then click the Movies tab.**

3. **Click the movie you want to add, and then drag it to the drop zone in which you want to place it.** iDVD displays a thumbnail of the movie in the drop zone.

4. **Add movies to any other drop zones in which you want to use movies rather than photos.**

5. **Click the Drop Zone button to return to the main menu, which now shows the movies you added in the drop zones.** Figure 12.17 shows an example in which only the first movie appears.

6. **Set the start point and end point of each movie you added:**

- If your menu screen plays movies in a single drop zone, drag the Motion Playhead along the playback bar across the bottom of the menu screen to make the drop zone display the right movie.

- Click the drop zone. iDVD displays a yellow-and-black border around it and opens the Movie Start/End panel (see figure 12.18).

- Drag the start marker to select the starting frame. The movie scrubs through the frames as you drag.

- Drag the end marker to select the ending frame.

- Click elsewhere to close the Movie Start/End panel and apply your changes.

- Repeat the procedure for each of the other movies.

Drop zone

12.17 The movies you added appear in the drop zones. This menu screen has only one drop zone (on the left), in which the movies play in succession.

12.18 Use the Movie Start/End panel to choose the frames at which to start and end the movie in the drop zone.

7. **If you want to turn off the movie intro, clear the Show/Hide Intro Movie check box.** Likewise, if you want to turn off the outro, clear the Show/Hide Outro Movie check box.

8. **Click the Motion button to loop through the movies in your drop zones and see how they look.** Click this button again to stop the playback.

Adding photos to a drop zone

Instead of a movie, you can add a still photo or a photo slideshow to a drop zone. Follow these steps:

1. **If the drop zone editor isn't open, click the Drop Zone button to open it.**

2. **Click the Media button to display the Media pane, and then click the Photos tab.**

3. **Click the photo you want to add, and then drag it to the drop zone in which you want to place it.** iDVD displays a thumbnail of the first photo in the drop zone.

4. **Click the Drop Zone button to return to the main menu, which now shows the drop zone to which you added the photos.**

5. Set up the slideshow to meet your needs:

● Click the drop zone once. iDVD displays a yellow-and-black border around it and opens the Photos panel.

● Click and drag the slider in the Photos panel to view the photos.

● If you need to rearrange the photos, click the Edit Order button in the Photos panel to open the photos in the slideshow editor. This is the same slideshow editor discussed earlier in this chapter, but when you create a slideshow for a drop zone, you can't add music or transitions or set slide durations.

● Rearrange the photos as needed by clicking and dragging them. You can also drag in other photos from the Photos pane if you want.

● Click the Return button. iDVD displays the drop zone editor.

● Click the Drop Zone button to return to the menu screen.

6. Click the Motion button to loop through the movies and slideshows in your drop zones and see how they look. Click this button again to stop the playback.

Change a menu's background and audio

To change the background and audio of a menu screen, follow these steps:

1. Click the Inspector Window button on the toolbar or choose View ⇨ Show Inspector to open the Menu Info window (see figure 12.19).

2. To change the background image for the menu screen, click a photo in the Photos pane and drag it into the center well in the Background area.

3. To change the duration of the loop, drag the Loop Duration slider.

4. To add audio to the menu, click a song in the Music pane and drag it into the Audio well. Drag the Menu Volume slider to set the volume.

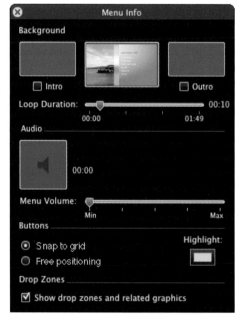

12.19 Use the Menu Info window to change the background of a menu and add audio.

5. **If necessary, change the menu's button:**

   ● If you want to reposition the menu's buttons freely, select the Free positioning option button instead of the Snap to grid option button. You can then drag the menu buttons to where you want them.

   ● To change the highlight color, click the Highlight button, and use the Colors window to pick the color you want. For example, choose a color that works better with the new menu background you've applied.

6. **Clear the Show drop zones and related graphics check box if you want to hide these items from view.**

7. **When you finish making changes, click the Inspector Window button on the toolbar again to close the Menu Info window.**

Checking Your Project's Status and DVD Space

To see how much of your DVD project iDVD has encoded, or to see how much space you have left on the DVD, choose Project ⇨ Project Info (or press Shift+⌘+I). iDVD displays the Project info window (see figure 12.20).

If necessary, you can also change the following settings:

● **Disc Name.** Just type the new name.

● **Video Mode.** Choose NTSC or PAL.

● **Aspect Ratio.** Choose Standard or Widescreen.

● **Encoding.** Choose Best Performance, High Quality, or Professional Quality, as needed.

● **DVD Type.** Choose Single-Layer or Dual-Layer.

If you change the setting in the Encoding pop-up menu from Best Performance to High Quality or Professional Quality, iDVD displays the Changing Encoding Mode dialog box to make sure you understand that iDVD must re-encode all the material it has already encoded. Click Yes if you're okay with this change; otherwise, click Cancel to restore the project's previous encoding.

When you finish using the Project Info window, close it by clicking the close button on its title bar or choosing File ⇨ Close Window.

12.20 The Project info window shows you how much space your material will occupy on the DVD and whether the components have been encoded.

Using Map View to Inspect Your DVD

iDVD's menu screens are neat, but they can make it hard to see exactly what your DVD contains and where all the content is. When you need to get a clear picture of what's on the DVD, click the Map button to display the DVD map (see figure 12.21).

If you can't see enough of your project, you can change the view in these ways:

- Drag the Zoom slider to zoom out (revealing more of your project) or zoom in.

- Click a sideways disclosure triangle to collapse the content underneath it. Click a downward disclosure triangle to expand its contents.

- Click the Vertical View button to switch the map to vertical view, or click the Horizontal View button to switch to horizontal view.

Project icon   Disclosure triangles

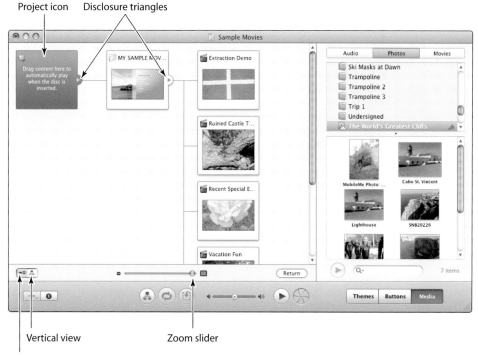

Vertical view   Zoom slider

Horizontal view

12.21 Use the DVD map to get a clear view of where all the files are in your DVD project and to add an autoplay movie.

These are the main actions you can take in the DVD map:

- **Delete an item.** Click the item and drag it outside the iDVD window, where it vanishes in a puff of smoke. Alternatively, click the item and then press Delete.

- **Add an item.** Click and drag a movie, photo, or album to a menu button. iDVD adds a new item to the menu.

- **Change a movie or slideshow.** Click and drag another movie, photo, or album to the button to replace its contents.

Genius

You can double-click a slideshow button in the DVD map to display the photos in the slideshow editor so that you can rearrange the photos, delete some, or add others.

385

● **Add an autoplay movie or slideshow.** Click and drag a movie or album to the project icon. If you drag an album, double-click the project icon button to open the Autoplay Slideshow editor and arrange the photos into your preferred order.

When you finish working in the DVD map, click the Map button to return to the menu screen.

Genius

If the DVD map shows a yellow triangle on an item, it means there's an error such as an empty drop zone. Position the mouse pointer over the yellow triangle to see the details of the error, and then visit the affected screen so that you can fix it.

Burning the DVD

When you finish adding content and have previewed the DVD project, you're ready to burn it to disc. Follow these steps:

1. **If your DVD project contains unsaved changes, press ⌘+S or choose File ⇨ Save to save them.**

2. **Click the Burn button on the toolbar.** iDVD prompts you to insert a recordable DVD.

3. **Insert a disc in your Mac's DVD drive.** If it's a drawer-style drive, close the drawer.

4. **Wait while iDVD burns the disc.** When it has finished, test the disc, remove it, and label it.

To create a disc image, choose File ⇨ Save As Disc Image. In the Save Disc Image As dialog box (see figure 12.22), type the filename, choose the folder in which to save it, and then click Save.

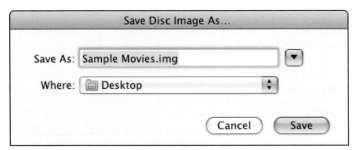

12.22 Save a DVD project to a disc image so that you can burn it to DVD multiple times using Disc Utility.

To create a VIDEO_TS folder, choose File ⇨ Save as VIDEO_TS Folder. In the Save VIDEO_TS folder As dialog box, type the file name, choose the folder in which to save the folder, and then click Save.

Creating a Disc Image or a VIDEO_TS File

Instead of burning your DVD project to a DVD, you can save it as a disc image or as a VIDEO_TS file.

- **Disc image.** If you create a disc image, you then have a file containing the completed DVD that you can burn to multiple DVDs using Disc Utility without having to encode it each time. This can save you a considerable amount of time over encoding the same DVD multiple times. Creating a disc image is also handy if you're working on a Mac that has no DVD burner. You can then transfer the completed disc image to a Mac that does have a burner.

- **VIDEO_TS folder.** A VIDEO_TS folder contains the video files for the DVD but not the DVD menus. You can play the contents of the VIDEO_TS folder using either DVD Player or third-party software such as the free VLC Media Player (www.videolan.org).

Creating a OneStep DVD

Do you ever find you have finished content on your DV camcorder that you need to burn to DVD? If so, you can use iDVD's OneStep DVD feature to quickly import the footage and burn it directly to DVD without putting it into iMovie first.

Here's how to use OneStep DVD:

1. **Open iDVD if it's not already running.** Leave it at the iDVD opening screen for the time being.

2. **Load the tape containing the movie footage.**

3. **Choose the starting point if necessary:**

   - If you want to capture only part of the footage on the tape, wind or play the tape until that point is ready to play.

   - If you want to capture all the footage on the tape, either rewind the tape or just let iDVD rewind it for you.

4. **Connect the DV camcorder to your Mac via a FireWire cable, just as you would for importing into iMovie.** Usually, you'll need a four-pin (small) plug at the camcorder end and a regular, six-pin plug at the Mac's end.

5. **Move the camcorder's switch to VCR mode or Playback mode (whichever the camera calls it).**

6. **In iDVD, click the OneStep DVD button on the opening screen.** iDVD notices the camcorder and prompts you to insert a recordable DVD disc.

7. **Insert a disc in your Mac's DVD drive.**

8. **iDVD displays the Creating your OneStep DVD screen (see figure 12.23).**

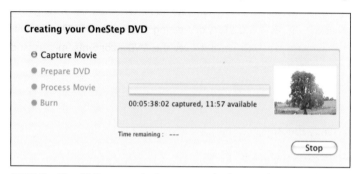

Creating your OneStep DVD

⊖ Capture Movie
● Prepare DVD
● Process Movie
● Burn

00:05:38:02 captured, 11:57 available

Time remaining :   ---

Stop

12.23 OneStep DVD automatically captures the footage from your DV camcorder and burns it to DVD.

9. **iDVD winds the camcorder's tape back to the beginning.** If you want to start playback from the point you chose, press the Play button on the camcorder immediately to prevent iDVD from winding the tape back.

Genius

You can also stop iDVD's capture at any point by clicking the Stop button in the Creating your OneStep DVD dialog box. If you let the capture run, it continues until it finds a 10-second blank section of tape or until the end of the tape.

10. **Wait while iDVD captures the video from the camcorder's tape, prepares the DVD, processes the movie, and then burns the DVD.** iDVD shows you its progress (see figure 12.23).

11. **When iDVD finishes the burn, it ejects the DVD and displays the Disc Insertion dialog box, prompting you to insert another DVD if you want to burn another copy.**

12. **Insert a blank DVD and repeat the recording process, or click Done to close the OneStep DVD window.**

Genius

If you like burning DVDs this easily, try the File ➪ OneStep DVD from Movie command to burn a DVD directly from a movie.

Jump-Starting a DVD with Magic iDVD

If you've played with the Magic GarageBand feature in GarageBand for creating custom songs in a snap, you'll grasp Magic iDVD at once: It gives you a way of creating a customized DVD with as little effort as possible, while providing you with control over the DVD's contents, menus, and appearance.

Here's how to create a DVD using Magic iDVD:

1. **Open iDVD if it's not already running.**

2. **Open the Magic iDVD window (see figure 12.24):**

   - **If you're looking at the iDVD opening screen, click the Magic DVD button.**

   - **If you have a project open in iDVD, choose File ➪ Magic iDVD.**

12.24 The Magic iDVD window looks like this when you open it.

3. **Select the default title (*My Great DVD*) in the DVD Title box and type the title you want.**

4. **In the Choose a Theme box, click the theme for the overall look of the DVD.** To see a different selection of themes, open the pop-up menu above the right end of the Choose a Theme box and choose the theme category you want. See the discussion earlier in this chapter for an explanation of the various categories of themes.

5. **Click and drag one or more movies from the Movies pane on the right to the wells in the Drop Movies Here box.**

   - You can click and drag movies from either of the Movies folders shown in the Movies pane.

   - You can also click and drag movies from the Movies folder in iTunes.

   - If your movies are in another folder, open a Finder window to that folder, and then click the movie and drag it to the well in iMovie.

Genius

If you need to delete a movie or slideshow from a well, simply click the well and then press Delete. You can also drag an item out of a well and drop it outside the iDVD window, where it vanishes in a puff of smoke.

6. **If you want to add one or more slideshows to the DVD, follow these steps:**

   - Click the Photos button in the upper right corner of the Magic iDVD window to display the Photos pane.

Genius

Adding a slideshow to a DVD with Magic iDVD is a bit weird because what you may want to do is add the slideshows you created in iPhoto. Frustratingly, you can't actually do this. What you do instead is create a new slideshow in iDVD by adding the photos and then (if you want) selecting music for them.

   - Select the photos you want. You can select an album, a group of photos you've selected, or a single photo.

   - Drag your selection to a photo well in the Drop Photos Here box. If you drag a single photo, you'll probably want to add others to its photo well; otherwise, it won't make much of a slideshow.

● To add audio, click the Audio button in the upper right corner of the Magic iDVD window to display the Audio pane. Click the song or playlist you want, and then drag it to the photo well for the slideshow.

7. **Click the Preview button.** iDVD assembles a preview of the project and displays it in the iDVD Preview window, together with an on-screen remote control. Use the controls on the remote to navigate the DVD. Click the Exit button to return to the Magic iDVD window, where you can add or delete content as needed.

Genius If you're satisfied with the project when you preview it, you can burn it directly from Magic iDVD. Simply click the Burn button, insert a blank DVD, and wait for the burn to take place.

8. **When your project has the contents you want, click Create Project.** Magic iDVD creates the project and then displays it in a window. You can now tweak the project as discussed earlier in this chapter, burn it to DVD, or simply leave it until later.

Index

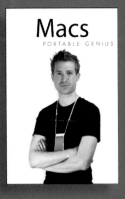

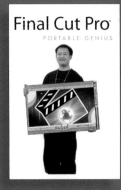